WORLD WAR II

WORLD WAR II

WORLD WAR II

THE BEST
OF
AMERICAN
HERITAGE

Edited and with an introduction by Stephen W. Sears

Houghton Mifflin Company
Boston
1991

The following article from *American Heritage* is reprinted by permission as noted:

"A Fateful Friendship," by Stephen E. Ambrose, Copyright © 1969 Stephen E. Ambrose. Reprinted by permission of the author.

PRINTED IN THE UNITED STATES

CIP data is available.
ISBN 0-395-61904-1

10 9 8 7 6 5 4 3 2 1

CONTENTS

vi   INTRODUCTION   *Stephen W. Sears*

1   THE DANGEROUS SUMMER OF 1940
                                             John Lukacs

13   THE BIG LEAK   *Thomas Fleming*

28   PEARL HARBOR: WHO BLUNDERED?
                                         Colonel T.N. Dupuy

60   THE DEFENSE OF WAKE   *Peter Andrews*

90   THE SPIES WHO CAME IN FROM THE SEA
                                          W.A. Swanberg

109 "I'VE SERVED MY TIME IN HELL"
                                        George McMillan

127 THE GALLANTRY OF AN "UGLY DUCKLING"
                                         Robert L. Vargas

138 SORRY, NO GAS   *Stephen W. Sears*

153 A FATEFUL FRIENDSHIP   *Stephen E. Ambrose*

168 THE BOMBING OF MONTE CASSINO
                                       Martin Blumenson

187 RETURN TO EAST ANGLIA   *John McDonough*

198 THE LONGEST WAIT   *John Lord*

211 HELL'S HIGHWAY TO ARNHEM *Stephen W. Sears*

227 LET SLIP THE BATS AND BALLOONS OF WAR
     I. The Fu-Go Project   *Carmine A. Prioli*
     II. Bats Away!   *Joe Michael Feist*

239 THE FIRST FLAG-RAISING ON IWO JIMA
                                       Richard Wheeler

253 THE AGONY OF THE *INDIANAPOLIS*
                                     Kenneth E. Ethridge

279 CONTRIBUTORS

INTRODUCTION

It has been called the Good War and (at least until 1991's Persian Gulf conflict) the Last Good War. In the pages that follow, a veteran of the 8th Air Force calls it (in marked contrast to Vietnam) "a war history will honor." This is not nostalgia speaking half a century after the fact. Certainly no surviving participant of World War II looks back on that titanic struggle and remembers it as a better time. Rather, for those like the 8th Air Force flier World War II represents a badge of honor, a time when there was no doubt and no question that the war had to be fought—and had to be won. The stakes were that high, and clear for all to see. President Roosevelt called America the Arsenal of Democracy, and General Eisenhower led what he called a Crusade in Europe; neither phrase rang hollow then nor do they echo hollowly today.

For nearly four decades *American Heritage* has made a particular point of insuring that the Second World War was indeed a war that history will honor. Its pages have portrayed the many dimensions of this greatest of twentieth-century conflicts and have cast the struggle in many perspectives, some of them unique. The war being a living memory for so many Americans, the editors appropriately enough have run war articles under such labels as "Before the Colors Fade," and "History at Middle Distance."

As this selection demonstrates, when it comes to World War II *American Heritage* has cast its net widely. Some authors have put the great battles in perspective, such as the epic fight for Guadalcanal or the mammoth airdrop at Arnhem. Others step behind the familiar and explore the little-known—the *first* flag-raising on Iwo Jima, for example, or the weird plot to raid Japan with bomb-carrying bats (while Japan was raiding America with paper balloons), or the case of the feckless Nazi saboteurs on Long Island.

There is no lack of controversy in this coverage. No press leak in the nation's history was larger than the one on the eve of Pearl Harbor that revealed America's most secret war plans. And on that day of infamy at Pearl Harbor, who blundered? What was the combination of mischance and incompetence that doomed hundreds of crewmen of the cruiser *Indianapolis* in the war's closing days? What military necessity was there to destroy the historic Italian monastery on Monte Cassino?

The fateful combination of events in the summer of 1940 that shaped American attitudes toward Europe's distant war is examined here. The rationing of gasoline (and much else) shaped the home front's attitude toward the conflict, and it was a matter of friendship that enabled Eisenhower to somehow keep the brilliant but eccentric Patton on the battlefield. Here is what it was like in East Anglia when the Fortresses and Liberators were there (and what it is like today), and here is chronicled the longest wait for the longest day; it is recorded that as the G.I.'s marched down to the Channel for the D-Day crossing, an elderly English woman stood by and kept saying over and over, "Thank you, lads, for helping us out."

Courage in war is seen here in a variety of ways. It is in the crew of the ugly duckling Liberty Ship *Stephen Hopkins* fighting to the death with a German raider. It is the defenders of Wake Island giving new definition to the phrase "forlorn hope."

All in all it is the stuff of history, in a war history will honor.

—*Stephen W. Sears,*
May 1991

THE DANGEROUS SUMMER OF 1940

by JOHN LUKACS

For a few weeks Hitler came close to winning World War II.
Then came a train of events that doomed him. However unsatis-
factory our world may be today, it almost was unimaginably
worse.

In the summer of 1940 Adolf Hitler could have won World War II. He came close to that. Had he won, we would be living in a world so different as to be hardly imaginable. So let us contemplate that dangerous summer. It was then that the shape of the world in which we now live began to take form.

There was a curious, abstract quality to World War II when it started. On the first day of September in 1939, Hitler's armies invaded Poland. In 1914 the Germans had gone to war not knowing what the British would do. In 1939 the British had given Poland a guarantee to deter Hitler, to make it clear that a German attack on Poland would mean a British (and a French) declaration of war against Germany. Until the last minute Hitler hoped that the British did not mean what they said. In a way he was right. The British and the French governments keep their word and declared war nearly three days after the German armies had driven into Poland. Yet the British and French armies did virtually nothing.

Before long the phrase "Phony War," invented by American journalists, came into the language. Poland was overrun: but in this war, it really was All Quiet on the Western Front. The French and the British troops spent the freezing winter that followed standing still, the French occasionally peering across the wooded German frontier from the concrete casemates of the Maginot Line. If not a phony war, it was a reluctant one.

There was a curious, abstract quality in the mood of the American people too. When World War I broke out in Europe, not one in ten thousand Americans thought that their country would ever become involved in it. In 1914 the American people and their President, Woodrow Wilson, took a naive kind of pride in their neutrality. When, on September 3, 1939, Franklin Roosevelt addressed the American people, he said the United States would stay neutral: but Roosevelt then added that he could not "ask that every American remain neutral in thought as well." Most Americans were not. They abhorred Hitler, yet they had no desire to commit themselves on the side of Britain or France or Poland. They followed the conflict on their radios: it was exciting to hear the voices of famous correspondents crackling through the transatlantic ether from the blacked-out capitals of Europe at war. Many Americans uneasily felt—felt, rather than said—that sooner or later their country would become involved in the war. They did not look forward to it.

Besides, the Phony War got curiouser and curiouser. It had started between Germany and Poland and Britain and France; but three months later the only fighting that was going on occurred in the snowy forests of Finland, a winter war between Finland and Russia. American sympathies for Finland arose. The British government noticed this. It was toying with the idea of coming to the aid of Finland, for many reasons, including the purpose of impressing American opinion. But the winter war came to an end. Churchill now wished to open a far-flung front against Germany, in Norway. Hitler forestalled him. On a freezing, raw morning in early April, his troops invaded Denmark and Norway. They conquered Denmark in a few hours and Norway in a few weeks.

Hitler's triumph in Norway—which he conquered nearly undisturbed by the British navy and largely unvexed by the hapless Allied troops put ashore and then withdrawn again— had an unexpected effect. The great portly figure of his nemesis had arisen—an old-fashioned figure of a man, whose very appearance rose like a spectral monument out of the historical mist. As a member of the Chamberlain government, Winston Churchill had been responsible for much of the Norwegian fiasco. Yet the representatives of the British people had had enough of Chamberlain's reluctant warfare. They helped Winston Churchill into the saddle of the prime ministership—by coincidence, on the very day when the German onslaught in Western Europe had begun.

It was the first of several great coincidences that summer: the kind of coincidences that people weaned on scientific logic dislike and others, with a touch of poetry in their souls, love. Or as the great Portuguese proverb says: God writes straight with crooked lines. But, as often happens in this world, we see the meaning only in retrospect. At the time, there was no guarantee that Churchill would last. He could have disappeared after a few weeks: a brave, old-fashioned orator, overtaken by the surging tide of the twentieth century, swept under by the wave of the future. When his horse is shot out under him, the best rider must fall.

O n the tenth of May, at dawn—it was a radiant, beautiful morning, cloudless across Europe from the Irish Sea to the Baltic—Hitler flung his armies forward. They were the winged carriers of an astonishing drama. Holland fell in five days; Belgium in eighteen. Two days after the German drive had begun, the French front was broken. Another eight days, and the Germans reached the Channel. Calais and Boulogne fell. Dunkirk held for just ten days. Most of the British Expeditionary Force barely escaped; all their equipment was lost. Five weeks from the day they had started westward, German regiments were marching down the Champs Elysées. Three more days, and a new French government asked for surrender.

Here was a drama of forty days unequaled in the history of war for centuries, even by the brilliant victories of Napoleon. Hitler himself had a hand in designing that most astonishing of successful campaigns. He also had a hand in designing an armistice that the French would be inclined to accept.

He hoped that the United States would stay out of the war. His propaganda minister Joseph Goebbels ordered the toning down of anti-American items in the German press and radio. When the German army marched into an empty Paris, its commanders made a courtesy call on the American ambassador, who, alone among the envoys of the Great Powers, chose to stay in the capital instead of following the torn French government during its sorry fight to the south. The Hotel

Crillon, headquarters of the German military command, was across the street from the American Embassy. The German general in charge received the American military and naval attachés at ten in the morning. He offered them glasses of what he described as "the very best brandy in the Crillon." His staff approached the American ambassador with calculated and self-conscious courtesies, to which William C. Bullitt responded with all the tact and reserve of a great envoy of classical stamp. Two months later Bullitt was back from France in his native city of Philadelphia, where, in front of Independence Hall, he made a stirring speech, calling the American people to rally to the British side against Hitler. His speech did not have much of a popular echo.

Hitler hoped that the British would think twice before going on with the war. Their chances, he said, were hopeless; and he repeated that he had no quarrel with the existence of the British Empire. He hoped that the British would make some kind of peace with him.

They didn't. Their savior Churchill had arisen; and behind Churchill—slowly, cautiously, but deliberately—rose the massive shadow of Franklin Roosevelt. In the summer of 1940—still a year and a half before Pearl Harbor and his declaration of war against the United States—Hitler already knew that his principal enemy was Roosevelt, whom he came to hate with a fury even greater that his hatred for Churchill (and, of course, for Stalin, whom he admired in many ways till the end).

Roosevelt and Churchill knew each other. More than that, they had, for some time, put their hopes in each other. For some time Franklin Roosevelt—secretly, privately, through some of his envoys, personal friends whom he trusted—had encouraged those men in London and Paris who were convinced that Hitler had to be fought. Foremost among these was Winston Churchill. In turn, Churchill knew what Roosevelt thought of Hitler; and he knew that what Britain needed was the support of the giant United States. The two men had begun to correspond, in secret. On the day German armor appeared on the cliffs across from Dover, an American citizen, an employee of the American Embassy in London, was arrested by detectives of Scotland Yard. This young man, Tyler Kent, was a convinced and committed isolationist. He knew of that secret correspondence and had tried to inform pro-Germany sympathizers in London.

A t that time—and for some dangerous weeks thereafter—
Winston Churchill's position was not yet fixed in
strength. He had, after all, a mixed reputation: yes, a great
patriot, but an enthusiast for losing causes. He had been flung
out of power during World War I because of his advocacy of
the failed Dardanelles campaign. There were many people
within his own Conservative party who distrusted him. When,
during the first eight weeks of his prime ministership, he
entered the House of Commons, they sat on their hands. King
George VI himself had not been quite happy to hand over the
reins to him on that tenth of May. John Colville, Churchill's
later faithful and admiring private secretary, reported in his
diary that day that "this sudden coup of Winston and his
rabble was a serious disaster and unnecessary one. . . . They
had weakly surrendered to a half-breed American whose main
support was that of inefficient but talkative people of a similar
type. . . ."

On the dark first day of the Dunkirk evacuation, there was
a near break between Churchill and the Foreign Secretary,
Lord Halifax. Halifax wanted to consider at least the possibility of some kind of negotiation with Hitler and Mussolini.
Churchill said no. "At the moment our prestige in Europe was
very low. The only way we could get it back was by showing
the world that Germany had not beaten us. If, after two or
three months, we could show that we were still unbeaten, our
prestige would return. Even if we were beaten, we should be
no worse off than we should be if we were now to abandon the
struggle. Let us therefore avoid being dragged down the
slippery slope. . . ." But he himself was not so far from the
edge of a slippery slope. All this looks strange and unreal now.
But it is the task of the historian to see not only what happened
but also what could have happened. At the end of May and
throughout June 1940, the continuation of Churchill's brave
position and leadership were still problematic. His great
phrases in his great public speeches had not fallen into the
void; but their meaning had yet to mature.

During that beautiful and deadly early summer of 1940,
Franklin Roosevelt, too, had to contend with a difficult
problem. This was the divided mind of the American people.
We have heard so much lately—because of nostalgic inclina-

tions due to the trauma of a divided nation during the Vietnam War—about World War II having been a Good War, when this giant nation was united in purpose and in concept. Even after Pearl Harbor this was not exactly true. During the summer of 1940 it was not true at all. There was a small minority of Americans that was convinced that the United States should abet and aid the nations warring against Hitler at almost any price. There was another, larger, minority of isolationists that wanted the United States to keep out of this war, at all costs. And there was a large and inchoate majority that did not like Hitler, and that was contemptuous of the Japanese, but their minds were divided: yes, the United States should oppose the enemies of democracy; no, the democracy of the United States should not engage in a foreign war. There were people who understood that these sentiments were contradictory. Others did not. Yet other Americans began to change their minds—slowly, gradually, at times imperceptibly. But not until after that dangerous summer of 1940.

There was a strange unreality in the American scene during the early summer. The few people from Europe and Britain who had landed in New York during those dazzling May and June days found themselves in quite another world— in the gleaming lobbies of the great New York hotels, among the glistening stream of automobiles and taxis, before the glowing glass windows of the incredibly rich department stores, around which flowed the masses of a confident, prosperous, largely undisturbed American people. It was as if the astonishing speed of the devolving events in Western Europe was too fast to grasp. It was not until the fall of France that the startling new specter of a German Europe cohered. The press, for example, including the internationalist newspapers of the East Coast, had not really prepared people for that. Until the fall of Paris its reporters gave undue credit to the resistance of the French and British armies: for the wish is the father of the thought, in newspaperdom as well as elsewhere.

There was another problem. A difficulty between Churchill and Roosevelt had arisen. In their confidential correspondence Churchill was wont to sign himself "Former Naval Person." Yet, oddly, of the two, Roosevelt was more of a naval person. Even after the fall of France, he believed, and said, that "naval power was the key to history," that Hitler, because of his naval inferiority, was bound to lose this war. For the

European theater, this was wrong in the long run. The internal-combustion engine had changed the nature of warfare; for the first time in five hundred years, armies could move faster on land than on the seas. Eventually Hitler's armies had to be destroyed on land, and mostly by the Russians. Had the German armies not been chewed up by the Russians, the Western allies, with all of their sea and air superiority, could not have invaded France in 1944.

W hat is more important, Roosevelt was wrong in the short run too. If worst came to worst, he thought, and told Churchill, the British navy could come across the Atlantic to fight on. But Churchill could not guarantee that. As early as May 15 he wrote Roosevelt that if American help came too late, "the weight may be more than we can bear." Five days later, when the Germans had reached the Channel, he repeated this: "If members of this administration were finished and others came in to parley amid the ruins, you must not be blind to the fact that the sole remaining bargaining counter with Germany would be the fleet, and if this country was left by the United States to its fate no one would have the right to blame those then responsible if they made the best terms they could for the surviving inhabitants." The day after Paris fell, Churchill let Roosevelt know that "a point may be reached in the struggle where the present ministers no longer have control of affairs and when very easy terms could be obtained for the British Islands by their becoming a vassal state of the Hitler empire." This was exactly what Hitler had in mind. As in the case of France, his plan called for a partial occupation of the British island, with the fleet in British ports but demobilized, and with a Germanophile British government somewhere within the reach of the German occupation forces.

Nevertheless, Roosevelt's inclinations were strong and clear. He tried to cajole and to warn Mussolini against entering the war on Hitler's side. Roosevelt knew that this kind of diplomacy represented another move away from neutrality and that Mussolini was still popular among the large Italian-American populations in the important cities of the East: but Roosevelt discounted that. When, on June 10, Mussolini chose to declare war on France and Britain, Roosevelt changed the draft of a speech he was to give at the University of Virginia in Charlottesville. He added a sentence: "The hand that held the dagger," he intoned, "has stuck it into the back of its neighbor." Few phrases could be more unneutral than that. When he heard this, Churchill growled with satisfaction. But Roosevelt's hands were, as yet, not free.

He had to prepare himself for an unprecedented nomination for an unprecedented third-term election as President. And against him a new American coalition had begun to gather: it came to be called America First, composed by all kinds of men and women who thought, and said, that American support to Britain was illegal, futile, and wrong. A leader of this movement was Charles A. Lindbergh, a great American hero. Its actual members were recognizable, while its potential popularity was not measurable. It is wrong to consider America First as if it had been a fluke, a conventicle of reactionaries and extremists. There were all kinds of respectable Americans who opposed Roosevelt and who were loath to engage themselves on the British side. They included not only Herbert Hoover but John Foster Dulles, with whom the Lindberghs were dining on the evening the French asked for an armistice—in other words, surrender. Anne Morrow Lindbergh was about to publish her book about the spirit of the times, entitled *The Wave of the Future*, arguing, by no means crudely or unintelligently, that the old world of liberal individualism, of parliamentary democracy, was being replaced by something new, before our very eyes. Another book, from the hands of a young Kennedy, a Harvard undergraduate, was also in the making. Its conclusions were more cautious than Anne Lindbergh's, but some of its underlying suggestions were not entirely different. His father was Roosevelt's ambassador to Britain. Joseph P. Kennedy, Sr., was no admirer of Hitler, but he was a convinced isolationist who loathed Churchill and believed the British resistance to Hitler was futile. His son, John F. Kennedy, was a secret contributor to America First.

Then came the second great coincidence. On the twenty-second of June the French delegates signed their capitulation to Hitler. It was his greatest triumph—and the lowest point in Britain's fortunes in a thousand years. Yet, that very week, the British cause was lifted by an unexpected stroke of fortune, in Philadelphia of all places. There the Republican party had met in convention and nominated Wendell Willkie for their presidential candidate: and Willkie was not an isolationist. There had been many reasons to believe that the Republicans would nominate an isolationist: perhaps Robert A. Taft from Ohio or Arthur H. Vandenberg from Michigan. The Midwest, with its large German-American and Scandinavian-American populations, mostly Republicans, was strongly isolationist. Willkie came from Indiana; and after Hitler's invasion of Scandinavia, some of that Scandinavian-American Anglophobe isolationism began to melt away. Yet the isolationist conviction was still a strong, unchanneled current among the milling Republican delegates on the floor, in that boiling arena of Philadelphia's Convention Hall. But a carefully orchestrated and arranged effort, with the galleries chanting, "We want Willkie," carried the day.

None of this would be possible in our day of the mechanized primary system. It was still possible half a century ago. It was the achievement of the internationally minded, anti-populist, financial and social leadership of East Coast Republicans, of the readers of the New York *Herald Tribune* over those of the Chicago *Tribune*, of Anglophiles over Anglophobes. The difference between the world view of Willkie and Roosevelt was one of degree, not of kind. Had the Republicans nominated an isolationist, Roosevelt would probably still have won, but the nation would have been sorely and dangerously divided; and Roosevelt would have been constrained to go slow, very slow; constrained to deny his very convictions and inclinations, to the mortal peril of the British, the sole remaining champions of freedom during that dangerous summer of 1940.

This Willkie business was a great help to Britain. Churchill knew that, and he had been smart enough to do nothing about it. He remembered the aggressive British propaganda in the United States during World War I. "We shall not dance attendance at American party conventions." He let Hitler do the job of turning the sentiments of Americans around, so that their captain could begin to change the course of the mighty American ship of state from armed neutrality to defiance and war.

Hitler now dawdled—for one of the very few times during the war. Europe lay at his feet. He went off on a vacation, touring places in northern France where he had soldiered during World War I. He made a short, furtive visit to an empty Paris at dawn. He suggested a European version of the Monroe Doctrine: Europe for the "Europeans," America for Americans. He did not draft the directive for the invasion of Britain until the middle of July— and even then with some reluctance. On July 19 he made a long and crude speed, offering a last chance of peace to Britain. In London the German "peace offer" was let drop with an icy silence, somewhat like a blackmailing note left at the door of a proud old mansion.

A proud old mansion: but would it stand? Could it stand? Above the gray seas patrolled the pilots, across the soughing waves drove the British flotillas, watching. Were the Germans about to come? And the Americans? There was a trickle of war goods moving eastward across the Atlantic, propelled by a current of American sympathy: but sympathy was not yet resolution, and that current was not yet a flood. The bombing of England that turned the hearts and minds of many Americans around had not yet begun. For six weeks after the fall of France, the Americans, as Churchill said later to a confidant, "treated us in that rather distant and sympathetic manner one adopts toward a friend we know is suffering from cancer." There were many people in America—not only isolationists but men high in the Army general staff—who doubted whether Britain would or could hold out against Hitler. In some of the country clubs around Boston and Philadelphia and New York, the members went around to collect secondhand shotguns for the British, whose Home Guard was still bereft of weapons. Some of the Home Guard were given old golf clubs and sticks, presumably to hit prowling Germans on the head. If and when the invasion came, "you can always take one with you," Churchill had planned to say.

Then came the third coincidence, so enormous and shattering in its consequences that, even now, many people, including a number of historians, are unaware of its ultimate portent.

Six weeks had now passed since France had fallen; and Britain still stood, inviolate, increasingly aglow with the spirit breathed by Churchill's words. Franklin Roosevelt made up his mind. He took an important step. He brought in a few confidants that assured him that he, in his constitutional capacity as Commander-in-Chief, could go ahead. This was at the very end of July. Two days later Roosevelt announced to his cabinet that the United States would "sell directly or indirectly fifty or sixty old World War destroyers to Great

Britain." Churchill had asked for such a deal in May. The destroyer were not, in themselves, as important as the gesture, the meaning of the act itself for the world. It meant *the* decisive departure from American neutrality. What Roosevelt did not know, and what Churchill did not know, was that, at the same moment, Hitler had taken his first decisive move in ordering the Germany army staff to plan for an invasion of Russia.

There was method in Hitler's madness. What did he say to the closed circle of his commanders on that day? "England's hope is Russia and America." Against America he could do nothing. But "if hope in Russia is eliminated, America is also eliminated," he said. He was not altogether wrong. Eliminating Russia would destroy British hopes for an eventual conquest of Germany in Europe, and it would strengthen Japan's position in the Far East. In the United States it would also strengthen popular opposition to Roosevelt. There were many Americans who hated and feared communism: the elimination of communist Russia would make Roosevelt's continued intervention on the side of Britain increasingly futile and unpopular. Russia, Hitler said on July 21, 1940, was not yet "a threat." But he was not sure about his prospects of conquering England. Air warfare against England was about to begin; but "if results of the air war are not satisfactory, [invasion] preparations will be halted." So at the end of July 1940, Hitler, after some hesitation, began to consider invading Russia at the very moment when Roosevelt, after some hesitation, made his decision to commit the United States on the British side.

This last day of July in 1940 was not merely an important milestone. It was the turning point of World War II. There followed the climax of the Battle of Britain in the air, which, for Hitler, was indecisive. So far as the American people went, the bombing of Britain solidified their gradually crystallizing inclination to stand by the British. Britain held out; and in November 1940 Roosevelt easily won the majority of his people for a third term. That was the first American presidential election watched by the entire world. When Mussolini attacked Greece at the end of October, Hitler berated him: he ought to have waited until after the American election. When Hitler agreed to invite Stalin's minion Molotov, the Soviet commissar for foreign affairs, to Berlin, Stalin set the date of the visit after the American election.

What followed—Lend-Lease, the Selective Service Bill, the Marines sent to Greenland and Iceland, Roosevelt's order to the Navy to shoot at any appearance of Axis naval craft—was a forgone conclusion. Hitler was shrewd enough to order German commanders to avoid incidents with the United States at all costs. He did not want to furnish Roosevelt with the pretext of a serious naval incident. Eventually his Japanese allies were to accomplish what he was reluctant to do. Five hundred days after that thirty-first of July came another great coincidence. In the snow-covered wasteland before Moscow, the Russians halted the German army just when, in the sunny wastes of the Pacific, the Japanese attack on Pearl Harbor propelled the United States into the war. The Germans and the Japanese would achieve astounding victories even after that: but the war they could not win.

O ne year before Pearl Harbor, Roosevelt had announced that the United States would be the "arsenal of democracy." Churchill had told the American people: "Give us the tools, and we will finish the job." Did he mean this? We cannot tell. It was far from certain that Hitler could be defeated by the supply of American armaments alone. What was needed was the employment of immense American armies and navies in the field. And even that would not be enough. Hitler's defeat could not be accomplished without the armed might of Russia, whereby victory in Europe had to be shared with Russia.

Churchill understood the alternative: either all of Europe ruled by Germany, or the eastern portion of it controlled by Russia. It was not a pleasant alternative. In world politics few alternatives are altogether pleasant. Yet half of Europe was better than none. Had it not been for Franklin Roosevelt during that dangerous summer of 1940, even this alternative would have been moot. Had the United States been led by an isolationist president in 1940, Hitler would have won the war.

—October 1986

THE BIG LEAK

by THOMAS FLEMING

So big was the leak that it might have caused us to lose World War II. So mysterious is the identity of the leaker that we can't be sure to this day who it was . . . or at least not entirely sure.

Blazoned in huge black letters across page one of the December 4, 1941, issue of the Chicago *Tribune* was the headline: F.D.R.'S WAR PLANS! The *Times Herald*, the *Tribune*'s Washington, D.C., ally, carried a similarly fevered banner. In both papers Chesley Manly, the *Tribune*'s Washington correspondent, revealed what President Franklin D. Roosevelt had repeatedly denied: that he was planning to lead the United States into war against Germany. The source of the reporter's information was no less than a verbatim copy of Rainbow Five, the top-secret war plan drawn up at FDR's order by the Joint Board of the Army and Navy.

Manly's story even contained a copy of the President's letter ordering the preparation of the plan. The reporter informed the *Tribune* and *Times Herald* readers that Rainbow Five called for the creation of a ten-million-man army, including an expeditionary force of five million men that would invade Europe to defeat Hitler. To all appearances the story was an enormous embarrassment to a President who when he ran for a third term in 1940 had vowed that he would never send American boys to fight in a foreign war.

It also made a fool or a liar out of Sen. Alben Barkley, the Senate majority leader. On August 18, 1941, after Roosevelt and Churchill had met in Placentia Bay, Newfoundland, Manly had written a story based on another leak, reporting, without documentation, plans for an American expeditionary force. The next day, Barkley had risen in the Senate and denounced Manly for writing a "deliberate and intentional falsehood."

In Congress antiwar voices rose in protest. Alarmed Democratic House leaders delayed consideration of the administration's $8.244 billion arms bill for more than two hours. Republican Congressman George Holden Tinkham of Massachusetts declared that the nation had been "betrayed" and received unanimous consent for his motion to put the story into the *Congressional Record*. "The biggest issue before the nation today is the *Tribune* story," said Republican Congressman William P. Lambertson of Kansas. "If it isn't true, why doesn't the President deny it?" In the Senate, Burton K. Wheeler, a Democrat from Montana and the leading antiwar spokesman, who had predicted Roosevelt would "plow under every fourth American boy," declared that the story proved everything he had been saying.

Although Hitler had crushed France and the rest of Europe except for Great Britain and was now advancing through Russia, most Americans felt no great desire to stop him. The threat from Japan seemed even more remote, although the Japanese were clearly on the march to dominate Asia. Since 1937 their war with China had given them control of virtually the entire Chinese coast. In the summer of 1941 they had seized French Indochina. A majority of Americans favored aid to China and Great Britain, but polls revealed that 80 percent were opposed to declaring war on Germany or Japan. Many viewed with great uneasiness Roosevelt's policy of escalating belligerence with Germany, which had U.S. Navy ships convoying war supplies as far east as Iceland and had already produced three clashes between U-boats and American destroyers.

Congress reflected this public ambivalence. On August 13, 1941, the House of Representatives had come within a single vote of refusing to extend the 1940 Draft Act. Only an all-out effort by the White House staff prevented a catastrophic political defeat. On September 11 Roosevelt reported that the *USS Greer* had been attacked by a German submarine and henceforth U.S. ships had orders to "shoot on sight" any Germany vessel in the proclaimed neutral zone west of Iceland. The President neglected to say that *Greer* had stalked the sub for three hours, in cooperation with a British patrol plan.

As recently as October 27, 1941, Roosevelt had been reduced to using a map, forged by British intelligence, purporting to be a German plan to conquer South America. Without this device he would never have persuaded Congress to relax the Neutrality Act to let American vessels carry arms to British ports.

If the *Tribune* story caused consternation in Congress, its impact at the War Department could be described as explosive. The man who has provided the most vivid recollection is Gen. Albert C. Wedemeyer. "If I live to be a hundred," he told me when I interviewed him in the spring of 1986, "December fifth, 1941, will still seem like yesterday." Although only a major in the War Plans Division, Wedemeyer had already been tabbed by his superiors as a man with a bright future. In 1936 they had sent him to Germany, where he spent two years studying at the German War College in Berlin. When Roosevelt ordered the preparation of the Rainbow Five, the forty-four-year-old major was given the task of writing it.

General Wedemeyer, still erect and mentally alert, recalled the atmosphere he encountered when he walked into the Munitions Building at 7:30 A.M. on December 5. "Officers were standing in clumps, talking in low tones. Silence fell, and they dispersed the moment they saw me. My secretary, her eyes red from weeping, handed me a copy of the *Times Herald* with Manly's story on the front page. I could not have been more appalled and astounded if a bomb had been dropped on Washington."

For the next several days Wedemeyer almost wished a bomb had been dropped and had landed on him. He was the chief suspect in the leak of Rainbow Five, which within the closed doors of the War Department was called the Victory Program. He had strong ties to America First, the leading antiwar group in the nation. Both he and his father-in-law, Lt. Gen. Stanley D. Embick, were known to be opponents of Roosevelt's foreign policy, which they thought was leading the United States into a premature and dangerous war.

Embick and Wedemeyer viewed the world through realpolitik and military eyes. They did not believe the United States should fight unless it was attacked or seriously threatened. They scoffed at Roosevelt's claim that Germany planned to invade South America, acidly pointing out that if Hitler were to land an army in Brazil, his reputed prime target, the Germans would be farther away from the United States than they were in Europe. Both men also knew that America was not prepared to take on the German and Japanese war machines.

At the same time, Wedemeyer and Embick were men of honor, true to their oaths of allegiance as officers of the United States Army. Although they disagreed with the President's policy, there was no hesitation to obey his orders. "I never worked so hard on anything in my life as I did on that Victory Program," Wedemeyer says. "I recognized its immense importance, whether or not we got into the war. We were spending billions on arms without any clear idea of what we might need or where and when they might be used. I went to every expert in the Army and the Navy to find out the ships, the planes, the artillery, the tanks we would require to defeat our already well-armed enemies."

One conclusion he drew from his research was particularly alarming. There was a minimum gap of eighteen months between the present U.S. military posture and full readiness to wage a successful war. To discover this secret splashed across the front pages of two major newspapers for the Germans and the Japanese to read was dismaying enough. But it was the "political dynamite" in the revelation that Wedemeyer dreaded even more.

His civilian boss, Secretary of War Henry Stimson, declared that the man who had leaked Rainbow Five was "wanting in loyalty and patriotism," and so were the people who had published it. Wedemeyer was summoned to the office of John McCloy, Assistant Secretary of War. He was not invited to sit down. He therefore stood at attention. "Wedemeyer," McCloy said, "there's blood on the fingers of the man who leaked this information."

Frank C. Waldrop, at that time the foreign editor of the *Times Herald*, contributes another recollection of that emotional morning in the Munitions Building. He visited the War Department offices in pursuit of another story and encountered a friend on the War Plans staff, Maj. Laurence Kuter. "Frank," a white-lipped Kuter said, "there are people who would have put their bodies between you and that document."

No less a personage than J. Edgar Hoover, the director of the FBI, was summoned to the office of Frank Knox, the Secretary of the Navy. Hoover called in the chief of naval operations, Adm. Harold R. Stark, and Rear Adm. Richmond

Kelly Turner, who had been in charge of preparing the Navy's portion of the Victory Program, and began interrogating them. Hoover asked if there was any dissatisfaction among naval officers with the plan. Turner, exhibiting his talent for political infighting, caustically informed him that all the Navy officers considered Rainbow Five "impractical of consummation" and "ill-advised."

Later in this tumultuous morning two FBI agents appeared in Wedemeyer's office and examined the contents of his safe. Their eyes widened when they discovered a copy of the Victory Program with everything that had appeared in the newspapers underlined. The sweating Wedemeyer explained that he had just done the underlining to get a clear idea of how much had been revealed. The two agents began an interrogation of Wedemeyer and other Army and Navy officers that continued for months.

Several Army staff officers said they strongly suspected Wedemeyer of being the leaker. An anonymous letter, obviously written by an insider and addressed to the Secretary of War, accused him and General Embick. Wedemeyer's prospects grew even bleaker when the FBI discovered that he had recently deposited several thousand dollars in the Riggs National Bank in Washington. He explained it was an inheritance and went on manfully to admit to the FBI that he knew Gen. Robert E. Wood, Charles A. Lindbergh, and other leaders of America First and agreed with some of their views. He often attended America First meetings, although never in uniform.

Agents hurried to Nebraska, the general's home state, to investigate his German origins. They were somewhat befuddled to discover his German-born grandfather had fought for the Confederacy. His Irish-American mother was interrogated and called him long distance to ask him what in the world he had done. She thought he was in danger of being shot at sunrise. General Wedemeyer smiles when he tells the story, but in 1941 he found nothing about his ordeal amusing.

Wedemeyer was not the only officer discomfited. The FBI reported that an Army Air Corps major, who knew Charles A. Lindbergh, sweated profusely, blundered into bad grammar, and displayed other signs of extreme nervousness. "It appears definite that [he] has been involved in some War Department politicking [*sic*] or sculduggery [*sic*] about which he is considerably worried," the agent concluded.

M eanwhile the White House was reacting to the leak in several ways. Although FDR "approved" Secretary of War Stimson's statement, the President refused to discuss the matter at a press conference on December 5. But he allowed reporters to question his press secretary, Stephen Early, who claimed he was not in a position to confirm or deny the authenticity of the *Tribune*'s story. Early blandly commented that it was customary for both the Army and the Navy to concoct war plans for all possible emergencies. Sensing that this was an absurd way to describe Rainbow Five, which included the President's letter ordering its preparation, Early stumbled on to comment that it was also customary to ask the President's permission to publish one of his letters.

The press secretary undercut himself again by admitting that this was an official, not a personal, letter, hence a public document. Then he lamely pointed out that the President's letter made no mention of an expeditionary force—although the report called for seven million tons of shipping and a thousand ships to bring five million men to Europe.

On only one topic did Early seem forthright. He said that the newspapers were "operating as a free press" and had a perfect right to print the material, "assuming the story to be genuine." It was the government's responsibility to keep the report secret. Almost in the same breath he added that other papers were free to print the story, too, depending on whether they thought such a decision was "patriotic or treason."

Obviously Early was practicing what contemporary Washington calls "damage control." After his histrionics with Major Wedemeyer, John McCloy coolly informed Clarence Cannon, the head of the House Appropriations Committee, and John Taber, ranking House Republican, that there were no plans for an American expeditionary force. They brought this assurance back to their colleagues; Cannon declared the whole story, which he implied was fictitious, was designed to wreck the appropriations bill. The next day the House voted the more than eight billion dollars to enlarge the Army to two million men.

In his diary Secretary of the Interior Harold Ickes recorded his outrage at the Manly story. At a cabinet meeting on December 6, Ickes urged the President to punish the *Tribune* and the *Times Herald*. Attorney General Francis Biddle said he thought they could be prosecuted for violating the Espionage

Act. Ickes recorded his bafflement that Roosevelt, although apparently angry, showed no real interest in prosecuting the *Tribune*.

Roosevelt was not motivated by any idealistic opinions about the First Amendment. Later, in June 1942, when a *Tribune* reporter printed certain censored details about the Battle of Midway, the President ordered Biddle to prosecute, and the Attorney General did so, even though he later admitted the case was so weak that "I felt like a fool." A grand jury was convened in Chicago to take up the Midway case, and the FBI at that time contributed more than a thousand pages of materials it had gathered on the Victory Program leak with a suggestion that the jury investigate it as well. In the middle of the hearings, the government dropped the entire case.

In other branches of the government, the reaction to the big leak was quite different. Far from exhibiting the slightest embarrassment, the Office of War Information decided to send the story abroad by shortwave radio as proof of America's determination to defeat the Axis powers. The British, hanging on by their fingernails against German air and submarine offensives, headlined it in their newspapers as a beacon of hope.

On December 7, 1941, the question of Rainbow Five's impact on American politics became moot. Japanese planes swooped out of the dawn sky to devastate the American fleet at Pearl Harbor. The Victory Program had envisaged devoting almost all of America's military strength to defeating Hitler. Japan, in that scenario, was to be handled by defensive strategies short of war. This posture reflected the perceived danger of a German victory over Russia and Great Britain if the United States did not intervene swiftly.

America's military leaders had been worried by Roosevelt's decision in June 1941 to embargo all shipments of oil to Japan when it seized Indochina, a cutoff that the Dutch and British imitated. The military feared that the Allies were goading Japan to the brink of war. When the Japanese sent negotiators to Washington to try to resolve the dispute peacefully, Gen. George Marshall, the Army's Chief of Staff, had urged the State Department to make concessions to keep peace in the Pacific. In his book *Going to War with Japan 1937–1941*, Jonathan G. Utley has described how Roosevelt and Secretary of State Cordell Hull attempted to negotiate a comprehensive agreement with Japan, including its withdrawal from China—a diplomatic goal far too ambitious in the context of the political and military realities of 1941.

After Pearl Harbor everyone in the United States except the FBI lost interest in the *Tribune* story. But the secret information revealed by Chesly Manly acquired a second life in Nazi Germany. On December 5 the German Embassy had cabled the entire transcript of the story to Berlin. There it was reviewed and analyzed as the "Roosevelt War Plan."

While his military advisers were ingesting it, Hitler wrestled with an immense political decision. Should he declare war on the United States? The Japanese attack on Pearl Harbor surprised him as much as it surprised Franklin D. Roosevelt. The Tripartite Pact signed by the Axis powers in 1940 had never been supplemented by specific agreements about coordinating their war aims. The German foreign minister, Joachim von Ribbentrop, had promised Hiroshi Oshima, the Japanese ambassador to the Third Reich, that Germany would support Japan if it became embroiled with the United States. But neither he nor Hitler envisioned the kind of aggressive assault launched by Japan at Pearl Harbor. Oshima urged Ribbentrop to make good on his promise. Hitler's reaction to Pearl Harbor made it clear that he had no overwhelming sense of obligation to declare war as a result of Ribbentrop's unauthorized assurances.

Theretofore one of Hitler's basic strategies had been to keep the United States out of the war by getting all possible leverage out of the strong isolationist sentiment in Congress and elsewhere. Even after Roosevelt had issued orders to American warships to "shoot on sight" at German submarines, Hitler had ordered Grand Adm. Erich Raeder, the navy's commander in chief, to avoid incidents that Roosevelt might use to bring America into the struggle. After the war Col. Gen. Alfred Jodl, Hitler's chief planner, said that Hitler wanted Japan to attack Great Britain in the Far East and the U.S.S.R. but not the United States. Hitler had wanted "a strong new ally without a strong new enemy."

On December 8, 1941, President Roosevelt seemed to confirm the wisdom of Hitler's policy in his speech to Congress, calling for a declaration of war against Japan. Condemning the attack on Pearl Harbor as a "day of infamy," FDR did not so much as mention Germany. Most historians agree that in the wake of Pearl Harbor, Roosevelt could not have persuaded Congress to declare war on Germany. The nation's rage was focused on Japan.

On December 6, just before Japan launched its attack, Admiral Raeder became a major player in the Reich chancellor's global decision. He submitted to Hitler a report prepared by his staff that pointed with particular urgency to the most important revelation contained in Rainbow Five: the fact that the United States would not be ready to launch a military offensive against Germany until July 1943. Raeder argued that this necessitated an immediate reevaluation of Germany's current strategy. He recommended an offensive on land and sea against Britain and its empire to knock them out of the war before this crucial date. He envisaged further incidents between American naval vessels and German submarines in the North Atlantic and admitted that this could lead to war with the United States. But he argued that Rainbow Five made it clear that America was already a "nonbelligerent" ally of Great Britain and the Soviet Union and that a declaration of war was no longer something Germany should seek to avoid by restraining its U-boats. Moreover, Raeder concluded that Roosevelt had made a serious miscalculation "in counting upon Japanese weakness and fear of the United States" to keep Nippon at bay. He was now confronted with a Japanese war two or three years before the completion of a two-ocean navy.

On December 9 Hitler returned to Berlin from the Russian front and plunged into two days of conferences with Raeder, Field Marshal Wilhelm Keitel, the chief of staff of the Oberkommando der Wehrmacht (usually referred to as the OKW), and Reich Marshal Herman Göring, the commander of the air force. The three advisers stressed the Victory Program's determination to defeat Germany. They pointed out that it discussed the probability of a Russian collapse and even a British surrender, whereupon the United States would undertake to carry on the war against Germany alone.

Meanwhile on December 9, Franklin D. Roosevelt made another address to the nation. It accused Hitler of urging Japan to attack the United States. "We know that Germany and Japan are conducting their military and naval operations with a joint plan," Roosevelt declared. "Germany and Italy consider themselves at war with the United States without even bothering about a formal declaration." This was anything but the case, and Roosevelt knew it. He was trying to bait Hitler into declaring war. On December 10, when Hitler resumed his conference with Raeder, Keitel, and Göring, the Führer's mind was made up. He said that Roosevelt's speech confirmed everything in the *Tribune* story. He considered the speech a de facto declaration of war, and he accepted Raeder's contention that the war with Japan made it impossible for the Americans to follow the grand strategy of defeating Hitler first that had been laid down in Rainbow Five.

On December 11 Hitler went before the Reichstag and announced that Germany and Italy had been provoked "by circumstance brought about by President Roosevelt" to declare war on the United States. His final decision, Hitler said, had been forced on him by American newspapers, which a week before had revealed "a plan prepared by President Roosevelt . . . according to which his intention was to attack Germany in 1943 with all the resources of the United States. Thus our patience has come to a breaking point."

With a little extra prodding from the White House, the *Tribune* story had handed Roosevelt the gift that he desperately needed to proceed with the program outlined in Rainbow Five. Contrary to Raeder's expectations, neither America's military leaders nor the President altered the Europe-first cornerstone of the Victory Program. "That's because it was sound strategy," says General Wedemeyer, who went on to plan Operation Overlord, better known as D-day.

But for a few weeks the big leak developed yet a third life in Germany. The German army—as distinct from the Führer—greeted the *Tribune*'s revelations as a gift from on high. Its offensive against Moscow and Leningrad was faltering in the freezing Russian winter. The generals seized on the Roosevelt war plan to reinforce a suggestion they had already made to Hitler: to pull back to carefully selected defensive positions and give them time to regroup and reinforce their decimated divisions.

In his book *Inside Hitler's Headquarters*, Col. Walter Warlimont, the deputy chief of the general staff, revealed how little information the generals had on the United States, which made Rainbow Five all the more important to them. He told of receiving a phone call from Jodl in Berlin on December 11, 1941.

" 'You have heard that the Führer has just declared war on America?' Jodl asked.

" 'Yes and we couldn't be more surprised,' Warlimont replied.

" 'The staff must now examine where the United States is most likely to employ the bulk of her forces initially, the Far East or Europe. We cannot take further decisions until that has been clarified.'

" 'Agreed,' Warlimont said. 'But so far we have never even considered a war against the United States and so have no data on which to base this examination.'

" 'See what you can do,' Jodl said. 'When we get back tomorrow we will talk about this in more detail.' "

On December 14 the OKW staff submitted to Hitler a study of the "Anglo-Saxon war plans which became known through publication in the Washington *Times Herald*." The analysts concluded that to frustrate the Allies' objectives, Germany should choose a "favorable defensive position" and terminate the Russian campaign. Next Hitler should integrate the Iberian Peninsula, Sweden, and France within the "European fortress" and begin building an "Atlantic wall" of impregnable defenses along the European coast. The "objective of greatest value" should be the "clearing of all British and Allied forces out of the Mediterranean and the Axis occupation of the whole of the northern cost of Africa and the Suez Canal."

Admiral Raeder and Reich Marshal Göring joined in this recommendation in the most emphatic fashion. They told Hitler that in 1942 Germany and Italy would have "their last opportunity to seize and hold control of the whole Mediterranean area and of the Near and Middle East." It was an opportunity that "will probably never come again." To everyone's delight Hitler agreed to these proposals. On December 16 the German Army's supreme command issued Directive No. 39, calling for the cessation of offensive operations against Russia and withdrawal to a winter line.

Between the time he approved these orders and their release by the supreme command, Hitler had returned to the Russian front, where he was astonished and enraged to find his armies reeling back under assaults from Russian armies whose existence his intelligence officers had failed to detect. When Directive No. 39 reached him, he flew into a rage and summoned Col. Gen. Franz Halder, the chief of staff of the German Army, and Field Marshal Walther von Brauchitsch, the commander in chief, and hysterically berated them. He declared that a "general withdrawal is out of the question" and insisted that Leningrad, Moscow, and the Don Basin had to be included in any permanent defensive line. On December 19 he fired Brauchitsch and took over command of the army.

If Hitler had stuck with his original decision and acted to frustrate the objectives of the Victory Program, he could have freed a hundred divisions from the eastern front for a Mediterranean offensive. Against this force the Allies, including the Americans, could not have mustered more than twenty divisions. Germany's best general, Erwin Rommel, was already in Egypt, demonstrating with a relatively puny force what he could accomplish against the British and Australians.

There is little doubt that Hitler could have turned the Mediterranean into a German lake and frustrated the Allied plan to seize Africa and attack Europe from the south. The catastrophic German defeat at Stalingrad would never have occurred, and the Allied attempt to invade Europe at any point, particularly across the English Channel, would have been much more costly.

In 1955 the historian and former intelligence officer Cap. Tracy B. Kittredge reviewed these probabilities in an article in *Proceedings of the U.S. Naval Institute*. From the evidence he presented one can conclude that the leak of Rainbow Five almost lost World War II. This may be overstating the case. But captured documents make it clear that some of the best brains in the German army and navy tried to use the information to alter the course of the war and that only Hitler's stubborn fury thwarted them.

One question remains unresolved. Who leaked Rainbow Five? General Wedemeyer survived the investigation unscathed and went on to high command. He attributes a good part of his salvation to his innocence. But he admits that Gen. George Marshall's trust in him, which never wavered, also had a lot to do with it.

In the ensuing years a good deal of information has surfaced. We now know that the man who passed Rainbow Five to Chesly Manly was Sen. Burton K. Wheeler. In his memoirs Wheeler says he got the plan from an Army Air Corps captain. Senator Wheeler's son, Edward Wheeler, a Washington attorney, recalls that the captain told his father, "I'm only a messenger." The same captain had come to Wheeler earlier in the year to feed him secret information about the appalling weakness of the U.S. Air Force. Senator Wheeler never had any doubt, his son says, that the man who sent the messenger was Gen. Henry H. ("Hap") Arnold, the chief of the Army Air Corps.

In 1963 Frank C. Waldrop published an article recalling his memories of the big leak. He told of having lunch after the war with the FBI man who had directed the investigation. The agent told him the bureau had solved the case within ten days. The guilty party was "a general of high renown and invaluable importance to the war." His motive was to reveal the plan's "deficiencies in regard to air power."

In a recent interview Waldrop added some significant details to this story. They FBI man was Louis B. Nichols, an assistant director of the bureau. Waldrop asked him, "Damn it, Lou, why didn't you come after us?" Waldrop and everyone else at the *Times Herald* and the *Tribune* had hoped that the government would prosecute. They had a lot of information about the way the White House was tapping their telephones and planting informants in their newsrooms that they wanted to get on the record. Nichols replied, "When we got to Arnold, we quit."

Murray Green, General Arnold's official biographer, has vigorously disputed Arnold's guilt. He maintained that all available evidence shows Arnold supported Rainbow Five, which did not, contrary to the imputation, scant a buildup of American air power. Even more significant in Green's opinion was General Arnold's continuing friendship with General Marshall. If the FBI had found Arnold guilty, Marshall would certainly have been told. The virtue Marshall valued above all others was loyalty. It was inconceivable to Green that Marshall could ever have trusted or worked with Arnold again. Forrest Pogue, General Marshall's biographer, seems inclined to agree with this judgment.

The twelve hundred pages of the FBI investigation, made available to this writer under the Freedom of Information Act, are an ironic counterpoint to what Nichols told Waldrop. A memorandum summarizing the investigation, sent to the Attorney General with a covering letter from Director Hoover, on June 17, 1942, concluded: "Owing to the number of copies [there were thirty-five copies of Rainbow Five distributed to the Army, Navy, and Army Air Corps] and the several hundred Army and Navy officers and civilian employees in both the War and Navy Departments having legitimate access thereto, it has not been possible to determine the source. . . ."

A wild card explanation of the mystery emerged in 1976. In William Stevenson's book *A Man Called Intrepid*, about the British spy William Stephenson, the author asserted that the leak was conceived and orchestrated by Intrepid as part of his plan to bring America into the war on Britain's side. "The Political-Warfare Division of the BSC [British Security Coordination, the secret group that Intrepid led, with President Roosevelt's knowledge and cooperation] concocted the Victory Program out of material already known to have reached the enemy in dribs and drabs and added some misleading information," Stevenson wrote. On November 26 James Roosevelt, the President's son, supposedly told Intrepid that the Japanese negotiations had collapsed and war was inevitable. The Army Air Corps captain was sent to Wheeler with the supposedly fake document to create a newspaper story that would provoke Hitler into a declaration of war.

The only verifiable fact in this version is the date, November 26, 1941. That was indeed the day that negotiations with Japan broke down. But it is clear from the reaction of Stimson and others in the War Department that they did not regard Rainbow Five as material already known to the enemy. The rest of Intrepid's story must be dismissed as fabrication.

Nevertheless, Stephenson's story suggests in a murky way the identity of the man who may have engineered the leak. "I have no hard evidence," General Wedemeyer told me, "but I have always been convinced, on some sort of intuitional level, that President Roosevelt authorized it. I can't conceive of anyone else, including General Arnold, having the nerve to release that document."

Not everyone accepts this idea. Forrest Pogue says he never got a hint of it from his many conversations with General Marshall, while writing his biography. Pogue says he is inclined to doubt high-level conspiracy theories. Frank Waldrop says, "I'd like to believe it, because that confrontation with Larry Kuter in the Munitions Building bothered me for a long time." Nevertheless, Waldrop finds it hard to believe that FDR would have "thrown gasoline on a fire." That was the way he and other isolationists regarded the political impact of the leak.

But no other explanation fills all the holes in the puzzle as completely as FDR's complicity. Although Intrepid's specific claim to have concocted the leak is preposterous, his presence in the United States and his purpose—to bring America into the war with Germany—are admitted facts. That he was here with the knowledge and connivance of the President of the United States is also an admitted fact. Would a President who had already used faked maps and concealed from Congress the truth about the naval war in the North Atlantic hesitate at one more deception—especially if he believed that war with Japan was imminent?

This explanation enables us to understand why General Marshall, who was told of the deception soon after it was launched, never blamed Arnold. It explains FBI Assistant Director Nichols's cryptic admission that the bureau "quit" when it "got as far" as General Arnold. Nichols would seem to have been implying that the FBI knew the real leaker was someone above Arnold in the chain of command. The explanation also makes sense of Marshall's continuing trust in Wedemeyer, on whom such dark suspicions had been cast. It also explains Roosevelt's reluctance to prosecute the *Tribune*. What Intrepid's story tells us is the purpose of the leak: to goad Hitler into that desperately needed declaration of war.

Only FDR and a handful of other men, all of whom have joined him in the shadows, could confirm this scenario. If it is true, it is an extraordinary glimpse into the complex game Franklin D. Roosevelt was playing on history's chessboard in the closing weeks of 1941.

—December 1987

PEARL HARBOR: WHO BLUNDERED?

by COLONEL T. N. DUPUY

Though war with Japan was expected momentarily, and four carriers of the Imperial Navy were ominously unaccounted for, no one thought to protect our most important Pacific base from surprise attack. Why?

Precisely at 7:55 A.M. on Sunday, December 7, 1941, a devastating Japanese aerial attack struck the island of Oahu, Territory of Hawaii. When it was over, the battleships of our Pacific Fleet, moored by pairs in their Pearl Harbor base, had received a mortal blow. Our army air strength in Hawaii—the Japanese found its planes ranged neatly wing to wing on airfield ramps—was a tangled mass of smoking wreckage.

The worst disaster in the military annals of the United States had ushered us into World War II. As in most wars, the political and diplomatic background was so complex and confused as to defy definitive analysis—though this has not prevented historians and others from making the attempt. But as to the disaster itself, the military record is clear.

A well-planned and brilliantly executed surprise attack by Japanese carrier-based aircraft was launched against the major American bastion in the Pacific. The United States government, its senior military leaders, and its commanders in Hawaii had had sufficient information to be adequately warned that an attack was possible, and had had time to be prepared to thwart or to blunt the blow. The information was largely ignored; the preparations were utterly inadequate.

Someone had blundered. Who? And how?

At the moment of the attack four professional military men filled posts of vital importance. In Washington, General George C. Marshall, Chief of Staff, was responsible for the entire United States Army and all of its installations. In a nearby office sat his Navy counterpart, Admiral Harold R. Stark, Chief of Naval Operations. On the Hawaiian island of Oahu, Lieutenant General Walter C. Short commanded the Hawaiian Department, the Army's most vital overseas outpost. Commanding the United States Pacific Fleet was Rear Admiral Husband E. Kimmel; his headquarters was also on Oahu, overlooking the great Navy base at Pearl Harbor.

Marshall, product of the Virginia Military Institute, had a well-deserved reputation for brilliant staff work under Pershing in France in World War I. Later he had taken a prominent part in developing the Army's Infantry School at Fort Benning, Georgia. Short, a graduate of the University of Illinois, had entered the Army from civilian life in 1901. Early in 1941 he had been chosen by Marshall to command the Hawaiian Department.

Both Stark and Kimmel had graduated from the United States Naval Academy at Annapolis—Stark in 1903, Kimmel a year later. Both had risen to their high positions in the Navy following exemplary command and staff service at sea and on shore. Close personal friends, both were highly respected by their naval colleagues.

The thinking and attitudes of these four men were shaped by two decades of unanimous opinion among American soldiers and sailors that someday Japan would clash with the United States in a struggle for predominance in the vast Pacific Ocean. All accepted without question the basic elements of U.S. doctrine for the defense of the Pacific in such a war.

The doctrine was that the United States Navy—and in particular its Pacific Fleet—was the essential element to American success in a Pacific war. Immobilization or destruction of that fleet would be the greatest damage Japan could inflict on the United States. Upon the Army lay the responsibility for furthering the offensive powers of the fleet by protecting its great Pearl Harbor base; by safeguarding the Panama Canal, the Navy's life line from the Atlantic to the Pacific; and by defending the advanced Philippine delaying position, which in military opinion was likely to be Japan's initial target.

Since 1939 the top military authorities of the nation,

including President Franklin D. Roosevelt, had understood the almost inexorable logic of events that pointed to our eventual involvement either in the conflict which Hitler had began in Europe or that in Asia between Japan and China—or both. And under Roosevelt's skillful guidance the nation, albeit grudgingly, was very slowly building up its military strength.

As 1941 rolled along it became apparent, even to the man in the street, that the most pressing danger lay in the Far East. Our diplomatic relations with Japan were worsening; by November they appeared to be almost at the breaking point. The long-continued diplomatic bickering between the two nations on a variety of subjects had resulted in the arrival in Washington of a special envoy, Saburo Kurusu, who—with Ambassador Kichisaburo Nomura—had on November 20 presented the State Department with a document that was practically an ultimatum.

Japan would acquiesce to our government's demands that she withdraw from Indochina only upon "establishment of an equitable peace in the Pacific area" and, further, upon "supply to Japan [by the U.S. of] a required quantity of oil."

In 1940 our cipher experts had cracked the Japanese secret codes—a cryptoanalytical procedure known in the War Department as "Magic." Hence our government knew that the envoys had received instructions to press for American acceptance of this "final proposal" by November 25. The ambassadors had been warned that for reasons "beyond your ability to guess" this was essential, but that if the "signing can be completed by the 29th" the Imperial Japanese government would wait. "After that things are automatically going to happen."

It was also known through Magic radio intercepts that a large proportion of Japanese military strength—land, sea, and air—was concentrating in the Indochina and South China Sea areas. No evidence of aircraft carriers had been found, however, either in those areas or in the Japanese mandated islands. Intelligence agencies, monitoring Japanese radio traffic, considered it probable that the carriers were still in their home waters, but they were not certain.

On this basis Marshall, Stark, and their respective staffs concluded that the Japanese were preparing to strike in Southeast Asia; this threat, of course, included the Philippine Commonwealth. Accordingly our Army and Navy commanders in the Philippines and at Guam had been specifically warned. The commanders in Hawaii, Panama, Alaska, and on the West Coast were kept informed of important developments.

This was the situation as Marshall and Stark saw it early on November 25. From that time on events succeeded one another with increasing rapidity, both in Washington and in Hawaii. This is how they unfolded:

Washington, Tuesday, November 25

Marshall and Stark attended a "War Council" meeting with the President, Secretary of State Cordell Hull, Secretary of War Henry L. Stimson, and Secretary of the Navy Frank Knox. Were the Japanese bluffing? Hull thought not; rejection of their terms would mean war. "These fellows mean to fight," he told the group. "You [Marshall and Stark] will have to be prepared."

Adequate preparation could not be guaranteed by either service chief. The great draft army was still only a partly disciplined mass. The Navy, better prepared for an immediate fight, was still far from ready for an extended period of combat. Marshall urged diplomatic delay. If the State Department could hold war off for even three months, the time gained would be precious, especially in the Philippines, where Douglas MacArthur's newly raised Commonwealth Army was only partly organized and equipped.

Perhaps the State Department's formula—*modus vivendi* they called it—which had been sent by cable to our British, Chinese, Australian, and Dutch allies for comment—could gain the needed time. This was a proposal for a three-month truce in Sino-Japanese hostilities, during which the United States, in return for Japan's withdrawal from southern Indochina, would make limited economic concessions to her.

It was evident to all concerned that otherwise hostilities were almost certain to break out within a few days. The President, noting Japan's proclivity for attacking without a declaration of war, impressed on all concerned that if war came, it must result from an initial blow by Japan. How, then, asked Roosevelt, could the United States permit this without too much danger to itself?

That evening Stark wrote a lengthy warning to Kimmel in Hawaii, informing him that neither the President nor the Secretary of State "would be surprised over a Japanese surprise attack," adding that while "an attack upon the Philippines would be the most embarrassing thing that could happen to us ... I still rather look for an advance into Thailand, Indochina, Burma Road areas as the most likely." Marshall reviewed the incoming and outgoing messages to overseas commanders, and busied himself with the almost numberless duties of his most important task: preparing our Army for combat.

Honolulu, Tuesday, November 25

Kimmel and Short had more than a passing interest in the status of our negotiations with Japan. Admiral Kimmel had been kept informed of the increasingly strained relations by frequent frank and newsy letters from Admiral Stark. One of these, dated November 7, had said in part: "Things seem to be moving steadily towards a crisis in the Pacific. ... A month may see, literally, most anything ... It doesn't look good."

Admiral Kimmel undoubtedly was thinking of that letter when he reread the official radio message which he had received the day before, November 24: "Chances of favorable outcomes of negotiations with Japan very doubtful ... A surprise aggressive movement in any direction including attack on Philippines or Guam is a possibility. Chief of Staff has seen this dispatch, concurs and requests action addressees to inform senior Army officers their areas. Utmost secrecy necessary in order not to complicate an already tense situation or precipitate Japanese action."

Admiral Kimmel promptly sent a copy of the message to General Short. He had standing instructions to show such messages to the Army commander: the most critical messages from Washington were usually sent over Navy channels because the Army code was considered to be less secure. The admiral saw no need for further action. After receiving a warning message on October 16 he had taken some measures for a partial alert and reported those promptly to Stark, who replied: "OK on the disposition which you made."

Admiral Kimmel and General Short had a cordial personal relationship, despite subsequent widespread but unfounded allegations to the contrary. They had frequently discussed, officially and personally, the possibility of a surprise Japanese attack and the measures to be taken to prepare for it and to thwart it if it should come. These plans had been approved in Washington. The Navy was responsible for long-range reconnaissance up to 700 miles, while the Army, with its land-based aircraft, was responsible for inshore reconnaissance for a distance up to twenty miles from shore. The Army's new radar would provide additional reconnaissance and air-warning service for a distance of up to 130 miles from Oahu. Periodically the commanders held joint maneuvers to test the plans and the readiness of their forces to carry them out.

They commanded large forces which might soon be called upon to fight, and it was essential that they maintain an intensive training schedule to assure the highest possible standard of combat efficiency. This was a formidable task, since many of their officers and men were inexperienced and untrained, having only recently been brought into our rapidly expanding armed forces. At the same time, as outpost commanders, both Short and Kimmel were well aware of their responsibilities for assuring the security of the fleet and of the island of Oahu.

Moreover, each commander assumed the other knew his business; each assumed the other's command was running on a full-time status. Each felt—as shown by later testimony—that to probe into the other's shop would be an unpardonable and resented intrusion. As a result, the liaison essential to any sort of joint or concerted operation—the daily constant and intimate exchange of details of command operations between Army and Navy staffs—was almost nonexistent. Each commander, then, was working in a partial vacuum.

On the single island of Oahu were concentrated most of the 42,857 troops that comprised the units of General Short's department. Carrying out the intensive training schedule was the bulk of two infantry divisions, less one regiment scattered in detachments on the other islands of the group. Also on Oahu were most of the antiaircraft and coast defense units of the Coast Artillery Command, and more than 250 aircraft, of the Army's Hawaiian air force. Some of these aircraft, aloft on routine training exercises, were being tracked by the inexperienced crews of six Army mobile radar units newly installed at different points on the island.

There was comparable activity at the great Pearl Harbor Navy Yard, on the southern coast of the island, close by the bustling metropolis of Honolulu. Quite a few vessels of the U.S. Pacific Fleet were in port. Here Kimmel, the fleet's commander in chief, had his headquarters, from which he and his staff closely supervised the intense training programs of their ships in Hawaiian waters. The fleet comprised eight battleships, two aircrafts carriers (with a total of 180 planes), sixteen cruisers, forty-five destroyers, twelve submarines, and slightly more than three hundred land-based aircraft. In addition another battleship, an aircraft carrier, four cruisers, and various smaller vessels were temporarily absent, many being in mainland yards for repairs.

The Navy Yard itself was the principal installation of the Fourteenth Naval District; both base and the district were commanded by Rear Admiral Claude C. Bloch, who was a direct subordinate of Kimmel both as base commander and as a Pacific Fleet staff officer—a setup which bred no little confusion and which was not helped by the fact that Bloch was Kimmel's senior in the service, though not in command. Kimmel properly held Bloch responsible for the functioning and local security of all the land-based installations of the fleet in Hawaii, while he himself devoted his principal attention to the readiness of the fleet to function offensively at sea. He considered Bloch to be Short's naval counterpart, so far as local protection of the fleet in Hawaii was concerned. Formal coordination of Army and Navy activities in Hawaii and nearby Pacific areas, however, was done at conferences—fairly frequent—between Kimmel and Short.

[On November 25 (Washington date line), Vice Admiral Chuichi Nagumo's First Air Fleet—six aircraft carriers and 414 combat planes, escorted by two battleships, two heavy cruisers and one light, and nine destroyers—put to sea from Tankan Bay in the southern Kurile Islands. Eight tank ships trailed it. Screening the advance were twenty-eight submarines which had left Kure a few days earlier.

This powerful naval striking force had long been preparing for a surprise attack on the United States Pacific Fleet at Pearl Harbor. It did not, however, have a final directive to carry it out. The First Air Fleet was to leave the Kurile Islands and steam slowly east into the North Pacific to await orders either to attack or, if negotiations with the United States reached a conclusion satisfactory to Japan, to return home.]

Washington, Wednesday, November 26

Before attending a meeting of the Army-Navy Joint

Board, both General Marshall and Admiral Stark had learned that Secretary of State Hull, with the full approval of the President, had made a momentous decision.

During the evening of the twenty-fifth and the early hours of the twenty-sixth, the State Department received the comments of our allies on the *modus vivendi* reply to the Japanese ultimatum. The British, Australians, and Dutch gave lukewarm approval to the proposal for a three-month truce, though in a personal message to the President, Prime Minister Winston Churchill remarked pointedly, "What about Chiang Kai-shek? Is he not having a very thin diet?"

Chiang, in fact, had protested violently against the truce proposal, which, with its relaxation of economic pressure on Japan, could only work to the psychological and military disadvantage of China. The protest, as well as information gleaned from more intercepted messages indicating that the Japanese would accept nothing less than complete agreement to their demands of November 20, caused Secretary Hull to doubt the wisdom of the *modus vivendi*. Obviously, these concessions were inadequate to satisfy Japanese demands, yet, because they would seem like American appeasement they would strike a major blow to Chinese morale.

Hull therefore recommended a different reply, which the President approved. After a calm but firm restatement of the principles which had guided the American negotiations, the new note proposed, in essence: withdrawal of Japanese military forces from China and Indochina, recognition of the territorial integrity of those countries, unqualified acceptance of the National Government of China, and, finally, negotiation of a liberal U.S.-Japanese trade treaty once the other conditions had been met.

At 5 P.M. on November 26 Secretary Hall met with the two Japanese ambassadors and presented this reply to them. Special envoy Kurusu read the note, then commented that his government would "throw up its hands" and that the American position practically "put an end to the negotiations."

By frequent phone calls, Secretary Hull had kept both Stimson and Knox informed of these rapid developments, and the two service secretaries had passed on the information to their senior military subordinates. So it was that when they met at a Joint Board conference the same day, Marshall and Stark were well aware of the course of events still in progress at the State Department. Agreeing that war was now almost certain, they both felt that it was incumbent upon them to remind the President once more of the dangerous weakness of the Army and Navy and particularly the grave danger of disaster in the Philippines if war were to break out before further reinforcements of men and matériel could reach General MacArthur. They directed their subordinates to have ready for their signatures the next day a joint memorandum to the President which would urge avoidance of hostilities for as long as possible consistent with national policy and national honor.

Late in the afternoon General Marshall held a conference with Major General Leonard T. Gerow, Chief of the War Plans Division, to discuss what should be done the next day, November 27. Marshall had planned to be in North Carolina that day to observe the final phases of the largest maneuvers in the Army's peacetime history; he felt he should carry out that intention, despite his concern about a report that a large Japanese troop convoy had moved into the South China Sea. The two officers discussed the grave implications of the growing Japanese concentrations in the Southeast Asia region. Even though he intended to be back at his desk on the twenty-eighth, General Marshall authorized Gerow to send overseas commanders a warning in his name if further information next day—the twenty-seventh—should point to the possibility of a surprise Japanese attack.

Honolulu, Wednesday, November 26

Admiral Kimmel received a report from the radio intelligence unit in Hawaii of a strong concentration of Japanese submarines and carrier aircraft in the Marshall Islands. This implied, but did not definitely prove, that some Japanese carriers were there as well. This information was perhaps inconsistent with a somewhat more definite report from the Philippines saying that radio traffic indicated all known Japanese carriers to be in home waters. Neither Admiral Kimmel nor members of his staff saw any need to inform General Short of these reports.

Short, meanwhile, had received an official message directing him to send two long-range B-24 bombers—due from the mainland—to photograph and observe the Japanese bases of Truk in the Caroline Islands and Jaluit in the Marshalls, reporting the number and location of all Japanese naval vessels. He was to make sure both planes were "fully equipped with gun ammunition." But neither mission was ever flown: only one B-24 reached Short, and it was not properly equipped.

[On the high seas, their bleak rendezvous at Tankan far astern, Nagumo's task force was steaming eastward. Radio silence was absolute. High-grade fuel kept smoke to a minimum. No waste was thrown overboard to leave telltale tracks; blackout on board was complete. Only the admiral and a handful of his staff knew their orders; the rest of the command buzzed with speculation like so many hornets.]

Washington, Thursday, November 27

General Gerow, summoned to Mr. Stimson's office, found Secretary Knox and Admiral Stark already there. The Secretary of War felt the time had come to alert General MacArthur in the Philippines. He told his listeners that Secretary Hull had warned him no peaceful solution was apparent. "I have washed my hands of it," Hull had said, "and it is now in the hands of you and Knox, the Army and the Navy."

Stimson added word of a telephone discussion with the President, who, agreeing that an alert order be sent out, desired all commanders to be cautioned that Japan must commit the first overt act of war. All four in Stimson's office then prepared drafts of alert messages to be sent to General MacArthur and Admiral Hart in the Philippines and to Army and Navy commanders in Hawaii, Panama, and on the West Coast.

Early in the afternoon Gerow sent out the warning: "Negotiations with Japan appear to be terminated to all practicable purposes with only the barest possibilities that the Japanese Government might . . . offer to continue."

The message then reiterated Mr. Roosevelt's desire that Japan commit the first overt act. But this, it was pointed out, "should not repeat not be construed as restricting you to a course . . . that might jeopardize your defense. *Prior to hostile Japanese action you are directed to undertake such reconnaissance and other measures as you deem necessary* [italics supplied], but these measures should be carried out so as not repeat not to alarm civil population or disclose intent. Report measures are taken . . . "

The message further directed that, should hostilities occur, commanders would undertake offensive tasks in accordance with existing war plans. It concluded with the caution that dissemination of "this highly secret information" should be limited to the essential minimum.

Stark's message to Navy commanders (as well as to our special naval observer in London, who was to advise the British) was sent at the same time; it opened bluntly: "This dispatch is to be considered a war warning." It related the end of negotiations and the expectation that "an aggressive move" might come within the next few days. Then, in contrast to the more general Army warning, it added the information that known military activities of Japanese indicated they probably intended to launch "an amphibious expedition against either the Philippines, Thai or Kra peninsula or possibly Borneo." Like the Army warning, it directed execution of existing war plans in the event of hostilities. Naval commanders in the continental United States, Guam, and Samoa were cautioned to take antisabotage measures.

If read together, these two messages definitely pointed a finger at Southeast Asia as the expected enemy target. This, of course, in no way excuses any of the subsequent actions of our commanders in Hawaii, whose paramount responsibility was the security of their post. But it must have influenced their thinking.

Honolulu, Thursday, November 27

The official warnings from Washington confirmed to Short and Kimmel the seriousness of the international situation. Short, who noted that he was expected to report the measures he was taking, sent the following reply: "Report Department alerted to prevent sabotage. Liaison with the Navy."

The Hawaiian Department plans provided for three kinds of alert. Number 1, which was what Short had ordered, was to guard against sabotage and uprisings—long a preoccupation of Hawaiian commanders because of the high proportion of Japanese in the Islands. Number 2 included security against possible isolated, external air or naval attacks. Number 3 was a full-scale deployment for maximum defense of the Islands, and particularly of Oahu—heart of the military organization. Only in the two higher states of alert was ammunition to be distributed to the antiaircraft batteries; in Alert No. 1 all ammunition was to be kept stored in the dumps. Under Alert No. 1, planes would be parked closely for easy guarding; under the others they would be dispersed.

General Short felt he was confirmed in his concern over sabotage when his intelligence officer—or G-2—presented a message from the War Department G-2, warning that "subversive activities may be expected."

In obedience to the instruction to make such reconnaissance as he might "deem necessary," Short did, however, order his newly installed radar stations to operate daily from 4 A.M. to 7 A.M.; these were the dawn hours when surprise attack was most likely. Further reconnaissance, he felt, was the Navy's responsibility. He didn't know that Kimmel was having troubles of his own in attempting any sustained offshore reconnaissance. Nor was Kimmel aware that Short's radar was operating only on a curtailed basis.

Kimmel pondered over what steps he should take. Though he was already alerted to some extent, he knew that for the moment he could do little in the way of "defensive deployment" in his war plan tasks—most specifically, raids into the Japanese mandated islands. Should he then prepare for an attack against Oahu? The Washington message implied that this was not a probability. Even so, he didn't have sufficient planes for a 360-degree, distant reconnaissance from Oahu.

In compliance with instructions from Washington, Kimmel was sending some Marine planes to Wake and Midway islands. He decided that the two carrier task forces he was ordering to carry out this instruction could, en route, conduct long-range searches to the west, over the direct route from Japan to Oahu.

Task Force 8, under Vice Admiral William F. Halsey, including the carrier *Enterprise* and three cruisers, was leaving that day. In conference with Halsey before departure, Kimmel showed him the "war warning" message. Halsey asked how far he should go if he met any Japanese ships while searching. "Use your common sense," was Kimmel's reply. Halsey, it is understood, commented that these were the best orders he could receive, adding that if he found as much as one Japanese sampan, he would sink it. Kimmel, by making no further comment, apparently acquiesced.

Pending the arrival of Halsey at Wake, Kimmel sent orders to a patrol plane squadron based on Midway to proceed to Wake and return, searching ocean areas and covering a 525-mile area around Wake itself.

Kimmel felt that he had done all he could in that line without completely halting fleet training and exhausting the pilots of his relatively weak air command. But he did order immediate attack on any and all unidentified submarines discovered in the vicinity of Oahu and other fleet operating zones. Neither then nor later, apparently, did he check on the local security measures undertaken by Admiral Bloch's command, nor did he suggest any coordination between Bloch and Short.

[Nagumo's force was steady on a course laid between the Aleutians and Midway Island, the carriers in two parallel rows of three each. Battleships and cruisers guarded the flanks, destroyers screened wide, and submarines were scouting far ahead.]

Washington, Friday, November 28

General Marshall, back from his North Carolina inspection, was briefed by Gerow on the previous day's happenings. He read and approved the joint memorandum, already signed by Admiral Stark, which urged on the President the need for gaining time, particularly until troops—some already at sea and nearing Guam, others about to embark on the West Coast—could reach the Philippines. He also approved the warning message Gerow had sent to the overseas commanders.

At noon he attended the President's "War Council" meeting at the White House. The implications of a large Japanese amphibious force, known to be sailing southward through the South China Sea, were discussed. British Malaya, the Netherlands East Indies, and the Philippines were potential targets, the invasion of which would immediately involve us in war. But unless Congress should previously declare war, the United States could not attack this force. It was agreed that the President should send a message to Emperor Hirohito urging him to preserve peace, and that Mr. Roosevelt should also address Congress, explaining the dangers being created by this Japanese aggressive action. The President then left for a short vacation at Warm Springs, Georgia, directing his advisers to have the two documents prepared in his absence.

Marshall, back at his desk, thumbed through a sheaf of radio replies to the "war warning" message. Lieutenant General John L. DeWitt, commanding on the Pacific Coast, reported instituting a harbor alert at San Francisco and similar precautions in Alaska in liaison with naval authorities. He requested permission to direct air as well as ground deployment of his far-flung command. It was a long message, contrasting sharply with Short's succinct report of sabotage defense measures in Hawaii. But the Chief of Staff didn't pay much attention; it would be Gerow's job to handle any necessary responses. So Marshall initialed most of the messages and then forgot about them.

Short's message, however, was not initialed by Marshall. He would later testify he had no recollection of ever having seen it, although it bore the routine rubber stamp, "Noted by Chief of Staff."

As for Admiral Stark, he was pushing off a long message to Navy commanders on the West Coast, and to Admiral Kimmel, quoting the Army alert message of the twenty-seventh, including its admonition that Japan must commit the first "overt act."

Honolulu, Friday, November 28

Kimmel read Stark's long quote of the Army's alert message. He was particularly interested in its stress that "if hostilities cannot . . . be avoided the United States desires that Japan commit the first overt act." This appeared to confirm his decision of the previous day: limiting defensive deployment to one patrol squadron cruising from Wake to Midway and sending carrier task forces for local defense of those outposts.

Admiral Kimmel received several other interesting reports. The U.S.S. *Helena* reported contact with an unidentified submarine. An intelligence estimate based on radio intercepts indicated Japanese carriers were still in their own home waters. Another report on intercepted Japanese messages established a "winds code," by means of which Japan would notify its diplomatic and consular representatives abroad of a decision to go to war: "east wind rain" meant war with the United States; "north wind cloudy, war with Russia; "west wind clear," war with England and invasion of Thailand, Malaya, and the Dutch East Indies.

It was all very interesting. However, the admiral never thought of mentioning any of these reports during his conference with General Short that day. They discussed mutual responsibility for security of Wake and Midway—in light of the mixed Army-Navy garrisons at both places. But neither thought of asking the other what action he had taken on the November 27 warnings, nor did either volunteer any information on matters he considered to be of interest to his own service only.

[Admiral Nagumo's fleet spent the day in attempts to refuel in a plunging sea—an operation which, as it turned out, would continue for several days under almost heartbreaking conditions of bad weather.]

Washington, Saturday, November 29

Both General Marshall and Admiral Stark received Magic copies of more intercepted Japanese messages. One of these from Premier Tojo in Tokyo to the ambassadors in Washington was quite ominous: "The United States' . . . humiliating proposal . . . was quite unexpected and extremely regrettable. The Imperial Government can by no means use it as a basis for negotiations. Therefore . . . in two or three days the negotiations will be de facto ruptured. . . . However, I did not wish you to give the impression that the negotiations are broken off. Merely say to them that you are awaiting instructions. . . . From now on, do the best you can."

To Marshall and Stark this was clear evidence indeed that the Japanese were stalling for time only long enough to get their forces ready to attack in the Indonesia-Southeast Asia area. It seemed now only a question of time, as more reports streamed in about Japanese convoys moving into the South China Sea.

For a good part of the morning Stark and Marshall were working very closely with Secretaries Knox and Stimson in preparing and revising drafts of the presidential messages to Congress and to Emperor Hirohito, in accordance with the agreement at the previous day's meeting of the War Council. Finally, about noon, the two secretaries were satisfied, and their proposed drafts were sent to Secretary Hull.

Late in the afternoon both read with considerable interest reports of a warlike speech which Premier Tojo had delivered that day (November 30, Tokyo time). The twenty-ninth had been the deadline established in the messages from Tokyo to the ambassadors. The speech, while violently warlike in tone, failed to give any indication of Japanese intentions.

Honolulu, Saturday, November 29
Things were generally quiet on Oahu and in the outlying waters, as the Army and Navy both began a weekend of relaxation after five days of strenuous training. There was considerable bustle, however, at the Army's headquarters at Fort Shafter, as well as at Navy headquarters at nearby Pearl Harbor. General Short approved a message in reply to the latest sabotage warning from Washington, outlining in detail the security measures which had been taken. Admiral Kimmel received another message from Washington reminding him once more that he was to be prepared to carry out existing war plans in the event of hostilities with Japan. Thus, once again, the two commanders were reminded of the alert messages they had received on the twenty-seventh, and once again they found themselves satisfied with the actions they had then taken.

[In the North Pacific Admiral Nagumo's fleet continued refueling.]

Washington, Sunday, November 30
General Marshall, returning from his usual Sunday morning horseback ride at Fort Myer, found another intercepted Japanese message awaiting him; the Foreign Ministry was cautioning its envoys in Washington to keep talking and "be careful that this does not lead to anything like a breaking-off of negotiations." He agreed with G-2's conclusion that the Japanese were stalling until their South China Sea assault was ready.

Stark, at his desk, was called that morning by Secretary of State Hull, gravely concerned about Premier Tojo's warlike speech. The Secretary told him he was going to urge the President's return from Warm Springs. A later call from Hull informed Stark that President Roosevelt would be back Monday morning; Stark must see the President and report on the naval developments in the Far East.

Honolulu, Sunday, November 30

General Short, in light of his instructions "not to alarm the civil population, "must have been annoyed to read the Honolulu *Advertiser* headlines that morning: "Hawaii Troops Alerted." There wasn't anything he could do about it, however; even the limited nature of his Alert No. 1 would draw newspaper attention in a critical time such as this. He also read that "Leaders Call Troops Back in Singapore—Hope Wanes as Nations Fail at Parleys" and "Kurusu Bluntly Warned Nation Ready for Battle."

Kimmel ordered a squadron of patrol planes to Midway, to replace temporarily the squadron which he had ordered to reconnoiter about Wake. He was also interested in an information copy of a Navy Department message to Admiral Hart, commanding our Asiatic Fleet at Manila, directing him to scout for information as to an intended Japanese attack on the Kra Isthmus of Thailand, just north of Malaya.

Kimmel didn't think that war could be delayed much longer. He wrote on the top of a piece of paper the words— "Steps to be taken in case of American-Japanese war within the next twenty-four hours," an *aide-mémoire* of the orders he must issue to his fleet.

[The Japanese First Air Fleet was still engaged in the arduous refueling job, while continuing its eastward course at slow speed.]

Washington, Monday, December 1

A busy day. Stark learned from his intelligence staff that the Japanese navy had changed service radio frequencies and call letters for all units afloat—a normal prewar step. He went to the White House with Secretary Hull and briefed the President.

In the afternoon both Stark and Marshall digested an unusual number of important Magic intercepts of Japanese messages. Japan's Foreign Minister was urging his ambassadors to prevent the United States "from becoming unduly suspicious, "emphasizing that it was important to give the impression to the Americans that "negotiations are continuing." Tokyo also had ordered its diplomatic offices in London, Hong Kong, Singapore, and Manila "to abandon the use of code machines and to dispose of them." Japan's ambassador at Bangkok reported his intrigues to maneuver Thailand into a declaration of war on Great Britain.

But most significant was an exchange between Japan's ambassador to Berlin and his foreign office. The ambassador reported that Foreign Minister von Ribbentrop had given him Hitler's unequivocal assurance that "should Japan become engaged in a war against the United States, Germany, of course, would join the war immediately." Tojo promptly told the ambassador to inform the German government that "war may suddenly break out between the Anglo-Saxon nations and Japan through some clash of arms. . . . This war may come quicker than anyone dreams."

And how quickly would that be? This was the question which sprang immediately to the minds of Admiral Stark and General Marshall, the men responsible for readying the armed forces of the United States for the coming clash of arms. They had no way of knowing that the answer lay in a brief uncoded message picked up by several American radio intelligence intercept stations just a few hours earlier. "Climb Mount Niitaka," was the message. No significance could be attached to it, so it never came to the attention of Marshall or Stark. Nor would it have meant anything to either of them.

Honolulu, Monday, December 1

Kimmel and Short held another routine conference. Presumably they discussed at some length the grave international situation. Supplementing the cryptic but alarming official intelligence reports and warnings were the headlines blazoning the Honolulu newspapers.

But neither Kimmel nor Short in their conversation discussed local security precautions or a possible threat to Oahu. Politely but inconclusively they continued discussion of the divided responsibility at Wake and Midway. Kimmel never thought to mention to Short that he had received another Washington warning about the "winds code" and that he had also been informed of the change in Japanese military frequencies and call letters. It never occurred to Kimmel that Short might not have been told about either matter.

Routine training continued in Army posts. General Short was quite pleased that his limited alert—which the War Department had apparently approved—had not interfered noticeably with training programs.

["Climb Mount Niitaka!"

Admiral Nagumo sucked in his breath as the message was laid before him this day. This was it; the prearranged code which meant "Proceed with attack."

Obedient to the signal flags broken out aboard the flagship, the gray ships came foaming about to a southeasterly course, vibrating to the thrust of increased propeller speed. Inside the steel hulls the mustered crews, learning the news, cheered, quaffed sake, and burned incense to the spirits of their ancestors.]

Washington, Tuesday, December 2

Additional Magic intercepts indicated further Japanese preparations for war, with the enemy's known offensive weight still massing in Southeast Asia.

Honolulu, Tuesday, December 2

Kimmel, discussing intelligence reports with his staff, noted the change in Japanese radio frequencies as related in the Navy Department's fortnightly intelligence summary, received late the previous day. The gist of it was that Tokyo was preparing for "operations on a large scale."

Then Kimmel called for intelligence estimates on the location of Japanese aircraft carriers. Captain Edwin T. Layton, his intelligence officer, gave estimated locations for all except Divisions 1 and 2—four carriers.

"What!" exclaimed Kimmel, "you don't know where [they] are?"

"No, sir, I do not. I think they are in home waters, but—"

Sternly, but with a suspicion of a twinkle in his eyes, Kimmel delivered himself of a masterpiece of unconscious irony. "Do you mean to say they could be rounding Diamond Head and you wouldn't know it?"

The conference ended after a discussion on the difficulty of locating a force operating sealed orders while preserving radio silence.

Short met Kimmel that day again. They continued debate over jurisdiction at Wake and Midway.

[Nagumo's fleet was steadily driving south toward Oahu. In

prearranged code—unintelligible to American Magic intercep-
tors—Tokyo had confirmed the target date: "X-Day will be 8
December"—December 7, Honolulu time.]

Washington, Wednesday, December 3

Along with other recipients of Magic information, General Marshall and Admiral Stark noted but attached no particular significance to a pair of intercepted messages made available to them that day.

One, dated November 15, was already old; its translation had been deferred for several days in order to take care of messages considered more urgent. It referred to an earlier message directing the Japanese consulate at Honolulu to make periodic reports on the location of American warships in Pearl Harbor, and requested the Honolulu consulate to step up these reports to twice a week.

No particular importance was attributed to this by Admiral Stark or his senior naval intelligence officers, since the Japanese had long been making efforts to obtain information about the activities and number of ships in harbor at other naval bases on the West Coast and at Panama. The fact that the Japanese wanted more complete data, including exact locations of specific vessels in Pearl Harbor, was assumed to be merely an indication of their thoroughness in evaluating intelligence on America's main Pacific combat force.

The other message was a reply by Prime Minister Tojo to the suggestion of his ambassadors at Washington that peace could perhaps be preserved through a high-level conference—they had proposed former Premier Prince Konoye as the Japanese envoy and Vice President Henry Wallace or Presidential Assistant Harry Hopkins for the United States—at "some midway point, such as Honolulu." Tojo's response, that "it would be inappropriate for us to propose such a meeting," seemed a less significant indication of Japan's immediate intentions than the continuing reports of her movements in and near Indochina.

Honolulu, Wednesday, December 3

Admiral Kimmel noted the continuing and surprising lack of information on Japanese carriers contained in the latest daily radio intelligence summary, which stated that "carrier traffic is at low ebb."

That day, too, he received Admiral Stark's letter of November 25. He agreed with Stark's view that "an attack on the Phillippines" might be embarrassing, but that "an advance into Thailand, Indochina, Burma Road area [was] most likely."

In the afternoon Short and Kimmel conferred. They soon got into a grim discussion of what they could do to carry out assigned war plans when and if war broke out. Both were thinking, of course, of planned naval and air raids into the Marshall Islands and of security measures for Wake and Midway. There was no mention of like measures for Oahu. Nor did Admiral Kimmel think to mention to General Short his latest intelligence reports about the burning of Japanese codes or the missing aircraft carriers.

[Nagumo's planners on the high seas were busy marking on their charts of Pearl Harbor the exact locations of six of the U.S. battle fleet—the Pennsylvania, Arizona, California, Tennessee, Maryland, *and* West Virginia. *The data came from Honolulu, relayed by radio through Imperial Navy Headquarters in Tokyo.]*

Washington, Thursday, December 4

A mixed bag of Magic intercepts available to both Stark and Marshall gave clear indication of Japanese intentions to go to war. Instructions came to Ambassador Nomura to completely destroy one of the two special machines for secret coding, but to hold the other and its cipher key—which should be in his personal possession—"until the last minute." One intercepted message, considered to be relatively insignificant, was to the Japanese consul at Honolulu; he was to "investigate completely the fleet-bases in the neighborhood of the Hawaiian military reservation."

Stark and Marshall concerned themselves with routine activities.

Honolulu, Thursday, December 4

Admiral Kimmel conferred with two of his senior task-force commanders, scheduled to sail the next day on combined training-alert missions. One, under Vice Admiral Wilson Brown, was to proceed to Johnson Island, 700 miles southwest of Oahu, on a joint Navy-Marine bombardment and landing exercise. The other, under Rear Admiral T. H.

Newton, included the carrier *Lexington*. This force was to go to Midway Island, fly off a squadron of Marine planes to reinforce the local garrison, and then rendezvous with Brown at Johnson Island. En route the *Lexington*'s planes would conduct routine scouting flights.

Kimmel's intention was that, should war break out, these forces would be available for raids into the Marshall Island group in accordance with existing war plans. Both task-force commanders understood their war-plan missions; both were aware in general of the tense international situation. Kimmel, therefore, felt he was under no obligation to inform either of Washington's November 27 "war warning" message.

The net naval situation on Oahu now was that the entire carrier force of the Pacific Fleet was either at sea or about to steam and that the approaches to the island from the west would be scouted for several days to come.

Kimmel felt that these steps would ensure a reconnaissance search of a large portion of the central Pacific Ocean, as extensive as his limited aircraft strength would permit. But, from the Hawaiian Islands north to the Aleutians, both sea and air were still bare of American reconnaissance.

Kimmel and Short did not meet that day.

[Admiral Nagumo, watching the intermittent refueling being carried on during the day, was intrigued to learn from Honolulu, via Tokyo, that watchful Japanese eyes were "unable to ascertain whether air alert had been issued. There are no indications of sea alert. . . ."]

Washington, Friday, December 5

Both War and Navy departments were busy compiling data for President Roosevelt on Japanese sea, land, and air strength concentrating in French Indochina and adjacent areas. In an intercepted Japanese message from Washington, Ambassador Nomura told Tokyo that in case of Japanese invasion of Thailand, joint military action by Great Britain and the United States "is a definite certainty, with or without a declaration of war." Another, from Tokyo, reiterated the previous instructions about destruction of codes and coding machines.

Admiral Stark, conferring with staff officers, decided no further warning orders need be sent to overseas naval commanders; the message of November 27 was adequate. All concurred.

Honolulu, Friday, December 5

General Short read with interest a cryptic message from G-2 in Washington to his intelligence officer, directing him to get in touch with the Navy immediately "regarding broadcasts from Tokyo reference weather." So Lieutenant Colonel George W. Bicknell, assistant G-2, gave the general all facts obtainable from his own office and from Kimmel's headquarters. Short was informed by Kimmel of the departure of the two naval task forces of Admirals Brown and Newton.

[While pilots and squadron leaders on board Nagumo's fleet studied and restudied their coming roles, the ships—900 miles north of Midway and 1,300 miles northwest of Oahu—slid slowly down the North Pacific rollers, far beyond the range of any American search plane.]

Washington, Saturday, December 6

Reports of increasing Japanese concentration and movements in Indochina, South China, and the South China Sea absorbed Stark and Marshall, as well as all the other members of the War Cabinet from the President down. Mr. Roosevelt, the service chiefs were glad to learn, had decided that he would personally warn Emperor Hirohito that further aggressions might lead to war and urge the Japanese ruler that withdrawal of his forces from Indochina "would result in the assurance of peace throughout the whole of the South Pacific area."

Late in the afternoon Magic plucked out of the air thirteen parts of a fourteen-part memorandum from Tokyo to the Japanese envoys. This much of the message summarized negotiations from the Japanese viewpoint, concluding that the American note of November 26 was not "a basis of negotiations." The envoys were instructed to handle it carefully, since "the situation is extremely delicate."

Distribution of this intercept was curious. Decoding was completed after office hours. General Sherman A. Miles, Army G-2, saw no need to disturb either the Secretary of War, General Marshall, or General Gerow at their homes. (In passing it might be mentioned that one didn't disturb General

Marshall at home without extremely good reason.) Some Navy people saw the message. Stark, who was at the theater learned of it when he returned home and found that he was expected to call the White House. The President had received the intercept, as had the State Department. The details of the conversation are not known, but presumably the President told Stark, as he had earlier said to Harry Hopkins: "This means war!"

Honolulu, Saturday, December 6

In the daily radio intelligence summary received that morning from Washington, Admiral Kimmel was again struck by the lack of information on the location of Japanese carriers. In other dispatches, however, there was considerable information about different kinds of Japanese activity. He received a copy of Admiral Hart's message reporting on the movement of the two convoys south of Indochina. And he received a message from Washington authorizing him, "in view of the international situation and the exposed position of our outlying Pacific Islands," to order the destruction of classified documents at these islands, "now or under later conditions of greater emergency." Neither the admiral nor any member of his staff saw any need to pass on any information to the Army. Presumably General Short was getting it all through Army channels.

Carefully checking the reported locations of all fleet units and projecting their planned routes for the next twenty-four hours, Admiral Kimmel again made his daily revision of his personal check-list memorandum: "Steps to be taken in case of American-Japanese war within the next twenty-four hours."

Over at Fort Shafter, Army headquarters, the daily staff conference was as usual presided over by Colonel Walter C. Phillips, chief of staff. General Short did not usually attend these meetings. Bicknell, assistant G-2, who seems to have been on his toes those days, reported the Japanese consulate in Honolulu was busily burning and destroying secret papers, significant in light of similar reports throughout the world already noted in the intercepts. The chief of staff and G-2 reported this information later to General Short.

And so Oahu drifted into another weekend: a time of relaxation for both Army and Navy. Short, however, was interrupted by Bicknell early that evening at his quarters while he and his G-2—Colonel Kendall Fielder—and their wives were about to drive to a dinner dance.

Bicknell, with some sense of urgency, reported that the local FBI agent had passed to him and to Navy intelligence a transcript of a suspicious long-distance telephone message. A Japanese named Mori, talking to someone in Tokyo, mentioned flights of airplanes, searchlights, and the number of ships in Pearl Harbor, along with cryptic reference to various flowers—apparently part of some sort of code.

Both the FBI man and Bicknell were alarmed at the implications of this flower code. Neither Short nor Fielder, was disturbed. Short, before they hurried to the car where their wives awaited them impatiently, told Bicknell he was, perhaps, "too intelligence-conscious." In any event they could talk about it again in the morning.

The district intelligence officer of the Navy decided that the transcript should be studied further by a Japanese linguist and so put the FBI report away until morning. Admiral Kimmel was not informed.

[Nagumo's fleet, the wallowing tankers now left behind, was churning southward at twenty-four-knot speed. By 6 A.M. next day it would be 230 miles north of Oahu with its planes thrusting skyward. And at dawn, five midget two-man submarines—disgorged from five large Japanese submarines gathered offshore that night—poked their way around Diamond Head, Pearl Harbor-bound.]

Washington, Sunday, December 7

By 8 A.M. the last part of the Japanese memorandum—Part Fourteen—had been intercepted, transcribed, and was ready for distribution. Both Army and Navy intelligence officers were slightly surprised at its mild tone: "The Japanese Government regrets . . . that it is impossible to reach an agreement through further negotiations."

Stark got it in his office. Marshall was taking his Sunday morning recreational ride at Fort Myer: the message would await his arrival—usually at about 11 A.M. All others concerned got it. Meanwhile two other messages had been intercepted by Magic, and Colonel Rufus Bratton, executive officer in G-2, was so upset by them he tried vainly to get them to the chief of staff.

One of the messages ordered the embassy to destroy immediately its one remaining cipher machine plus all codes and secret documents. The other read: "Will the Ambassador please submit to the United States Government (if possible to the Secretary of State) our reply to the United States at 1 P.M. on the 7th, your time."

It will be remembered that General Marshall did not take kindly to interruptions in his off-duty hours. So, despite the limited area of his ride—an automobile or motorcycle from Fort Meyer headquarters could have intercepted him in fifteen minutes at most—not until his return to his quarters at ten-thirty did Marshall learn that an important message was awaiting him. He reached his office in the Munitions Building at about 11:15, to find General Gerow, General Miles, and Colonel Bratton there. Bratton handed him the three intercepted messages—the memorandum, the instructions to destroy codes and papers, and the instruction to deliver the Japanese answer at 1 P.M. precisely.

Marshall read quickly but carefully, as was usual with him. Then— "Something is going to happen at one o'clock," he told the officers. "When they specified a day, that of course had significance, but not comparable to an hour."

He immediately called Stark, who had read all three messages. A warning shall be sent at once to all Pacific commanders, Marshall felt. Stark hesitated; he felt all had already been alerted. Marshall stated that in view of the "one o'clock" item he would apprise Army commanders anyway.

Hanging up, he reached for a pencil and drafted his instruction to DeWitt, Western Defense Command; Andrews, Panama Command; Short, Hawaiian Command; and MacArthur, Philippine Command. It took him about three minutes. He read it to the group: "The Japanese are presenting at 1 P.M. E.S.T. today, what amounts to an ultimatum. Also they are under orders to destroy their code machine immediately. Just what significance the hour set may have, we do not know, but be on alert accordingly."

As he was ordering Bratton to send it out at once, Stark telephoned back. Would Marshall please include in his dispatch the "usual expression to inform the naval officer"? Marshall quickly added the words "Inform naval authorities of this communication." He sent Bratton on his way, instructing him to return as soon as the message had been delivered to the message center.

Bratton was back in five minutes; he had delivered the message personally to the officer in charge of the message center, Colonel French.

Marshall, obviously more perturbed than any of those present had ever before seen him, asked Bratton how much time would be consumed in enciphering and dispatching the message. Bratton didn't know. So back he was rushed to find out.

Marshall, it developed, was pondering whether or not he should telephone a warning—especially to MacArthur. Time was running out; not much more than one hour remained. Marshall had a "scrambler" phone on his desk, which permitted secure long-distance conversations with similar phones in the headquarters of overseas commanders; eavesdroppers would hear only unintelligible gibberish. Marshall, however, must have had some private reservations as to the efficacy of the scrambler mechanism, and apparently feared that the Japanese might have some way of deciphering the conversation. A telephone call which could not be kept secret might precipitate Japanese action; it would almost certainly indicate we had broken their secret code. Would it be worth it?

Bratton reported back that the process would take about thirty minutes.

"Thirty minutes until it is dispatched, or thirty minutes until it is received and decoded at the other end?"

Business of rushing back to the message center again, while the big office clock ticked away. Bratton, charging back, announced that the message, decoded, would be in the hands of the addressees in thirty minutes. It was now precisely noon. In Hawaii is was only 6:30 A.M. Marshall, satisfied, made no further follow-up.

Had he done so he would have found out that Colonel French at the message center was having some troubles. To San Francisco, Panama, and Manila the warning sped without delay. But the War Department radio, so Colonel French was informed, had been out of contact with Hawaii since 10:20 that morning. French decided to use commercial facilities: Western Union to San Francisco, thence commercial radio to Honolulu. This was a normal procedure; usually it would mean but little further delay. French never dreamed of disturbing the chief of staff by reporting such trivia. So Marshall's warning was filed at the Army Signal Center at 12:01 P.M. (6:31 A.M. in Hawaii); teletype transmission to San Francisco was completed by 12:17 P.M. (6:47 A.M. in Hawaii), and was in the Honolulu office of RCA at 1:03 P.M. Washington time (7:33 A.M. in Hawaii). Since that was too early for teletype traffic to Fort Shafter, RCA sent it by motorcycle messenger. He would, as it turned out, be delayed through extraordinary circumstances.

Honolulu, Sunday, December 7

Extraordinary circumstances had become almost commonplace on and near Oahu as early as 3:42 A.M. At that hour the mine sweeper *Condor*, conducting a routine sweep of the harbor entrance, sighted a submarine periscope. This was a defensive area where American submarines were prohibited from operating submerged. The *Condor* flashed a report of the sighting to the destroyer *Ward*, of the inshore patrol. For two hours the *Ward* searched the harbor entrance in vain; meanwhile the *Condor* and another mine sweeper had entered the harbor at about 5 A.M.; for some reason the antisubmarine net, opened to permit the entrance of the mine sweepers, was not closed.

At 6:30 the U.S.S. *Antares*—a repair ship towing a steel barge—was approaching the harbor entrance when she sighted a suspicious object, which looked like a midget submarine. The *Antares* immediately notified the *Ward*. At 6:33 a Navy patrol plane sighted the same object and dropped two smoke pots on the spot. The *Ward* hastened to the scene, spotting the sub—her superstructure just above the surface—at 6:40, and promptly opened fire. At the same time the patrol plane dropped bombs or depth charges. The submarine keeled over and began to sink, as the *Ward* dropped more depth charges. Shortly after 6:50 the destroyer sent a coded message that it had attacked a submarine in the defensive sea area.

At about 7:40 Admiral Kimmel received a telephone call from the staff duty officer, reporting the *Ward*-submarine incident. Kimmel replied, "I will be right down." Quickly he completed dressing and left for his headquarters.

Meanwhile, the Army's six mobile radar stations on Oahu had been on the alert since 4 A.M. in compliance with General Short's Alert No. 1 instructions. At 7 A.M. five of these stations ceased operations, in accordance with these same instructions.

At the remote Opana station at the northern tip of the island, Privates Joseph Lockard and George Elliott kept their set on while waiting for the truck which was to pick them up to take them to breakfast. Lockard, an experienced radar operator, planned to use this time to give Elliott a bit more instruction. At this moment an unusual formation appeared at the edge of the screen; Lockard checked the machine, found it operating properly, and at 7:02 A.M. concluded that a large number of aircraft, approximately 130 miles distant, was approaching Oahu from the north. For fifteen minutes Lockard and Elliott observed the approach formation, debating whether they should report it. Finally, at 7:20, Lockard called the radar information center. The switchboard operator informed him that the center had closed down twenty minutes before, that everyone had left except one Air Corps officer, First Lieutenant Kermet Tyler. Lockard reported the approaching flight to Tyler, who thought for a moment; the flight was undoubtedly either a naval patrol, a formation of Hickam Field bombers, or—most likely—a number of B-17's due from the mainland. "Forget it," he told Lockard.

Twenty minutes later—about 7:50—there was a bustle of activity on the decks of the ninety-four vessels of the Pacific Fleet in Pearl Harbor. It was almost time for morning colors on each vessel, and white-garbed sailors were briskly preparing for the daily flag-raising ceremony. Except for one destroyer, moving slowly toward the entrance, each ship was motionless at its moorings.

At 7:55 boatswains' whistles piped, and the preparatory signal for the colors ceremony was hoisted on each ship. At the same moment a low-flying plane, approaching over the hills to the northeast, swooped low over Ford Island, in the middle of the harbor. A bomb dropped on the seaplane ramp, close by the eight battleships moored next to the island. As the plane zoomed upward, displaying the red sun emblem of Japan, it was followed closely by others. By 9:45 some 260 Japanese planes had flashed that emblem over Oahu, and when the dreadful 110 minutes were over, 2,403 Americans—mostly sailors on battleships—were dead or dying; 1,178 more had been wounded; the battle force of the Pacific Fleet had been destroyed, with four battleships sunk or capsized and the remaining four damaged, while several smaller vessels were sunk or damaged severely. The Japanese lost twenty-nine planes, five midget submarines, and less than a hundred men.

One small further incident is pertinent to our assessment of United States leadership in high places just before Pearl Harbor.

The Nisei RCA messenger boy carrying General Marshall's message speedily found himself involved in trouble. Not until 11:45 could he thread his way through traffic jams, road blocks, and general confusion to reach the Fort Shafter signal office, which was itself swamped in traffic by this time.

Not until 2:58 P.M. Hawaiian time—9:58 that evening in bewildered Washington—was the message decoded and placed on Short's desk. He rushed a copy to Admiral Kimmel, who read it, remarked—perhaps unnecessarily—that it was not of the slightest interest any more, and dropped it into the wastebasket.

It had been a pretty long thirty minutes.

Who was responsible?

No disaster of the magnitude of Pearl Harbor could have ever occurred without the failure—somewhere and somehow—of leadership. A total of eight separate official investigations searched for scapegoats, and found them. The disaster remained a political football long after the last three of these investigations. And much confusion and argument still exist.

Yet through this welter of discord, some facts and conclusions stand out. They hold important lessons.

It makes no difference, in assessing responsibility, that exceptional Japanese military skill, shrouded by deceit and assisted by almost incredible luck, accomplished its mission. Nor, indeed, does it matter that—as adjudicated in the always brilliant light of afterthought—Japan might well have inflicted defeat upon our Pacific Fleet and our Army forces in Hawaii regardless of how well alerted they may have been on December 7, 1941.

It makes no difference, so far as responsibility for the disaster itself was concerned, whether the war could have been prevented by wiser statesmanship or more astute diplomacy— though this would have required a wholehearted and unified national determination which did not exist in America in 1941 and the years before. It makes no difference that on December 7 the President and the Secretary of State—like the civilian Secretaries of War and Navy—had their eyes fixed on the Japanese threat in Southeast Asia. They had repeatedly warned the military men that war had probably become unavoidable.

What *does* matter is that the civilian statesmen—however deft or clumsy, shrewd, or shortsighted—performed their difficult tasks of diplomacy and of administration confident that the military men would carry out their professional responsibilities by doing everything humanly possible to prepare for a war so clearly impending. They had every right to expect that—within the limits of scanty means available—the Armed Forces would be ready for any contingency.

The confidence and expectations of civilian leadership and of the nation were tragically dashed that Sunday morning.

Military failures were responsible for Pearl Harbor.

In Washington the most important of these were the following:

1. The War Department staff, over which General Marshall presided, was at the time a complicated but "one-man" shop, where delegation of responsibility was the exception rather than the rule. When Marshall was absent, the operational wheels tended to freeze. This situation was to some extent due to cumbersome organization, to some extent due to the personality of the chief of staff.

2. General Marshall, in a letter to General Short on February 7, 1941, stressed that "the risk of sabotage and the *risk involved in a surprise raid by air and submarine* [italics supplied] constitute the real perils of the [Hawaiian] situation." Yet, although definitely warning General Short on November 27 of the threat of war, and ordering him to report the measures he would take in response, Marshall did not check up on those measures; moreover, he was unaware that Short had done no more than to take routine precautions against sabotage. And General Gerow, heading the War Plans Division of General Marshall's General Staff—as he testified later in taking full responsibility for this slip—had not made any provision for following up operational orders. The net result was that both Marshall and Short remained the whole time in blissful ignorance of a vital misinterpretation of orders.

3. Marshall and Admiral Stark—and indeed all members of their staffs who knew the situation—permitted themselves to be hypnotized by the concrete evidence of the aggressive Japanese build-up in Southeast Asia which threatened our Philippines outpost. This theme, it will be remembered, ran as

background to nearly all the warnings sent Hawaii. Thus succumbing to the illusory diagnosis of "enemy probable intentions," both top commanders ignored the danger implicit in our inability to locate at least four Japanese carriers.

4. Finally, on December 7, having indicated his full realization of the significance of the "one o'clock" intercept—that less than two hours now separated peace and war—and having decided not to use his "scrambler" telephone, Marshall failed to require surveillance and positive report on the delivery of his final warning.

These certainly were grave lapses in leadership. Yet in fairness, it should be noted that the consequences might not have been disastrous if all subordinate commanders had taken adequate security measures on the basis of the instructions, information, and warnings which they had received. To General Marshall's credit one must also chalk up his ability to profit by his mistakes. In less than three months after Pearl Harbor, he completely reorganized the War Department, decentralizing the mass of relatively minor administrative and executive matters that choked major strategical and tactical decisions. His newly created Operations Division of the General Staff—which he aptly termed his "command post"—ensured coordinated action and direction of Army activities in theaters of war all around the globe. On Oahu the situation was less ambiguous: military leadership at the top failed utterly.

The story of the Pearl Harbor disaster has more significance than mere passing memorials to the brave men who lost their lives that day. If the lessons are heeded, our surviving descendants may never again have to commemorate another "day of infamy."

—February 1962

THE DEFENSE OF WAKE

by PETER ANDREWS

Their High Command abandoned them. Their enemy thought they wouldn't fight. But a few days after Pearl Harbor, a handful of weary Americans gave the world a preview of what the Axis was up against.

The Japanese attack on Pearl Harbor on December 7, 1941, was only one blow in an offensive without parallel in warfare. Within hours after the bombs had crashed into Battleship Row, Japanese forces struck at twenty-nine targets along a three-thousand-mile front that stretched from the central Pacific to the South China Sea. Destroyers shelled American installations on Midway Island, and airplanes spilled their bombs over Clark and Iba airfields in the Philippines, wiping out half the American air forces there in a single raid. On December 8 the Japanese army seized the international settlement in Shanghai, invaded Malaya in a drive toward Singapore, and marched into Thailand. Bangkok fell without opposition on the following day just as Japanese troops were landing on Tarawa and Makin in the Gilbert Islands. The operational plans of the Japanese High Command called for the swift occupation of the Philippines, Guam, Hong Kong, Malaya, Burma, the Bismarck Archipelago, Java, Sumatra, Borneo, Celebes, and Timor as its first major conquests.

Well down on the list of secondary objectives was Wake, a scruffy atoll in the central Pacific that the Japanese planned to use as an advanced base for patrol planes to support their thrust at Midway. In allotting forces to the task, the Japanese assigned 450 assault and garrison troops under the command of Rear Adm. Sadamichi Kajioka. If the force was small, it was considered adequate. Wake's three square miles were known to be manned by a scattering of inexperienced Marines. And throughout the Far East the Americans were not putting up much of a fight. The Marine detachments at Peking and Tientsin in China had already been herded off to detention camps without firing a shot. The 153 Marines on Guam, having nothing heavier with which to defend themselves than four .30-caliber machine guns, had surrendered after a few hours of disorganized scuffling. On the same day that Guam had toppled into the Japanese harvest basket, two landings on Luzon in the Philippines had been virtually unopposed. The Japanese naval command, which had not suffered a reversal or lost a ship of the line since the Russo-Japanese War, expected the reduction of Wake to be little more than a brisk afternoon's work.

Until the development of the long-range airplane, Wake was a desolate point of land in the central Pacific that held scant interest for a major, internationally minded power. Formed by the rim of a submerged volcano, Wake consists of three tiny atolls: the main island, shaped like a ragged *V*, with two smaller spits trailing a few yards behind the northern and southern ends. Seen from the air, Wake gives the appearance of a broken wishbone tossed aside after Thanksgiving dinner. It has a mean altitude of twelve feet and affords neither fresh water nor edible vegetation. It was discovered in 1586 by the Spanish explorer Alvaro de Mendaña, who apparently thought so little of his find that he did not bother to name it. That honor was left to a British sea captain named William Wake, who came upon the main island in 1786. The smaller atolls, Wilkes on the north and Peale on the south, were named after members of an American expedition that conducted a brief geological survey there in 1841. (Following military usage, "Wake" refers to the grouping while "Wake Island" refers only to the main island.) The United States claimed this dreary triptych for itself in 1899, when the gunboat *Bennington* sent a landing party ashore, raised the flag, fired off a cannon, and sailed away. Except for the occasional party of Japanese hunters shooting birds or the storm-lost mariner searching for water he would not find, Wake, in the three and a half centuries since its discovery, heard only the roar of the surf.

Useless to vessels of sail or steam, Wake, located 1,025 miles from Midway and 1,300 miles from Guam, suddenly emerged as an important link in the American air route across the Pacific. Pan American Airways obtained a permit to build a seaplane refueling stop there for the China Clipper traffic to the Philippines. By the time Pan American started flying passengers between San Francisco and Manila in 1936, the airline had built a twenty-four-room hotel, put in a system of catchments to store rainwater, and started work on a "bathtub garden" for growing fresh vegetables. The accommodations were crude, and to help its overnight passengers kill time, Pan American provided air rifles and ammunition for shooting the particularly hardy breed of long-legged rats that throve on the island.

If Wake was an essential element in America's western reach to the Orient, it was also neatly situated on a line from Tokyo through Iwo Jima and Marcus Island for Japan's anticipated thrust into the central Pacific. In the prewar planning of both Japanese and American strategists, Wake increasingly represented a risk and an opportunity. By 1941 the U.S. Navy had wheedled sufficient money from a parsimonious Congress to build a permanent airfield there. A civilian construction team of 80 men arrived on January 8 to start building an airstrip and base facilities. The crew, which eventually grew to 1,150, was a tough and experienced bunch, many of whom had learned their trade putting up the dams at Boulder and Bonneville. The project foreman was an ex-football player from the University of Washington named Dan Teters. He was reckoned a good boss who kept the work moving with a dollop of Irish charm or a clenched fist, whichever seemed appropriate at the time. Most of the men agreed they had a sweet deal. At a time when a Marine corporal with five years of service was paid twenty-eight dollars a month, a workman could plan on banking at least two hundred dollars. There were morale problems, however. Wake was a desperately lonely place with few pleasures. Liquor was effectively forbidden, and women were generally seen only on the screen at the outdoor movies that were shown six nights a week. Almost every supply ship that left Wake carried workers who had broken their contracts to get off the island. One man went berserk and drowned himself in the ocean.

During February of 1941, Adm. Husband E. Kimmel, an

experienced battleship sailor who had been jumped over thirty-two more senior officers to get the job, took command of the Pacific Fleet. A meticulous, by-the-book officer, Kimmel insisted on neat sailing formations and precise drills. He was not an officer given to great leaps of imagination, but he could recognize a ripe tactical opportunity when he saw one. Wake, with its new and undefended airstrip, was a prize the Japanese would surely reach for in the first days of a war. Kimmel calculated that if an invasion force could be held long enough in the waters off Wake, it would offer a rewarding target for counterattack. At his direction a Marine defense battalion was authorized to be assembled at Wake with orders to dig in and wait.

The battalion commander was Maj. James P. S. Devereux, an eighteen-year veteran of the corps who had seen garrison service in China and Nicaragua. With his balding pate, floppy ears, and a moustache that drooped under a beaked nose, Devereux did not cut a figure out of an enlistment poster. Indeed, he admitted he had been a poor student in school and had enlisted in the Marines because he fancied the red stripe that ran down the trouser leg of the uniform. Nevertheless, Devereux was a tough, no-nonsense commander who bore down on details. One fellow officer said, "He's the kind of guy who would put all the mechanized aircraft detectors into operation and then station a man with a spyglass in a tall tree."

At Wake there were no mechanized aircraft detectors—radar had been assigned, but the equipment never got there—and no tall trees. Devereux made do with what he had. He put his men to work twelve hours a day, building up the tactical defenses of Wake, until his troops said the first three initials of his name stood for "Just Plain Shit," a sobriquet that did not disturb Devereux in the slightest.

Throughout the autumn of 1941 personnel arrived at Wake like officials summoned to a hastily arranged meeting whose function was not clear to the participants. Even Devereux may have been misdirected as to his real mission. Kimmel obviously had a major operation in mind for Wake, but Devereux had been briefed only to prepare against small raiding parties. Although there were no planes based at Wake, by November the buildup had progressed to such a state that the complex was officially designated a naval air station and required a Navy officer as commandant. On the twenty-ninth, with his golf clubs among his luggage, Comdr. Winfield Scott Cunningham landed at Wake to take charge. Cunningham was a somewhat unprepossessing officer who had so little time to familiarize himself with his new command that many Marines never knew he was there until long after the war was over. This unfortunate failure to make his presence felt later led to a bitter and needless dispute among the survivors of Wake in allotting credit for its defense. Officially Cunningham was in overall command of Wake, while Devereux and his battalion were charged with its tactical defense. But in such a small operation, especially when there was nothing to do but fight off the enemy, the niceties of command structure became blurred. As a practical matter the main burden for the defense of Wake fell to Devereux.

On December 4 Wake became as operationally ready as it was going to become with the arrival of Marine Fighting Squadron 211, a dozen Grumman Wildcats under the command of Maj. Paul Putnam. VMF-211 was a microcosm of American military preparedness in 1941. Although the Wildcats had the stubby, pugnacious look that was to become a famous American fighting image of the war, these F4F-3 models were not ready to wage serious battle. They were both new and obsolescent at the same time. Just issued to the fleet, they were strange beasts to the pilots, who were still learning their flight characteristics on the trip out. They did not carry armor plating or self-sealing fuel tanks. The retractable landing gears had to be operated by old-fashioned hand cranks, an annoyance that on a routine flight could fracture a pilot's wrist but something that might kill him in combat. Once the planes had touched down on Wake's crushed coral runway, there were other deficiencies to deal with. The bomb racks did not accommodate the ordnance stored there. No spare parts had been sent ahead, and there were no experienced mechanics in the ground crews. There were no revetments or dispersal areas for the aircraft, and the underground storage area for aviation fuel had not been completed. Putnam could do little but park his planes in the middle of an open runway and complain.

There was much to complain about throughout the command: the list of Wake's inadequacies was a long and dispiriting one. Communications wire had been strung, but most of it was old and frayed. Worse, it was above ground and vulnerable to attack. A fair amount of defensive weaponry had been positioned. It included six five-inch coastal guns, two at each end of the Wake triangle, and a dozen three-inch antiair-craft batteries. But none of these guns had been test-fired or calibrated. Although Wake was supposed to be an observation post for the Pacific Fleet, no long-range reconnaissance aircraft had yet been assigned. But the most debilitating shortage was simple manpower. On paper a battalion called for 43 officers and 939 men. Devereux had less than half of that: 27 officers and 422 men. As a result, much of Wake's armament was useless. The antiaircraft batteries were only partly manned, and there were crews for only half the machine guns. Still, Devereux could take pride in what his men had accomplished. From being defenseless in August, Wake could now muster the firepower equivalent to that of a Navy destroyer.

Following a particularly sharp drill on December 6, Devereux felt he could let up on the seven-day-a-week schedule that had been in effect since he arrived. Sunday, December 7 (Wake, being on the opposite side of the international date line, was twenty-two hours ahead of Pearl Harbor), was holiday routine.

A few minutes before 7:00 A.M. on December 8, Devereux was shaving in his tent when he heard that the Japanese were bombing Pearl Harbor. As he raced to his office, he ordered the battalion bugler to sound general quarters. Alvin Waronker was, by all accounts, an indifferent bugler. He had gone to music school just to avoid being shipped to Alaska. Waronker rarely got the notes right, and this morning he couldn't remember them at all. He went through the whole catalog of Marine music, including pay call, church call, and fire call, until he happened on the correct one. The Marines turned out in considerable disarray, and a few appeared with sand buckets and fire fighting equipment. But Devereux passed the word that this was no drill, and within thirty minutes all posts reported ready for action.

The men at Wake were in the war, but no one knew when or how that war would reach them. Devereux and Teters did not want to halt vital construction because of an unconfirmed radio broadcast, so military and civilian work parties resumed while Marine guards stayed on alert. Major Putnam faced the hardest decision. He had twelve new Wildcats bunched on the runway. If he dispersed his planes onto open ground, some of them would certainly be damaged, and without any spare parts a damaged Wildcat was no different from a destroyed one. He took the risk of leaving eight planes on the runway while four stayed aloft, patrolling the area. If Putnam had a week, even a few days, he might have been able to protect his planes on the ground. He had less than four hours.

In war, bad luck is the inevitable lot of the ill-prepared. Shortly before noon, as four Wildcats, commanded by Capt. Henry Elrod, were beginning the northern leg of their scouting run at twelve thousand feet, thirty-six Japanese medium bombers, unseen by anyone in the air or on the ground, broke through the clouds at two thousand feet. To achieve maximum surprise, the Japanese cut their engines and glided silently toward the target. They need not have bothered. The crashing of the surf on Wake was so constant that no one ever heard an approaching airplane until it was upon him. As the Japanese came in over the airstrip, they found a bombardier's delight waiting for them: eight parked Wildcats stuffed with aviation gas. On their first pass the Japanese tripped their bombs and transformed the airfield into a fire storm of exploding planes and burning gasoline. Several Marine pilots tried to take off, but it was futile. Lt. Frank Holden was cut down before he got more than a few feet. Lt. Robert Conderman almost got to his plane before he was hit by machine-gun fire. Knowing he was dying, Conderman refused aid, telling the medics to look after men who had a chance of surviving. Lt. George Graves managed to climb into his plane, but before he could get the Wildcat cranked up, it exploded from a direct hit. The Japanese raiders split up and methodically began laying waste the island. They leveled the Pan American hotel and touched off stores of aviation gas maintained above ground. As at Pearl Harbor, the Japanese bombing was surgical in its neatness. The bomb craters were a systematic fifty feet apart, but almost none of the bombs landed on the runway. Clearly the Japanese wanted to use it for themselves once they occupied Wake in force.

It was all over in a few minutes. Without suffering a single casualty, the bombers re-formed, waggled their wings in a banzai sign of triumph, and headed back to their home base in the Marshall Islands.

The air section suffered most heavily. Of its fifty-five

officers and men, twenty-three were killed outright or died by the next morning. Eleven more were wounded. Whatever tools, tires, and assorted parts had been around had been blown away. Bad luck continued to plague the airmen of Wake even after the raid was over. When the flight patrol returned, still unaware of the attack, Captain Elrod badly jarred his plane on landing and skewed the propeller. Four days before, Marine Fighting Squadron 211 had arrived with twelve new planes. Now the entire air defense of Wake consisted of three serviceable Wildcats, two damaged ones, and seven flaming wrecks.

Wake faced an enormous damage-control job and turned to Dan Teter's work crew. The record of the civilians at Wake is mixed. Most of the workers did what untrained, unarmed men usually do when they suddenly find themselves in the middle of a battlefield. They hid. Figures are imprecise, but it appears that at least 700 civilians sat out the Battle of Wake hunkered down in the scrub, coming out only to steal food. But immediately after the first raid, about 185 civilians volunteered to serve in any capacity. Some offered themselves for combat duty and scoured the wreckage of the Pan American hotel, looking for weapons with which to arm themselves. Eventually perhaps as many as 400 offered to take their chances along with the Marines at least some of the time. Their contribution was invaluable. Working all day and through the night, crews set about digging foxholes, scooping out bomb shelters, and repairing communications wire. By dawn eight bombproof revetments had been completed to protect the remaining Wildcats. Meanwhile, Lt. John Kinney and Tech. Sgt. William Hamilton, by scavenging parts from destroyed planes, were able to make one more Wildcat serviceable.

C alculating the next Japanese air attack was a question of simple, stark mathematics. If the bombers took off from the Marshall Islands at dawn, they could be expected sometime after 11:00 A.M. They arrived at 11:45. But this time they were spotted by a ground lookout, and three rifle shots fired in quick succession—the only effective air-raid warning system Wake ever had—alerted the defense. Lt. David Kliewer and Sergeant Hamilton, flying the morning patrol run, saw twenty-seven bombers coming in and flung themselves on the formation. One bomber wobbled out of formation, burst into flame, and spun into the ocean. Wake had its first kill. The day before, the Japanese had come in low. This day they stayed up at eleven thousand feet. This was a mistake, because Wake's three-inch batteries, ineffective at low altitudes, could be deadly at a decent height against the tight, well-disciplined formations flown by the Japanese. One bomber was shot down, and four others turned away smoking. But again the Japanese scored heavily. The hospital was destroyed, and the naval air station was badly damaged. Until radio equipment could be transferred to an empty powder magazine, Wake's only communications link to Pearl Harbor was an Army radio truck. Wake was learning to hit back, but it was still taking a beating.

Devereux tried to guess the next Japanese move. He figured that after hitting the air defense and base facilities, they would strike at the antiaircraft batteries, particularly the guns at Peacock Point on the leading edge of Wake Island. Devereux ordered the battery moved, and it took a hundred civilian workmen all night to drag the eight-ton guns six hundred yards away and set up dummies in their place. Devereux's hunch was a good one. The next afternoon the Japanese wasted a bombing run going after the fake guns at Peacock Point and lost two planes to Captain Elrod's attack.

The Japanese had struck at Wake three times by air. Now they would try by sea.

It was about three in the morning on December 11 when sentries staring out to sea first spotted movement on the darkened horizon. As the predawn light grew, Devereux could just begin to make out the shapes of the Japanese invasion force: three light cruisers, six destroyers, four troop transports. It was not an armada, but it seemed enough to do the job. Devereux calculated that the light cruisers carried at least six-inch guns. If the enemy wished to, he had only to stay beyond reach of Wake's five-inch coastal guns and batter the island to rubble at his leisure. Wake's only hope was to sit tight and let the invaders stray into range. Devereux passed the word to hold fire until ordered. He checked with Putnam, who had four Wildcats ready to go at dawn. "Don't take off until I open fire," Devereux said. "I'm trying to draw them in and the planes would give the show away."

By five the Japanese had closed to within eight thousand

yards. We cannot know the mind of Admiral Kajioka standing on the bridge of his flagship *Yubari* as he headed for Wake. He may have been concerned that in attempting a landing without air cover to support the landing force and protect its ships, he was violating a primary rule of amphibious operations. But probably he was confident. His intelligence reports claimed that half of Wake's coastal guns as well as its airplanes had been put out of action. The *Yubari* opened fire at five-thirty as the flotilla cruised from opposite Peacock Point on Wake Island to Wilkes. When there was no response, the *Yubari* closed to six thousand yards and sailed back, casually hurling shells at a moribund enemy. A few minutes after six the invasion force turned once again toward the shore to begin its third firing run.

Cpl. Robert Brown, Devereux's radio talker, could hear batter gunners calling their commander "every kind of dumb son of a bitch" for letting the enemy come so close without giving them a chance to shoot back. But Devereux continued to hold. By six-ten the morning sun had made the sea bright as Japanese flanking destroyers closed to forty-five hundred yards. Devereux gave the command to commence firing.

The five-inch guns at Peacock Point and Wilkes opened up almost simultaneously. The gun crews did not have proper range finders or fire-control equipment, but they had been silently tracking the big ships for almost an hour. Lt. Clarence Baringer stood out on the roof of his post at Peacock Point, directing fire at the *Yubari*. The first salvo was over, and Baringer ordered the range down five hundred. Then he had the cruiser straddled. The *Yubari* turned to run, but at fifty-five hundred yards Peacock's battery caught it with two shells, as gunners like to say, "between wind and water." A destroyer coming up to give support to the flagship took a hit in the forecastle. Together they steamed through their own smoke and beat it for safer water.

The battery at Wilkes, commanded by Lt. John McAlister, had its choice of targets: three destroyers, two light cruisers, and two transports. McAlister took aim at the lead destroyer, *Hayate*. He missed with his first two salvos, but the third scored a direct hit with both shells. For a moment the *Hayate* was covered in a cloud of roiling mist and smoke. As the cloud cleared away, the gunners could see that the ship had been smashed into two pieces. Both halves disappeared beneath the waves with all hands in less than two minutes. McAlister's crew was jubilant with backslapping self-congratulation until Sgt. Henry Bedell, a warhorse who had seen service in China, recalled them to their duties. "Knock it off, you bastards, and get back to the guns. What d'ya think this is, a ball game?" Later the gunners liked to tell each other that the Japanese had retired in such haste because they thought Sergeant Bedell was yelling at them.

Confused and badly mauled, Admiral Kajioka's force regrouped in deep water and headed for home in Kwajalein. It was the first and only time during World War II that an invasion was successfully repulsed by shore batteries. The admiral had little time to muse on the historical significance of his defeat. His battle was not over. Major Putnam's four Wildcats jumped off the runway at the first sound of American gunfire. Their primary mission was the air defense of Wake, and they searched the sky for incoming Japanese airplanes. Surprised to find none there, Putnam went to the attack.

Rigged with pairs of hundred-pound bombs attached to homemade racks, the Wildcats caught up with the retreating ships fifteen miles southwest of Wake. Each pilot dived in, dropped his bombs, and hurried back to rearm and take off again. In all, Putnam's men flew ten sorties. Captain Elrod and Capt. Frank Tharin scored hits on the cruisers *Tenryu* and *Tatsuta*, while Capt. Herbert Frueler set the transport *Kongo Maru* aflame. Captain Elrod had the biggest score. He crashed a bomb on the deck of the destroyer *Kisargi*, which was carrying a load of depth charges topside. The *Kisargi* was consumed in a giant fireball, and then, like the *Hayate*, it simply disappeared.

The hot fighting took its toll on the squadron. Captain Freuler brought his plane back with its engine shot up beyond repair. The fuel line of Captain Elrod's Wildcat had been severed, and the engine cut out just as he was nursing it home. Elrod managed to crash-land among the boulders on the beach, but his craft was demolished. When Devereux and Putnam raced to pull him out of the wreckage, they found the pilot apologetic. "Honest, sir," he said, "I'm sorry as hell about the plane."

When the day's fighting score was added up, the Japanese had lost two ships, suffered damage to several more, and left as many as seven hundred men in the water. Incredibly the Marines had suffered only four minor casualties. As Corporal Brown commented to Major Devereux, it had been "quite a day."

The bloody nose suffered by the Japanese at Wake forced them to rethink the schedule so carefully worked out in Tokyo. Admiral Kajioka's force limped back to Kwajalein to be refitted with more men and more ships so that it could return to attack again. In the meantime, the Japanese would rely on aerial bombardment to soften up this unexpectedly difficult target. Weather permitting, and it usually did, they would bomb Wake twice a day. In the face of this, Wake's ability to defend itself was dwindling. After December 11 the effective air force of Wake was down to two airplanes.

It is a truism of war that winners tell the truth while losers make up stories. Except for the stolid defense of Wake, the Americans were losing badly elsewhere. Accordingly, press reports of the early days of the war were larded with unusually large doses of fiction. One of my most vivid memories of when I was a child listening to the radio was that of a broadcaster saying that Japanese firepower was so poor that soldiers on Bataan were actually fielding mortar shells with baseball mitts. We thrilled to reports of the Battle of Lingayen Gulf, in which a large invasion force was repulsed by the 21st Division of the Philippine Army, leaving the beaches strewn with Japanese bodies. The invasion force turned out to be a single Japanese motorboat on patrol. Every American child knew about the exploits of Capt. Colin Kelly, who, as the legend grew, won the Medal of Honor for flying his B-17 into the smokestack of the battleship *Haruna* and sending it to the bottom off the Philippines. In truth, Kelly had dropped a bomb on a large transport ship. And although he had done enough to earn any honor the nation might wish to bestow—at the cost of his own life Kelly had stayed at the controls of his stricken B-17 so his crew could jump to safety—he had seen no battleship; the *Haruna* at the time was fifteen hundred miles away in the Gulf of Siam.

In the first days of the war, with the American military position collapsing throughout the Pacific, the stand at Wake became a light of hope. Its troops were compared to the men who had fought at the Alamo, as Americans, thirsting for stories of gallantry and heroism, looked to Wake. But no information was forthcoming except what had been processed by public relations officers. Since they didn't know what was going on themselves—the only communications coming out of Wake were Cunningham's desperate requests for supplies and equipment—they, not surprisingly, provided legends.

In one of the most famous anecdotes of the war, Devereux, asked if he needed anything at Wake, shouted, "Send us more Japs!" The roar of defiance embodied the dogged spirit of beleaguered American troops everywhere. The story became so much a part of the fabric of the war that as late as 1945 *The New York Times* was still taking it seriously and editorialized that it demonstrated a fierceness not shown even by kamikaze pilots. The only thing known for certain about the celebrated line is that no one at Wake ever said it. The Marines at Wake had all the Japs they wanted. When they heard the story over the shortwave radio, they wondered how anyone could say something that stupid. After the war the official version of how the quote got around was that it was all a mistake. In sending a coded message from Wake to Pearl Harbor, Cunningham's communications yeoman went through the usual procedure of padding the message with nonsense material and sent out a communiqué reading "SEND US . . . NOW IS THE TIME FOR ALL GOOD MEN TO COME TO THE AID OF THEIR PARTY . . . CUNNINGHAM . . . MORE JAPS."

According to Duane Schultz, an energetic chronicler of the Wake saga, "someone in Honolulu seized upon the opening and closing words of the padding and a propaganda legend was born." Research as thorough as scanty records and fallible memory can provide offers no proof of this explanation, and it strikes me as even less plausible than the folklore version. In my opinion it is more likely the great quote was an inspired piece of flackery from a Marine public information officer no closer to Wake than the bar at the Royal Hawaiian Hotel—if it had been a Navy officer, he would have attributed the quote to Cunningham. But, as Devereux commented after the war, no one knows for sure.

Following the battle of December 11, real life on Wake settled into a deadly routine. For the next week the Japanese bombing was constant and methodical. A morning raid by land-based planes and a smaller one at dusk by seaplanes kept punishing Wake's defenses. The men on the ground worked to save their precious Wildcats. Technically each plane had been destroyed twice over, but the ground crews became expert scroungers. By taking propellers and spare parts from one plane and slapping them into another, they managed to keep something flyable. Once the crews actually wrenched a hot engine out of a crashed plane while the fuselage burned around them.

Next to Japanese bombardment, the greatest enemy faced by the Marines was simple fatigue. Devereux figured he never got more than two hours' sleep at any one time during the entire siege. Officers and men suffered from exhaustion as one day blurred into the next, punctuated only by bombing raids and burial details. Devereux recalled, "The men became so punch-drunk from weariness that frequently a man would forget an order almost as soon as he turned away, and sometimes it was hard for you to remember."

In their weariness everything seemed to conspire against the Marines. The birds that flocked around Wake suddenly seemed full of dark menace, and the men frequently mistook them for incoming bombers and sounded the alarm. Even in their foxholes there was little rest for the Marines as the island rats became more voracious, digging into shelters, looking for food and safety from the bombing.

Inevitably tempers became taut. It is unlikely that Cunningham and Devereux could have worked comfortably together even in garrison duty. Each man had a nice appreciation for the prerogatives of his rank and a good measure of the vanity common to men accustomed to exerting authority over their fellows. The memoirs of both men make obvious the fact that they didn't like each other. The strain of combat in close quarters made a thorny situation worse. Devereux had his hands full conducting the tactical defense of Wake, and he resented reporting to an officer so inexperienced in such matters that he did not know the gunnery characteristics of the weaponry in use. Battle is not a good time to be instructing your commanding officer in ballistics. Cunningham, in turn, was in a nightmarish situation. On November 29 he had come to Wake to be responsible for a brand-new naval air station, and two weeks later his command was being blown to pieces and there was nothing he could do to stop it. Cunningham, according to one reviewing Marine officer, "appears to have taken refuge from his own lack of experience and technical capacity by enveloping himself in authority. He attempted to supervise every detail of the defense exactly as the captain of a man-of-war would fight his ship, even down to an attempt to select precise moments for opening and cessation of fire." Cunningham was clearly beyond his depth at Wake, and as early as December 15 headquarters at Pearl Harbor had decided to relieve him with a Marine colonel, if he could be somehow be transported out there.

Bad weather kept the Japanese away on December 20, but that afternoon a PBY, a craft that was said to be "so big and ugly and stupid it didn't know it couldn't fly in rough weather," lumbered through the overcast and splashed down in the lagoon. A young ensign, James Murphy, in starched khakis, emerged and asked for directions to the Pan American hotel. He was shocked to be directed to a pile of debris.

Murphy brought mail to Cunningham and Devereux as well as an official dispatch containing the most blessed news a besieged commander can hope for. A Navy relief force with men and planes and matériel had already set sail from Pearl Harbor and was on its way to Wake. The dispatch apparently did not tell Cunningham that his replacement was also aboard.

When Admiral Kimmel had made his original plans for a counterattack at Wake, he had assumed, along with every other senior officer and civilian official in Washington, that he would be sailing against Japanese surface vessels in an openly declared war. The raid at Pearl Harbor had changed all that. With much of his fleet sunk in the harbor, Kimmel's trap had been unsprung, and he was just feeding the mice. Now the offensive-minded admiral intended to retrieve the bait and still slap the Japanese hard.

Considering the losses suffered at Pearl Harbor, Kimmel's plan was astonishingly bold. Conceived as early as December 9, it called for the deployment of all three fast carrier forces then available. Task Force 11 with Adm. Wilson Brown aboard the *Lexington* would make a diversionary raid on Jaluit in the Marshall Islands while Adm. William Halsey took the *Enterprise* and Task Force 8 west of Johnston Island with the double mission of covering the approach to Hawaii and lending support to the main attack. The job of leading the strike force heading straight for Wake was given to Adm. Frank Jack Fletcher. Fletcher's command was a pickup fleet that had never sailed as a unit before; it included nine destroyers, three heavy cruisers—*Astoria, Minneapolis,* and *San Francisco*—and the venerable carrier *Saratoga,* holder of several speed records between California and Hawaii, and which was then steaming toward Pearl Harbor from San Diego at twenty-one knots. Fletcher's ships held everything that Wake needed: two hundred Marines aboard the *San Francisco* and a fresh squadron of fighter planes on the *Saratoga.* Even if Fletcher's ships were too late to effect the relief of Wake, they were heading for a hell of a fight. Kimmel's plan involved considerable risk, but it was a good one. With speed, a little luck, and a Nelson on the bridge, it might have succeeded. It had none of these.

Skipper of the *San Francisco,* Fletcher was a solid officer. He had been graduated high in his class at Annapolis and seen service as a destroyer commander in World War I. He held the Medal of Honor from Veracruz. But Fletcher had no experience as a carrier force commander and had been given the assignment because he was the senior flag officer of the group. Adm. Aubrey Fitch, commander of the *Saratoga* and the most knowledgeable carrier admiral in the Navy, was relegated to a secondary role when Fletcher came aboard.

The expedition was plagued by misfortune and delay from the outset. The *Lexington* could not be fueled because of bad weather and did not get under way until the fourteenth; the *Saratoga* did not leave until the sixteenth. Worse, the *Saratoga,* which should have been dashing for Wake at top speed, was slowed to a crawl by the decrepit oiler *Neches,* which could put out only twelve knots. On the seventeenth, the *Lexington,* steaming toward Jaluit, held an antiaircraft gun drill and discovered that none of the ammunition aboard its cruisers worked. By then the relief expedition had lost its guiding spirit. Admiral Kimmel had been relieved of his command on the sixteenth and hustled into retirement until he could be court-martialed after the war for his part in the disaster at Pearl Harbor. Adm. Chester Nimitz was named to replace him, but Nimitz was still in Washington and could not take command for two weeks. In the interim the job would be held by Adm. William Pye, temporarily on the beach since his battleship *California* had been sunk on December 7. The rights and wrongs of Kimmel's court-martial are not within the scope of this article, but it should be noted that on December 15, 1941, Admiral Kimmel's principal thought was to seek out the Japanese and engage them wherever they could be found. His replacement's chief aim was to preserve the fleet and not turn a large butcher's bill over to the new commander in chief.

Pye was a careful officer. Nimitz, the kindest and most gently spoken of great war admirals, once described him as a "great brain but no guts." In an operation where other men saw opportunity, Pye was the sort of man who naturally saw difficulties. In looking over the operational plans of the departed Kimmel, Pye saw difficulties aplenty. In a single gambler's toss Kimmel, who had lost much of the Pacific Fleet in one afternoon, was sending the rest of it piecemeal into waters that the Navy did not control to engage an enemy whose position and strength he did not know. No, Pye didn't like the plan at all. Prudently he ordered Admiral Brown's *Lexington* to turn north away from the Marshalls to give Fletcher closer support. More cold water was thrown on the plan from Washington on December 20 when the chief of naval operations, Adm. Harold Stark, confided to Pye that Wake was considered more of a liability than an asset and left the relief of Wake up to Pye's "discretion," a universally understood shorthand in the military meaning the commander would be held responsible for any failure. In his heart Pye wanted to call off the project then and there. It was only when several staff officers begged him with tears in their eyes to keep the fleet on course that he agreed. The *Sea Hawk* spirit that had animated the project gave way to a sense of foreboding and concern. Still, the Navy was steaming for Wake. If the Marines there could hold for another four days, they might yet be saved.

Back at Wake, the men pumped Ensign Murphy for whatever information he had about Hawaii. Most of the news was bad. The devastation at Pearl Harbor was greater than any of them could have imagined. But they were tickled to hear that a Japanese radio in Shanghai had announced Wake had surrendered on December 8. The Marines, Devereux recalled, "felt pretty good that night."

The next day Maj. Walter Bayler, a communications officer with standing orders to leave for Midway by the first available transport, boarded the PBY and took off, bearing official reports and as much personal mail as the men had been able to scribble during the night. Although Bayler was destined to be known as the "last man off Wake Island," there should have been two passengers aboard the departing PBY. Through a mischance of war Herman P. Hevenor, a civilian analyst with the Bureau of the Budget, happened to be at Wake going over Dan Teters's books, checking construction costs, when the island was bombed. Although the needs of the defenders were great, they did not include a budget analyst, and Mr. Hevenor was granted permission to depart with Major Bayler. As he was about to embark, however, someone pointed out there was no life jacket or parachute available for him as required by Navy regulations. Since it was not considered safe for Mr. Hevenor to fly in a PBY, he was left on Wake.

Two hours after the PBY had taken off, Wake was struck again by air. The bombing and strafing were no more severe than the Marines were used to, but this raid carried a chilling message. Instead of land-based planes from the Marshalls, these attack bombers had flown off the decks of the Japanese carriers *Soryu* and *Hiryu*, which had taken part in the raid on Pearl Harbor. Two fleets were heading toward Wake, and the Japanese were closer.

The string was running out for the defenders. Diarrhea swept through the ranks. The men made rude jokes about it, as troops always do, but it was ferociously debilitating, and as many Marines were turning up in the sick bay because of illness as combat. As a result of thirteen days of bombing, the air defenses of Wake had diminished to the vanishing point: one antiaircraft battery of four three-inch guns and two effective airplanes, one of which was a balky starter. Throughout it all there was the harassing voice of headquarters back at Pearl Harbor. Cunningham sent a daily communiqué outlining the long litany of Wake's defense needs: men, airplanes, medical supplies, sandbags, disk clutches, fire-control equipment—the lot. In return it seemed they were getting nothing but idiotic messages and requests for useless information. On December 17 Cunningham was asked to report on the progress of dredging operations in the lagoon and other improvements scheduled to be made in base facilities. He replied by pointing out that half his trucks and engineering equipment had been destroyed along with most of his diesel oil. The garage, construction warehouse, and machine shops all had been blown away. He added laconically that daylight hours for construction work were "limited." Devereux found himself receiving little tips on having his men keep their sleeves rolled down and the suggestion that if glass was not available for windows in the barracks, seismograph paper was an adequate substitute.

Major Putnam's fliers made their last aerial show on the morning of December 22. Lt. Carl Davidson took off on the noon patrol, but Captain Frueler's cranky Wildcat wouldn't start. It took almost an hour of cursing and banging to get the engine to turn over. Davidson was covering the northern approach when he spotted thirty-three attack bombers and six Zeros storming in for their afternoon attack. Davidson called Freuler, whose Wildcat was wheezing up from the south, but without waiting for help, he bore in among the attackers alone. Freuler came as quickly as his plane allowed and found himself in a formation of bombers. He pulled up firing, and one of the bombers started exhaling smoke and fluttered into the sea. Freuler had no time to enjoy the exhilaration of the kill. He forced his faltering plane into a flip turn and went after a Zero only fifty feet away. It exploded into a fireball, showering Freuler's plane with hot steel fragments. Thrown out of control by the blast, Freuler's plane could just barely fly. The manifold pressure started to drop, and the controls were wooden. Looking about, Freuler could see Davidson caught in a deadly daisy chain, Davidson pouring machine-gun fire into a retreating bomber while a Zero, locked onto Davidson's tail, began a firing run of its own. A Zero hit Freuler's plane with a long burst, ripping bullets into Freuler's back and shoulder. Freuler tried to wriggle out of the line of fire, but he couldn't turn. There was only one thing left to try. He kicked his plane into a power dive and headed for the water. He pulled out at zero altitude and sputtered home over the wave tops. There was no question of landing in the normal sense; he didn't have the strength to operate the landing-gear crank. He bounced in on his belly and spun crazily to a stop. The plane was a total wreck.

Freuler did not know at the time whom he had shot down. Indeed, he didn't know what he had shot down. Plane recognition in the early days of the war was haphazard, and Freuler thought the bomber was a Zero. But postaction reports analyzed after the war indicate that his kill was the Nakajima B5N (Kate) that had been credited with sinking the *Arizona* at Pearl Harbor.

Davidson was aboard the last flyable airplane Wake owned. Ground crews stood out on the beach all afternoon until long after the outer limits of his fuel capacity had been passed, but no comforting speck appeared on the horizon. VMF-211 was finished. But there was still some fighting to do, so Putnam gathered up the remainder of his squadron, perhaps twenty able-bodied men, and marched them to Devereux's command post, where they reported in as infantry.

Devereux had great need of ground troops. He assumed the Japanese would attempt to land on the southern sides of Wake Island and Wilkes as they had done on the eleventh. The offshore coral reefs that surrounded Wake were closest to the beach on the lee side, giving the invaders the shortest stretch of water to get through. But knowing where an enemy will strike does not give a commander the resources to stop him. Devereux could put perhaps eighty men on Wilkes, and he had approximately two hundred Marines, sailors, and civilian volunteers to defend Wake Island. However, most of them were needed to man the gun crews. Even putting rifles into the hands of his grounded air force and stripping Peale to a small observation post, Devereux could dole out only eighty-five men to defend four and a half miles of beach. The major ordered some of the three-inch batteries broken down into individual units and depressed into the sand so they could be angled down and used as beach defense weapons. He put Lt. David Kliewer and three men in a dugout with a generator connected to dynamite charges laced into the runway. Lieutenant Kliewer's orders were to wait until the last minute, but if it looked as if the Japanese were going to overrun the airstrip, he was to blow it up. Lt. Arthur Poindexter had command of Wake's entire mobile reserve: two trucks for eight line Marines, fifteen sailors, and a smattering of civilians. For the rest, it was a matter of digging foxholes a little deeper and waiting. In fact, tactics and traditional concepts of coordinated defense would count but little in the battle for Wake. When a battle is neatly drawn up on a map or executed on a sand table, it is usually won by taking the high ground or key defense positions through adroit maneuver. There was no high ground at Wake and little cover. After two weeks of bombing, Wake Island was nothing more than a single strip of runway surrounded by scrub and beach. There was not much room to maneuver when the outer perimeter was much the same as the last redoubt. The fight would be a series of struggles in the dark, scrabbling for a patch of wet sand or a single gun emplacement. That called for close-up work by individual men with guns and bayonets.

"If they want this island," said Cpl. Hershal Miller, "they gotta pay for it." Miller had not been trained in the complexities of command, but like most good troopers who had seen a bit of combat, he had become a shrewd judge of the demands of battle. The Marines were preparing for a fight they knew they could not win unless they got support from the Navy relief column. In the meantime, they would sell themselves dearly.

A dmiral Kajioka returned to Wake in the dark early morning of December 23 with fresh troops and new ships but not much in the way of fresh ideas. This time his big ships would stay out of range of Wake's coastal guns, and instead of waiting until dawn, his invasion force would make its way to the beach in the darkness. But essentially it was the same plan that had failed twelve days before, only more so. A great deal more so. Kajioka's landing force had more than two thousand men in assault and reserve troops. If they were not enough to settle the matter, the admiral was prepared to run two destroyers straight onto the reefs and have their crews spill out onto the island. On December 11 Kajioka correctly assumed the American Navy would not be able to pull itself together after Pearl Harbor soon enough to be a bother to him. Twelve days later he could not be so sure. He stationed Cruiser Division 6, led by four heavy cruisers, to the east, covering the landing and ready to engage any approaching American surface vessels while the *Soryu* and *Hiryu* were to the north within air-strike range. The Japanese were determined to have Wake, and they were willing to pay Corporal Miller's price.

The vagaries of a major amphibious operation at night are many, however, and the second invasion of Wake got off to a poor start. Hoping to divert attention from the southern approach, Kajioka sent two destroyers, *Tenryu* and *Tatsuta*, northern to bombard Peale. The vessels lost their bearings in a gusty rainsquall and missed Peale by several miles. The first shells of the last battle for Wake were hurled into a turbulent ocean, and the aimless cannonade served only to alert the garrison.

Devereux refused to bite for a ruse so ineptly carried out, and for the next hour and a half he strained to peer through the sheeting rain, looking for a sign of ships to the south.

It was close to 2:00 A.M. when Japanese special naval landing-force personnel, some of whom in Bushido bravery had wrapped white sashes across their chests and helmets, struggled into their landing crafts and pushed off for the shore. Gunnery Sgt. Clarence McKinstry, at his battery position on Wilkes, was the first to pick out the sound of a barge motor through the crash of the surf. He called the island commander, Capt. Wesley Platt.

"Can you see anything?" Platt asked.

"Not a damned thing, but I'm sure it's there."

"Then fire."

McKinstry squeezed his .50-caliber machine gun, sending pink tracers into the night, and Platt slammed on the searchlight. The light had been damaged in one of the air raids and had not functioned properly since. It stayed lit for less than a minute, but that was enough to reveal landings under way on both Wilkes and Wake Island. The Japanese were already ashore at Wilkes and moving up. There was no distance for the three-inch battery. McKinstry had it loaded with high-explosive shells cut to muzzle-burst and fired into the oncoming shadows. As good soldiers do, the Japanese moved toward the flashing gun and began grappling hand to hand with the Marines. In the dark melee the Japanese pressed forward, lobbing grenades at the gun. It was hot work, and McKinstry saw his men would be overwhelmed if they tried to hold their ground any longer. He stripped the firing locks of the three-incher and yelled to his men to pull back and form a skirmishing line. The Japanese started to pursue until sharp rifle fire pinned them where they were. For the moment they contented themselves with holding the gun position.

On Wake Island Devereux's coastal guns were off the board from the start. Even if they could have seen the ships at sea, they could not reach them, and the guns could not bear as well on the beach area where two patrol craft had run up on the reef. During the brief flare of light, Lt. Robert Hanna saw one unmanned three-inch gun in the scrub line that might be able to do some damage. He pulled together a scratch crew and led it to the weapon. The gun had no sights, but at this range it didn't matter. Hanna opened the breech and sighted the target by looking through the barrel. Quickly he pumped fourteen shots into the near ship and set it ablaze.

Lieutenant Poindexter was one of those few men who really enjoyed getting into a good fire fight. His men said he was either "crazy as a bedbug or the bravest guy alive." He was eager to be in the fight, and when he saw the boats hung up on the reef, he took his chance. Poindexter and three men grabbed hand grenades and waded into the ocean to pitch them into the landing craft. They all fell short, and Poindexter went back for more. But it was too late. The resolute landing party had already gotten ashore and was fanning out over the island, looking for targets.

Devereux didn't want to lose the most effective gun he had on the beach and ordered Putnam and his crew to lend Hanna support. As they were about to pull out, John Sorenson and a group of civilians offered to help. Putnam tried to wave them off. Unarmed civilians didn't stand much of a chance on a battlefield, and if they were captured, it might go particularly hard with them. Sorenson, who was twenty years older than Putnam, and considerably larger, smiled genially. "Major, do you think you're really big enough to make us stay behind?" Sorenson and his men appointed themselves ammunition carriers and scurried off in the dark with the Marines. Putnam formed a horseshoe skirmish line on the beach in front of Hanna. It was a wild, screaming fight, so close that when Putnam shot one Japanese with this .45 automatic, the helmets of the two men clanged together. As on Wilkes, the Japanese swarmed over the defenders. Putnam gave ground slowly until he and the five men left in his command had been backed up to Hanna's smoking gun. "This," he shouted, "is as far as we go." And it was.

During the close fighting Sorenson repaid some of the debt incurred by his fellow workers hiding in the scrub. He was throwing rocks at the enemy when they shot him down. Sorenson and nine other civilians were killed defending Hanna's gun position.

On Wilkes the situation stabilized. Platt, who was later killed in Korea, didn't like stable situations and slipped out of his command post to reconnoiter. He crawled through the bush for a half-hour until he reached the gun position given up earlier. The Japanese, preoccupied with sporadic gunfire from McKinstry's squad, had neglected to set up a perimeter defense. Without even a single sentry to watch their rear, they all were facing east. Here was the kind of textbook situation an officer rarely finds on a cluttered battlefield. Platt gathered up a detail of Marines and worked back to within fifty yards of the Japanese. The predawn light was just enough for Platt to set up a neat line of skirmishers flanked by machine gunners. Platt opened fire and moved forward as McKinstry and a pickup squad led by Lt. John McAlister pushed in from their side. The Japanese, shocked to be attacked on two sides in a battle they thought had already been won, panicked. The men not cut down by the initial bursts scrambled for safety where there was none. About thirty tried to duck under the searchlight truck and were shot where they hid. In a few minutes of crossfire the invasion force was annihilated except for two prisoners. A Japanese afteraction report on the battle for Wilkes noted tersely, "In general, that part of the operation was not successful."

On Wake Island things were going more to their liking. The Japanese had landings on the beach and were moving inland. Shortly after three, when the struggle was just developing, Devereux's communications almost totally blanked out. The Japanese were cutting wire wherever they found it, and it is likely there was a major malfunction near the major's command post at the same time. Now totally isolated in his little igloo hut, Devereux began to lose effective control of his battle. He sent his executive officer, Maj. George Potter, and a detachment of men culled from the ranks of clerical personnel and telephone operators to set up a picket line a few hundred yards in front of his headquarters to stop a move against the sparsely defended north side. But the major was just guessing. He didn't know where the Japanese were or where they were heading. When he did get the news, it was usually bad. Once during the night a civilian, who had been cut off from Poindexter's group near the airstrip, stumbled into Devereux's post, sobbing, "They're killing them all! They're killing them all!"

By five, a half-hour before dawn, Devereux still did not know much for certain. He did not know about Platt's great success on Wilkes at all. But he did know the Japanese had established beachheads on Wake Island too strong for him to dislodge with the forces he had at his disposal.

Cunningham had disturbing news of his own. After the landings had been sighted, he radioed the submarine *Triton*, known to be in local waters, to help out by attacking the invasion force. *Triton* did not answer. It had left for Pearl

Harbor two days before. But at 3:19 A.M. Cunningham received a startling message from Admiral Pye informing him that no friendly vessels were in his area and none could be expected for at least another twenty-four hours. After conferring with Devereux at five, Cunningham sent a message to Pearl Harbor. "ENEMY ON ISLAND." Cunningham's mind went back to a phrase in an Anatole France novel, *The Revolt of the Angels*, which he had read many years before: "for three days . . . the issue was in doubt." And he added, "ISSUE IN DOUBT."

There was not much doubt in Pye's mind any longer. He had never liked the plan in the first place, and Cunningham's message indicated it was too late to relieve Wake anyway. But should he let the *Saratoga* force sail on and engage whatever enemy could be found? Pye didn't like that idea much either. A captain sailing into a sea battle ought to have some idea what he was getting into, but as one staff officer commented, "we had no more idea than a billy goat" what was going on at Wake. Pye radioed Fletcher, telling him to break off and return to port.

Fletcher was 425 miles from Wake when he got Pye's message. His task force had already suffered several frustrating delays. Had Fletcher made straight for Wake, he probably would have arrived about the same time as Kajioka, but not wanting to steam into battle with half-empty destroyers, he had paused to refuel. The refueling was snafu from the start. Seven oil hoses ruptured, and a number of towlines parted in the rolling seas. In ten hours only four destroyers were filled while the fleet actually drifted farther away from Wake. During the voyage Pye sent Fletcher a series of conflicting dispatches, each more cautionary than the previous one. It is likely Fletcher was glad to finally get a direct, explicit order from Pearl Harbor. He complied swiftly.

When word of the withdrawal reached Washington, CNO Stark couldn't bring himself to break the news to President Roosevelt and asked Secretary of the Navy Frank Knox to do it for him. Roosevelt, a former Undersecretary of the Navy and a keen yachtsman in his youth whose heart was always with the seafaring services, was devastated. Knox reported back to Stark that the President said it was "worse than Pearl Harbor."

The American people did not know a fleet had been ordered to Wake until much later, so there was no public reaction to the withdrawal. But within the Navy and Marine Corps, the reaction was immediate and bitter. Officers on the *Saratoga*, some of them weeping, pleaded with Fletcher to put Nelson's blind eye to the telescope and sail in spite of orders. The talk became so heated that Admiral Fitch left the bridge of his own ship because he did not want officially to hear his officers speaking in terms that were close to mutinous, particularly when they expressed sentiments he agreed with. One officer aboard the *Enterprise* scribbled furiously in an unofficial log, "It's war between two yellow races."

The incident marred Fletcher's long and honorable naval career. He was frequently referred to thereafter as "Fueling Jack Fletcher" and chastised for lack of resoluteness in combat. In fairness Admiral Fletcher did not win the Medal of Honor because he was squeamish about fighting, and to divide one's forces in the face of a numerically superior enemy, as he was to do five months later at the Battle of Midway, is not the mark of a timid admiral. The worst that can be said about Fletcher is that he was not Nelson.

On Wake Island the fighting had degenerated into a series of separate melees. Poindexter put up a good show. As first light was breaking, he found the Japanese had slipped past his flank during the night and were between his troops and the airstrip. He and his men charged through the scrub and sand for about five hundred yards. That was the last ground taken by the Marines at Wake Island. Now it was the Japanese who were defending the airstrip, and they set up a solid picket line, blocking Poindexter's way. Throughout the rest of the island American men and matériel began to break down. True to his word, Putnam had retreated no farther. But defending Hanna's gun had been costly. Captain Elrod, who was to be awarded the Medal of Honor, had been cut down during the night, trying to throw a grenade. Putnam was shot through the cheek and neck. He recalled later that he didn't realize he had been hit. He merely thought it was odd that he should suddenly feel sleepy during the middle of a fire fight. He passed out for a moment, came to, cursed his weakness, and passed out again.

Lieutenant Kleiwer's dugout had been under constant attack almost from the start. The Japanese repeatedly charged him with bayonets and grenades, but Kliewer's sharp fire beat them back. At first light Kliewer was surrounded, but incredibly all four men had survived the night. Several times Kliewer had been tempted to detonate the airstrip and try to cut his way out. But although his telephone link to Devereux had been dead for almost three hours, his last orders from the major were clear: Don't destroy the runway until the Japanese seize it. If the relief force should arrive, the strip would be need to receive planes from the *Saratoga*. As Kliewer began to make out shapes in the early dawn, he could see Japanese position flags around and in back of him. He reached over to push the generator button to blow up the strip. It didn't work. The night rains had flooded the motor.

As the morning sun broke clear over Wake, the defenders looked to the ocean for a sign of the relief force. They saw twenty-seven Japanese warships prowling the water. At seven, carrier planes from *Soryu* and *Hiryu* screamed down, shooting up the beaches.

With Devereux in his command post on the north side of Wake Island near the airstrip and Cunningham in his post farther up the island near Peale, the defense of Wake had become an absurdity. An officer who could not see the battle was reporting to one who could not comprehend it. Devereux and Cunningham had a telephone conference about seven-thirty, and the major filled in his superior officer as best he could with the spotty information he had. He told him that Wilkes was gone (in this Devereux was wrong, but it didn't matter—if he could not hold Wake Island, he could not hold Wilkes); the Japanese were securely on the island in at least three places; they had Peacock Point, and some were already on the airstrip.

Adm. Raymond Spruance, whose mildly professorial air belied the fact that he was one of the most effective sea fighters of the war, once defined battle in the simplest terms. "All operations," he said, "are like a woman going to shop. For you must ask two questions: 'What is it going to cost you and what is it worth to you?' "

This homely equation bore in heavily on Cunningham. He still had some capital to spend in the lives of a few more of his men, but he couldn't buy anything with it. The demands of military command are harsh. Throughout the defense of Wake, Cunningham's inexperience in tactical matters made him little more than a fretful observer. Now he faced a decision that only he had the authority to make.

"Well," he said, "I guess we'd better give it to them."

Devereux was still hoping. "Let me see if there isn't something I can do down here." He asked if the commander could spare any of his men for combat, but Cunningham's personal defense force consisted of five Army communicators freshly equipped with old rifles they didn't know much about. There wasn't anybody else.

"I'll pass the word," said Devereux. He cranked up his field telephone and told all units who could hear him to cease firing and destroy their weapons. The fight was over.

Cunningham sent another message to Pearl Harbor. "ENEMY ON ISLAND—SEVERAL SHIPS PLUS TRANSPORT MOVING IN—TWO DDS AGROUND." Although Cunningham's message and his decision to surrender were made within minutes of each other, he apparently didn't have the heart to tell Pearl Harbor he was giving up. He had the radio pulled down, and Wake went silent.

While Cunningham went back to his quarters to change into a dress blue uniform, Devereux had a sergeant tie a white rag to a mop handle, and together they moved out to effect the surrender of Wake. As the Japanese cautiously emerged from cover into the sunlight, the defenders of Wake got their first good look at the enemy they had fought for so long. One civilian, John Burroughs, was surprised to see how short they were. Their split-toed sneakers, he noted, gave them the appearance of having cloven hooves.

A Japanese combat correspondent, Ibushi Kayoshi, who landed on Wake, reported the capture "was so heroic that even the gods wept." The Japanese High Command issued a brief bulletin saying its forces "resolutely carried out landing operations against enemy opposition, brushing aside stubborn resistance, and completely occupied the island at 10:30 A.M.

The Japanese had Wake, but for most of the occupying forces it proved to be their burial ground. Tokyo's plan to use Wake as an advanced aerial reconnaissance station was wrecked by the disaster at Midway the following June. As the war swirled through the South Pacific, Wake became lost in a backwater of the conflict. Able to be supplied only by submarine and subjected to repeated attacks from American bombers and surface ships, the garrison at Wake slowly, inexorably perished. Some 750 Japanese were killed by American gunnery, and 1,500 starved to death. Near the end of the war, daily rations were cut to thirty-seven grams of rice, and the men who stayed alive could summon only enough energy to work one hour a day. The Japanese commandant, Adm. Shigematsu Sakaibara, was a cruelly effective officer who once had a man beheaded for pilfering liquor. As his command was dying, Sakaibara was faced with the problem of what to do with the 98 civilians who had been left behind to labor for the Japanese. By 1943 there was nothing for them to build, and they were eating rations Sakaibara needed for his own men. On October 7, after trumping up an excuse he himself could not have believed—that the civilians were in contact with American units and leading bombers to Wake—Sakaibara had all of them rounded up with their hands tied behind their backs and blindfolded. The men were marched to the north side of Wake Island, lined up in a long row on the beach, and machine-gunned. After the war Admiral Sakaibara was tried as a war criminal and hanged.

The four hundred Marines who were taken prisoner at Wake began their long endurance of the terrible capriciousness of captivity. One captor would offer cigarettes and as much camaraderie as the situation permitted, and the next a bayonet in the rib cage. Usually it was a bayonet. The prisoners were shipped to Shanghai by way of Yokohama aboard the freighter *Nitta Maru*. Between Japan and China five men were brought up on deck, where a lieutenant read to them in Japanese from a piece of paper while the crew formed up in a semicircle. It was just as well the Americans did not understand what the lieutenant was saying. In some kind of crazed Bushido ritual of revenge, they had been selected at random to atone for the deaths of Japanese troops on Wake. The Japanese forced the Americans to kneel down on mats and cut off their heads with samurai swords. Then they bayoneted the bodies and tossed the mutilated corpses into the sea.

For almost four years the Marines were shuttled in a dismal odyssey between various prison camps in southern China. To give the men something to do to break the monotony of hard labor and tedium, Devereux turned the prison cells into classrooms. He established classes in English, mathematics, and history and started up a vocabulary club. He was particularly strict with his junior officers. He had seen many a veteran of World War I coasting through the rest of his military career on decorations won at Belleau Wood and

Soissons. He told his officers to maintain and develop their skills and not to expect a free ride after the war was over because of their service on Wake. Always a stickler for decorum, Devereux insisted on the proper observance of all forms of courtesy. When he entered a room, all personnel had to rise for their commanding officer just as they had done at Wake. He continued to put enlisted men on report for minor infractions even though the reports weren't going anywhere. Soldiers in captivity measure out their victories in the tiniest of margins, and the battle to maintain pride in themselves as an existing military unit was clearly won when a Japanese guard querulously told them, "You don't act like prisoners."

By May 1945 the war had got too close for the Japanese prison keepers, and they put their charges on a train for Fengtai, near Peking. En route Lts. John McAlister and John Kinney, joined by two Marine officers from the North China Station and a Flying Tiger pilot, worked their way out of a boxcar and jumped free. They groped about in the countryside until they made contact with elements of the Communist Chinese 4th Army, who led them to an airfield where an American C-47 flew them home.

During their imprisonment the remaining Americans received little news from the outside, although a homemade radio built by Lieutenant Kinney brought them tantalizing snatches of information on the progress of the war. It was not until they were shunted from a camp in Pusan to the home islands of Japan that they realized their suffering must soon be over. In the summer of 1945, while being shipped by train across Japan to work scrabbling for coal in a mine in Hakodate, they stopped briefly outside Tokyo. The guards told them anyone caught looking outside the window would be shot, but Pfc. Henry Chapman decided to risk it. He saw a dull-eyed Japanese woman standing by the tracks holding a dead baby in her arms. Behind her Tokyo was a smoldering trash heap.

On September 5 the war was over for both captives and captors as the prison guards at Hakodate were disarmed.

The next day, Major Devereux had the members of the Marine 1st Defense Battalion fall in and led them in close-order drill.

—August 1987

THE SPIES WHO CAME IN FROM THE SEA

by W. A. SWANBERG

Wartime America's nerves were jumpy. One foggy night on a deserted Long Island beach a young coastguardsman heard the muffled engines of a submarine offshore, and suddenly shadowy figures loomed up out of the mist.

Few Americans remember even hazily what they were doing on the night of June 13, 1942. John C. Cullen remembers exactly what he was doing. He remembers with special vividness his activities at around twenty-five minutes past midnight. At that moment of time he was patrolling the lonely Atlantic beach near Amagansett, Long Island, 105 miles east of New York City. He did this every night—a six-mile hike. At that moment he was coming out of a thick patch of fog to run head-on into what seemed to be a Grade B movie thriller, but which turned out to be real life, with intimations of real death.

Cullen was twenty-one, a rookie coastguardsman, un-armed. America, at war with the Axis powers more than three thousand miles away, was yet worried enough about invasion, sabotage, and sneak attacks that houses were blacked out and coastlines were watched. Many good citizens thought this an excess of caution. Cullen himself says now that the last thing he expected to encounter was a party of invading Nazis just landed from a German submarine.

(Twenty-eight years later, a substantial family man of forty-seven who represents a large Long Island dairy coopera-tive, he retains a sense of having participated in a chunk of history so implausible that one would doubt it were it not all down in the records. "I suppose I've rehashed the story a thousand times," he says. "I had no weapon more dangerous than a flashlight and a Coast Guard flare gun, and I still feel lucky I got out of it alive.")

A man emerged from the mist—not too surprising, for some fishermen stayed out all hours in the summer. Cullen shone his torch on the stranger's face. "Who are you?" he asked.

The man—middle-sized, neither young nor old, gaunt, and with cavernous eyes—smiled. "We're fishermen from Southampton and ran aground here," he said. He identified himself as George Davis. Three of his companions were visible only as dark blobs in the mist. One of them came closer and shouted something in a foreign language that Cullen thought was German, and which angered Davis. "Shut up, you damn fool," he growled. "Everything is all right. Go back to the boys and stay with them."

("That jarred me, made me suspicious," Cullen recalls. "And I could see that this fellow was very nervous. Why should he be so nervous if he was O.K.?")

From then on events took a turn melodramatic enough to make a young coastguardsman believe himself gripped by fantasy. He suggested that Davis accompany him to the Amagansett Coast Guard station less than a quarter of a mile away. Davis refused. "Now wait a minute," Davis said. "You don't know what this is all about." He became quietly menacing, asking Cullen if he had a father and mother who would mourn him and saying, "I don't want to kill you." He reached into his pocket, but instead of a pistol he produced a wallet and offered Cullen $150, which he quickly raised to $300, to forget what he had seen. Cullen took the money to be agreeable, knowing he had no chance against four men, and also because it occurred to him that no one would believe his story unless he had evidence to prove it. For all he knew, guns might be covering him in the darkness. Cullen heard Davis murmur, "Forget about this," and then he headed back toward his station. ("I made it in record time," he recalls.)

Boatswain's Mate Carl R. Jenette, acting officer in charge, listened to this story with understandable incredulity. He counted the money and found that Cullen had been shortchanged—two fifties, five twenties, and six tens, totalling $260. He telephoned the station's commander, Warrant Officer Warren Barnes. While Barnes hurriedly dressed, Jenette armed Cullen and three other "beach pounders" and raced with them over the dunes to the scene of the improbability.

Davis and his companions were gone. The coastguardsmen could smell fuel oil and could hear a throbbing engine; offshore they could see the superstructure of a submarine splashed by wavelets. It was the *U-202* under Lieutenant Commander Lindner, which had run lightly aground and was freeing herself, moving eastward. ("She had a blinker light," Cullen remembers. "We ducked behind a dune, not wanting to get shelled, until she slid away.")

A search of the beach in the morning disclosed: an empty pack of German cigarettes; four heavy, waterproof oaken boxes buried in the sand; a gray duffel bag, also buried, containing four soggy German marine uniforms. The boxes contained brick-sized blocks of high explosives, bombs disguised as lumps of coal, bomb-timing mechanisms of German make, and innocent-looking "pen-and-pencil sets" that were actually incendiary weapons.

By this time the affair looked decidedly sinister. The Federal Bureau of Investigation took charge, trying to pick up the trail of "George Davis" and his men, hoping to prevent a repetition of the disastrously efficient German sabotage of World War I that had demolished the Kingsland arsenal and the Black Tom munitions plant in New Jersey. Ira Baker, the Long Island Railroad's Amagansett station agent, remembered four men, one of them answering Davis's description, buying tickets for the first morning train to New York City. Now the four men were swallowed up by the metropolis.

Behind this menacing business lay a curious Nazi seminary of sabotage at Quentz Lake, forty miles west of Berlin near Brandenburg. Established by the *Abwehr*, the German military intelligence headed by Admiral Wilhelm Canaris and Colonel Erwin von Lahousen, the school had received a direct order from Hitler to train specialists for the destruction of vital factories and communications in America. It was a crash program representing German fear of American industrial might. Perhaps this was why its high requirements for secret agents—men who not only qualified in intelligence and courage but who also spoke English and were familiar with the United States—were sometimes allowed to slide. Indeed, George Davis, whose real name was Georg Johann Dasch, was hardly the kind of operative one might meet in the pages of John Le Carré.

Born in Speyer-am-Rhein in 1903, Dasch landed in Philadelphia as a stowaway in 1922. Familiar with German and French, he soon learned English, but he became disgruntled because he could find work only as a waiter. He followed this calling at hotels and restaurants in New York, Miami, Los Angeles, and San Francisco. After his marriage in 1930 to Rose Marie Guille, a Pennsylvania-born hairdresser, he visited Germany with his bride. When they returned to America, Dasch again was seen at some fairly good restaurants, but only as a man with a tray.

Meanwhile the propaganda coming out of the Fatherland confirmed his belief that he was meant for better things. The beginning of the European war in 1939 made up his mind. He haunted the German consulate in New York, begging them to get him back into Germany. His passage was arranged in March of 1941, and in Berlin, Dasch met thirty-six-year-old Lieutenant Walter Kappe, a Nazi intelligence officer who from 1925 to 1937 had worked as a newspaperman in Chicago and Cincinnati and had wound up in New York as press chief for the Hitler-loving German-American Bund. Dasch's English was good, so Kappe landed him a job monitoring American broadcasts. In February 1942, when Kappe was selected to superintend the "American branch" of the Quentz Lake school for saboteurs, he picked Dasch as his first pupil. Among others in the student body were seven who figure in this account, all of whom had spent years in America:

Violin-playing Ernest Peter Burger, from Augsburg, was only seventeen when he joined Hitler's gang in the abortive Munich beer-hall putsch of 1923. Immigrating to America in 1927, he worked as a machinist in Milwaukee and in Detroit, joined the Michigan National Guard and also the German-American Bund, and in 1933 became a citizen; but he returned to Germany that same year when Hitler became chancellor. He rose swiftly to become an aide to Captain Ernest Röhm, head of the storm troopers—a connection that became a liability when Röhm was liquidated in the 1934 blood purge. Thereafter Burger had the inevitable troubles with the Gestapo. In 1940 he was imprisoned for seventeen months, occasionally tortured, and his pregnant wife was grilled so mercilessly that she had a miscarriage. After his release, however, his standing was partially restored, and he became a student at Quentz Lake.

Edward Kerling, born in Wiesbaden in 1909, had joined the Nazi party in 1928 and yet had gone to America the following year. He worked in a Brooklyn packing plant, then became a chauffeur, handling the wheel for Ely Culbertson, the bridge expert, and other wealthy people. He married, but soon separated from his wife. A loyal Bundist, he also kept up his dues-paid membership in the Brown Shirts, so that when he returned to Germany in July 1940 he had considerable seniority.

Richard Quirin, a Berliner, was nineteen when he came to the United States in 1927. He worked as a mechanic in Syracuse, Schenectady, and New York City and joined the Bund. His return to the Fatherland in 1939 came about because he was out of work at the time, Germany had started a policy of paying the return fare for the faithful, and the news about *Der Führer* excited his feelings of nationalism.

Heinrich Heinck, born in Hamburg in 1907, had entered the United States illegally in 1926. After working in New York City as a handyman, then as a machinist, he was swept away by the stirring rites of the Bund, and in 1939 he also leaped at the "free return trip" offer.

Hermann Otto Neubauer, born in Hamburg in 1910, had been a cook and hotel worker in Hartford and Chicago from 1931 until 1940, when his Bund-inspired Nazi loyalty drew him back home.

Werner Thiel, born in Dortmund in 1907, came to America at twenty to work as a toolmaker and in other jobs in Philadelphia, Detroit, and Los Angeles. He followed the pattern in his wholehearted embracing of the Bund (Dasch was the only nonmember) and in accepting a German-paid return trip after the war began in 1939.

Herbert Hans Haupt was brought to America by his parents from Stettin as a five-year-old, grew up in Chicago, and became an optical worker there. He had little recollection of Germany, but his father, although naturalized, was such a loyal Nazi that he might as well have been in Prussia. Young Haupt drilled with the Bund in an Illinois cornfield. Still, his return to Germany was motivated by prudence as well as national feeling. Discovering that his Chicago girl friend was pregnant, he fled to Mexico in June of 1941. The German consul in Mexico City, regarding him as useful timber, gave him money and arranged his passage to Germany by way of Japan. Haupt, born in 1919, was the youngest member of the student body and a lady-killer.

During April and part of May 1942 these eight men were hurry-up classmates at Quentz Farm, where their teachers were experts—two of them doctors of philosophy—in explosives, chemistry, electricity, and allied arts useful in destruction. In the surrounding fields small bridges and lengths of railroad track had been built, and here the students could lay practice demolition charges under the supervision of their instructors. They were expected to study the American newspapers and magazines passed around among them and to be posted on current American news, slang, and song hits. Finally they were taken to factories in Berlin, Bitterfeld, and Aachen and shown how the destruction of one vital production process could knock out a whole plant. They were saluted with a "graduation" dinner complete with wines, and their mission was designated Operation Pastorius, after Franz Pastorius, the first German immigrant to America, who landed in 1683.

Each man (except for the two American citizens, Burger and Haupt, who could safely use their own names) was given a fictitious identity and forged papers to support it—passport, draft card, ration coupons, and driver's license. Each of the fraudulent six memorized a fake past history.

On May 22, 1942, Lieutenant Kappe and the eight took the express train to Nazi-occupied Paris, where they had a two-day binge—theatres, night clubs, women—courtesy of the Third Reich. Thence they traveled to the submarine base at Lorient, the take-off point. Dasch, the leader of one four-man team, had with him Burger, Quirin, and Heinck. Kerling, the other leader, had under him Neubauer, Thiel, and Haupt. To each team Kappe gave about ninety thousand dollars in United States currency, the leader carrying the bulk of it—a sum intended to cover possible bribes as well as expenses. Each team leader was also given an ordinary white handkerchief on which was written, in invisible ink that could be brought out by ammonia fumes, the names and addresses of a Lisbon mail drop that would reach the *Abwehr*, and two dependable sources of help in the United States. On the night of May 26 Kerling and his men boarded the *U-584*, under

Lieutenant Commander Deeke, and soon were plowing west-ward in the Atlantic, bound for Florida. Two nights later Dasch and his group were off in the *U-202* for Long Island.

The landing of the saboteurs near Amagansett was made in an inflated rubber boat with the aid of sailors from the *U-202*. The four were clad in German marine fatigue uniforms on the theory that if captured at once they would be treated as prisoners of war (that is, interned) rather than being shot as spies. They quickly changed into mufti, buried their cache, and after the brush with coastguardsman Cullen, went on to New York, where Dasch and Burger took rooms at the Governor Clinton Hotel across from Pennsylvania Station. Heinck and Quirin registered at the Hotel Martinique.

Now the men and their mission took on a complexion of *opera bouffe*. They lacked the close acquaintance and implicit trust that was essential for the success of an assignment of such high risk and long duration. The morale of the three of them had sagged during the sixteen-day submarine voyage—a Spar-tan journey made fearful when the U-boat had to hit bottom to escape American destroyers and was shaken, though not damaged, by depth charges. They actually disliked each other. Burger, the solid one of the group, had ice in his veins and was equal to any risk; but he was not forgetting what the Gestapo had done to him, and besides, he had lost all faith in Dasch. Quirin tended to be moody and quarrelsome. Heinck had already exhibited a weakness for liquor and loose talk that was potentially fatal. Dasch himself was undergoing the cold shivers. Their narrow escape from the Coast Guard had been a vivid reminder of the dangers they faced. The psychological pressures peculiar to those most isolated of all creatures, secret agents, were oppressive.

They had too much time to think, for their orders were to spend about ninety days in preparation before launching any sabotage. They were loaded with more money than any of them had ever seen before; they spent it on snappy American summer clothes and on food that seemed Lucullan after the leaner German war rations. Dasch, the knowing ex-waiter, escorted his crew to restaurants he liked—the Swiss Chalet, the Kungsholm, Dinty Moore's, and an Automat near Macy's.

On Sunday morning, only some thirty hours after they had landed, Dasch and Burger had a long talk at their hotel during which Dasch dropped subtle hints of his own doubts in order to determine whether his sidekick felt the same way and could be trusted. It must have been instantly apparent to Burger that with the leader in such a frame of mind the mission would surely fail, and he had better get clear. Reassured at last, Dasch said he intended to betray the whole plot (and his accomplices) to the F.B.I. According to the two men's later testimony, they agreed to this at once. Dasch felt that by exposing the plot he would become an American hero celebrated in headlines and honored by the President.

At 7:51 on Sunday evening, with Burger standing near the telephone booth, Dasch called the New York F.B.I. office and talked with Agent Dean F. McWhorter. Identifying himself as Frank Daniel Pastorius, he said he was recently from Germany. "I want you to know," he said, "that I shall get in touch with your Washington office next Thursday or Friday. I have some important information." When McWhorter asked what the information was, the caller said it was of such moment that only J. Edgar Hoover himself could have it, and then hung up. McWhorter, accustomed to crank calls, nevertheless made a record of the conversation.

Dasch then indulged in a period of dawdling that he later explained was motivated by the conviction that the other six saboteurs should be given their own opportunity to save their skins by surrender. It was not until Thursday afternoon that Dasch boarded a train for Washington, still determined to see Hoover personally. He checked into Room 351 in the Mayflower Hotel.

On Friday morning, June 19, he telephoned the F.B.I. and was connected with Agent Duane L. Traynor. He must talk with Mr. Hoover, he said, finally disclosing that he was the leader of a group of German saboteurs. Traynor, who knew of the discovery of explosives at Amagansett and the hunt for the missing men, told Dasch firmly to stay right there in Room 351. Dasch did. A group of agents arrived with almost miraculous speed and escorted him to headquarters at the Department of Justice. Here, when he became persuaded that Hoover was not at leisure, he told his story to others. He gave them his handkerchief with the invisible writing. He jolted them with the news that there was a second sabotage group slated to land with explosives at Ponte Vedra Beach, Florida. They were to take two years, he said, to complete their work of destruction. Their major objectives were centered most heavily on aluminum production, transportation, and power stations.

The ingenious bombs masquerading as lumps of coal were to be tossed into coal cars serving industrial plants and seagoing vessels, eventually to find their way into furnaces— with disastrous results. The saboteurs were instructed also to destroy civilian morale by spreading incendiary devices in large department stores and by leaving time bombs in lockers at hotels, railway stations, and other places where crowds congregated.

So inattentive a student was Dasch that he had forgotten which chemical would bring out the message on the handkerchief—a problem the F.B.I. laboratory quickly solved. One of the addresses on it was that of a New York German whose house could be safely used by the saboteurs as a meeting place. Indeed, when the G-men got on the trail of Dasch's henchmen in New York, they discovered not only that the other four had already landed at Ponte Vedra on June 17 but that two of them—Kerling and Thiel—had also come to New York. What with the information obtained from Dasch and the handkerchief, it was a simple matter to arrest Burger, Quirin, Heinck, Kerling, and Thiel. That left only Haupt and Neubauer to be apprehended. Kerling was escorted by agents to Ponte Vedra, twenty-five miles southeast of Jacksonville, where he glumly pointed out the spot where he and his men had buried four German uniform caps and four boxes of explosives identical to those found at Amagansett.

The G-men worked in utter secrecy. Not a word had been given to the newspapers—a precaution that was continued, since publicity might hamper the arrest of the remaining saboteurs. The case contained elements so ominous that Hoover kept his boss, Attorney General Francis Biddle, posted on it from the start. Biddle, in turn, reported to President Roosevelt, who was following developments with keenest interest.

Herbert Haupt, on leaving Florida, had gone to his home city of Chicago, with Hermann Neubauer following him in a later train. For the time being, young Haupt forgot about sabotage and devoted himself to movies, fun, and romance. Unknown to him, his skylarking was being watched by federal agents, who knew his home address and were waiting for him to lead them to Neubauer. When agents zeroed in on Neubauer at the Sheridan Plaza Hotel on June 27, both men were arrested.

Biddle telephoned the good news to President Roosevelt, who was determined that a speedy example be made of the eight in order to discourage further conspiracies. The President, in a memorandum to Biddle, gave his opinion that the two saboteurs who were American citizens were guilty of high treason, that the other six were in the category of spies, and that all deserved the death penalty.

This sort of punishment could be decreed only by a court-martial. In civil law, if one bought a gun with intent to shoot someone, it was not murder until the fatal shot was fired; and if someone arrived in the United States with heavy explosives but had not got around to using them, it was not sabotage. If the eight were tried in a civil court, they might get off with two or three years' imprisonment.

"I want one thing clearly understood, Francis," the President said. "I won't give them up . . . I won't hand them over to any United States marshal armed with a writ of habeas corpus."

Now at least it was safe to release the story—that is, part of the story. J. Edgar Hoover's statement to the press told briefly of the two landings, the buried explosives, the plan to cripple key industries and to kill and demoralize, and the eight men arrested. He did not say *how* they were apprehended. Nothing was said about the defections of Dasch and Burger, not only to prevent possible retaliation against them by their six comrades, or Nazi retaliation against their families in Germany, but also because there was no desire to enlighten the enemy about how the men had been caught. If Berlin believed that our counterespionage was superhuman, Berlin might think twice before repeating such efforts.

The press and the public seized on the story as they would have embraced a great victory in battle. *The New York Times* gave it an unprecedented triple-banner headline and declared that the nocturnal landings from U-boats only a few hundred yards off our shores seemed like "a fantastic plot borrowed from the movies." The spectacle of the eight saboteurs sneaking across the Atlantic only to run into the arms of the waiting G-men contained perfect ingredients for national satisfaction. It made the Germans look comic and the F.B.I. heroic.

Not for days to come did the news leak out about the role

played by Cullen and the Coast Guard at Amagansett. However, the actual facts of the capture still remain unknown. Cullen was promoted to coxswain (he later was awarded the Legion of Merit), while some observers urged that dogs be used to aid in beach patrols.

As for Georg Dasch, he was appalled to discover that instead of being hailed as a national hero, he was a prisoner along with the seven others. He was in the familiar plight of the squealer, a man useful to the law but held in some contempt because his talebearing seemed dictated by expediency rather than idealism.

On July 2 President Roosevelt announced that the accused men would stand trial before a military commission composed of seven general officers—three major generals, three brigadiers, and the president, Major General Frank R. McCoy, Retired. The prosecution would be in the hands of Attorney General Biddle and the Army judge advocate general, Major General Myron Cramer. The defense was entrusted to Colonel Kenneth C. Royall and Colonel Cassius M. Dowell. More than a majority vote of the commission—five of the seven—was required for conviction and sentence. The rules of evidence would not be as restrictive as those protecting civilian rights. The President himself, as commander in chief, would make the final decision on the sentence on the basis of the commission's recommendation, and there would be no appeal.

Extraordinary efforts were made to keep the eight prisoners in good health until they faced the summary fate the public expected for them. They were placed in a second-floor wing of the old District of Columbia jail. Each man was kept in a tiled, ever-lighted cell with an empty cell on each side of him. He was clad only in pajamas, was allowed no writing materials, and ate his meals with fiber spoons off paper plates so that there was no opportunity for suicide. Only his counsel was permitted to visit him, and he could not communicate with the other accused men. He was guarded constantly by members of a detail of four officers and thirty soldiers. As Brigadier General Albert M. Cox, who as wartime provost marshal general of the District was custodian of the prisoners, later put it, "Whenever a man requested a smoke, he was handed one cigarette. His guard lit the match. . . . Every instant for thirty-five days and nights, at least one pair of eyes was glued to each prisoner."

Reporters were excluded—an order that brought a howl from the press. Elmer Davis, the former newsman and radio commentator who had just been appointed director of the brand-new Office of War Information, had been promised full authority over censorship. He protested to Secretary of War Henry L. Stimson. Stimson, seventy-five and tart, let him know that the Army was in charge and that secrecy was vital. Davis next went to Roosevelt, urging that he allow censored accounts. The President relented only enough to permit a brief daily communiqué from General McCoy—a distinguished officer who would prove himself an execrable newspaperman.

Attorney General Biddle felt that the secrecy was overdone, that the public could have been informed far more completely without danger to the national interest, and that indeed virtually the only things that had to be concealed were the voluntary confessions of Dasch and Burger.

The most immediate menace to the attorney general and his colleague General Cramer was a man named Milligan, who was long dead. In 1864 a Confederate sympathizer, Lambdin B. Milligan of Indiana, was arrested for pilfering munitions from Northern arsenals and sending them to Rebels. Denied a civil trial, he was speedily condemned to death by the military. However, President Lincoln was assassinated before he could sign the death warrant. Thereafter Milligan's attorneys fought the case through to the Supreme Court. The Court unanimously awarded Milligan a writ of habeas corpus. But five of the justices did more than that. Going well beyond the scope of the case at issue, they ruled that if a statute had permitted trial of a civilian by a military commission, the statute would have been unconstitutional. The military could not try a civilian as long as the civil courts were functioning. Only if actual invasion had driven out the courts could the military take over, and Indiana had not been invaded.

Biddle, knowing the caliber of the defense attorneys, was sure that they would exhume *Ex parte Milligan*. When they did, would the President of the United States and two of his cabinet officers be humiliated, and would sabotage be virtually sanctioned, and would the American public be outraged, by the removal of the case to the civil courts, where the eight men who had come to destroy would receive punishment of a kind given to purse snatchers?

The trial opened on July 8 in a long room on the fifth floor of the Justice Department building. The windows were swathed with blackout curtains. All of the defendants—who had confessed after their exhibitions of innocence and their fictitious identities had failed them—pleaded not guilty. The two turncoats, Dasch and Burger, testified that they had intended to betray the plot from the very beginning in Germany. Dasch, whom Mr. Biddle described as "an interminable talker who made a poor witness," tended to irritate the judges, whereas the stalwart Burger made a better impression. He, after all, had good reason for his course. After the Gestapo's mistreatment of his wife and his own imprisonment and torture, he had vowed to betray Hitler (whom he had known personally) at the first opportunity. Even now he was worried that news of his collaboration with the prosecution might leak out and that his wife would suffer as a result.

As for the unlucky six, their bitterness against Dasch—and to a lesser extent against Burger—was quiet but evident. They were all caught in the same net. The law rewarded the quick squealer. They had not confessed as quickly as the other two and would be condemned for it. They were sure that no real effort would be made to defend them and indeed that their attorneys, Royall and Dowell, were actually spies for the prosecution. The two colonels had worked hard to win their trust, but they did not get it until they were able to arrange for the detested Dasch to be defended by another soldier-attorney, Colonel Carl M. Ristine. From then on the accused men came to understand more strongly with every succeeding day that they were being defended to the very limit of energy and resourcefulness by attorneys of superlative skills who knew all about *Ex parte Milligan.*

For each day's session the eight men were shaved by barbers, since a razor in their own hands might be used suicidally. They traded their pajamas for the clothing they had bought with Nazi money and were whisked by armored cars guarded with Tommy guns from their cells to the court over routes that changed with each trip. In the courtroom they sat diagonally across from the seven generals who would judge them—generals whose shoulders glittered with a total of twenty-two stars. Each of the unlucky six, though admitting he had arrived secretly by submarine from Germany with TNT and other explosives, gave the only argument open to him—that he had been trapped by fate or fear or military duty.

Young Haupt, pimply but dashing, swore that he had gone along with the plot only through fear of the Gestapo but that never in the world did he intend to carry out any sabotage. The curly-haired, solemn-faced Quirin said that he was actually afraid of explosives and would not have used them in this country or anywhere else. Heinck, the stolid machinist, pointed out that in Germany it was dangerous to refuse such an assignment, but disclaimed any intention to put his training to use here. The balding Thiel said he thought Quentz Farm was a training center for propagandists and was appalled when he learned the truth. These four pictured themselves as deluded about Germany. They said they had seized upon the sabotage plan as the only means of getting back to an America they now appreciated and that they had arrived here somewhat in the nature of refugees from Nazidom.

Biddle left these arguments in shreds. He suggested that they might have received a welcome here instead of a trial had they only made all this known sooner. Instead they followed every Nazi order, told no one about their doubts, moved stealthily about the country, registered at hotels under fictitious names, carried fraudulent papers, and lived comfortably on Nazi money until the moment of their arrest—after which they still tried to maintain the fiction until they saw it was impossible.

Only Kerling and Neubauer (although they also doubted that they could have carried the plot through) took the defense of a soldier's duty. The handsome, bushy-haired Kerling said that for him to have disobeyed orders would have been cowardly, while the burly Neubauer testified, "As a soldier you are not supposed to think; and I did not. I just got the order and I didn't know what for."

Colonel Royall knew that however necessary these assertions were, they would never save his clients' necks. His second line of defense was that even if the defendants could be shown to be guilty of clandestine conduct, that was the extent of their crime. They had not even attempted any spying or violence, much less achieved any. But the last line of defense was *Milligan.*

Had newsmen been present, they would have depicted

the drama between the two men charged with most of the oral presentations, Francis Biddle for the prosecution and Kenneth Royall for the defense. Biddle, eight years the senior, was a tall six feet two, Royall a towering six-five. Each had studied law at Harvard, and each had sharpened his abilities under a titan of jurisprudence—Royall under Felix Frankfurter at college, Biddle as secretary to Associate Justice Oliver Wendell Holmes after graduation. Each had become an eminent attorney, Biddle in Philadelphia, Royall in his native North Carolina. Each in his lifetime would be a cabinet member, Royall slated to become the first secretary of the same army whose executioner's efforts he was now trying to thwart. And now each was serving the country in a wartime role that brought them into sharp, but always courteous, legal collision.

Royall made it clear at the start that he would challenge the legality of the President's proclamation and that all his arguments in the military court would not imply any concession that the military was competent to try the prisoners. This course brought an anguish of doubt to his defense colleague, Colonel Dowell. Unlike Royall, Dowell was a Regular Army man, with forty years of service behind him. He could not entirely quell a feeling that it would be insubordination for him to question a proclamation of his commander in chief. While he did not oppose the move, his uncertainty was so strong that he could not actively support it either, which left it up to Royall.

The Supreme Court was in summer adjournment, its members scattered. Royall cleared the way by applying to the district court for leave to file petitions of habeas corpus—a plea immediately refused. He talked with the attorney general. The next day Royall and Biddle flew together to Chester Springs, Pennsylvania, where Associate Justice Owen J. Roberts was vacationing on his farm with Associate Justice Hugo L. Black as his guest. There, over country cheese and crackers, the two jurists listened at length to the callers. Roberts ended by telephoning Chief Justice Harlan Fiske Stone at Sugar Hill, New Hampshire, where he was spending the summer. The next day the nation learned that the Supreme Court would convene at all speed for the sake of men who were described by some commentators as "saboteurs, bomb-throwers, and killers." While a few of the justices were within reasonable distance, Justice James Byrnes was in South Carolina, Justice

Frankfurter was in Connecticut, Justice Frank Murphy was an Army colonel training in North Carolina, and Justice William Douglas was in Oregon.

To a lawyer, appearing before the Court is equivalent to a pietist meeting the choir of angels. It is never easy, even for one like the attorney general, who had done it repeatedly. The younger Royall had done so only once before. The two attorneys, though they had expert aid in research, got little sleep as they prepared their opposing presentations. This was the biggest spy case in American history. It was the first time the Court had broken its summer recess in twenty-two years. It would hardly do to present arguments not well founded in law.

Although there were many precedents involved (Biddle cited forty-eight, Royall sixteen), the Milligan ruling was at once the most striking and the one that seemed most promising for the defense. Royall portrayed the analogy to the Court, one of whose members was his old professor Frankfurter. No more so than Milligan's Indiana, he said, could the beaches of Long Island and Florida be called "zones of military operation." There was no combat there; there was not even a threatened invasion, much less an actual one. The civil courts were functioning, Royall went on to argue, and they were the proper places to try the prisoners.

But the two days before the Court, the thousands of words spoken by the opposing counsel, and the many questions asked by the justices demonstrated among other things that Milligan was not the man he once had been. The attorney general declared that the old case no longer applied—that time and technology had wiped out its relevance: "The United States and Nazi Germany are fighting a war to determine which of the two shall survive. This case is . . . part of the business of war." The swift total war of 1942 was as different from the static land warfare of 1864 as a Stuka bomber was from a musket. This war was everywhere—on land, in the water and air, and in our factories and civilian morale as well as on the battlefield. The saboteurs, arriving secretly in enemy submarines, had penetrated our defenses, bringing explosives. Like spies of all ages—like Major André and our own Nathan Hale—they had removed their uniforms and come in disguise. The universally accepted law of war was that spies should be tried by military tribunals and executed if guilty.

As for Chief Justice Stone, he was able to distinguish the case from *Milligan* because the saboteurs were belligerents from a foreign country. He was more troubled by the secrecy of the trial, and he wanted to show that the law of the land still governed. Yet the President had already been chided by this very hearing, and it was difficult to say that he had violated the Articles of War, which were not entirely clear and perhaps were never intended to bind him. On July 31 the Court, which tends to support the President in time of war, upheld the attorney general unanimously.

Although the decision merely meant that the military trial would continue, it was the end of the line for the saboteurs. On August 3 the generals gave their verdict—death for all eight defendants—to President Roosevelt as the court of last resort. He followed Biddle's recommendation in commuting the sentences of Dasch to thirty years and of Burger to life imprisonment as rewards for their aid. It was the duty of General Cox, as provost marshal general, to inform the eight individually of their fate. The six condemned to die, he later reported, "seemed stunned and turned pale although they kept silent." The cool Burger, who was lying on his cot reading the *Saturday Evening Post* when Cox entered, looked up long enough to get the news of his life term, said, "Yes, sir," and returned to his reading. Dasch, whose disillusionment had been painful ever since his arrest, was outraged at his sentence. He wrote to President Roosevelt declining to accept the verdict—a dissent that was entirely rhetorical, for he was bundled off with Burger to the federal prison at Danbury, Connecticut.

Astonishingly, the doomed six signed a statement expressing appreciation for having been given a fair trial and adding, "Before all we want to state that defense counsel . . . has represented our case . . . unbiased, better than we could expect and probably risking the indignation of public opinion. We thank our defense counsel . . . "

The electric chair on the jail's third floor was readied for use. On August 8, in strictest secrecy, the six men, starting in alphabetical order with Haupt, were executed one by one. "Haupt was seated in the electric chair at one minute past noon," General Cox recorded. "The last of the six was pronounced dead at four minutes past one." It established a gruesome statistic—ten and one-half minutes per man, the swiftest multiple electrocution ever carried out.

The watchful press had learned of the electrical prepara-tions, and reporters were standing outside in the rain. As *Time* put it: "In the courtyard, in the drizzle, six sheeted bodies on stretchers were loaded in ambulances . . . Steel-helmeted sol-diers, with bayonets and machine guns, kept a little crowd of the curious away. The ambulances swung out slowly on the wet pavement, took the bodies to the Walter Reed Hospital for autopsy. . . . The U.S. still knew less about the case than about any one of its daily, tawdry crimes of passion."

In fact, not even the press knew until weeks later that the six men were buried in the District of Columbia Potter's Field at Blue Plains. The headstones consisted of unpainted boards bearing only the numbers from 276 to 281.

If it was true that newsmen and some libertarians were offended by the heavy cloak of secrecy, this policy did succeed in concealing for the war's duration the fact that Dasch and Burger had betrayed the plot to the F.B.I. This seemed to have one salutary effect: The Nazi *Abwehr* was stunned by the quick failure of its enterprise. At the time of the arrest of the eight, Colonel von Lahousen noted in his diary, "Since early morning we have been receiving [radio] reports . . . announcing the arrest of all participants in Operation Pastorius." The diary also disclosed that Hitler, in a rage at the debacle, gave the colonel and Admiral Canaris a tongue-lash-ing. So impressed were the Germans by the skill of the F.B.I. that they made only one further effort at sabotage in the United States during the war—a minor one that failed.

In 1948 Dasch and Burger were released from prison and deported to Germany. The garrulous Dasch had never stopped projecting a picture of himself as a loyal American who had risked death to foil a Nazi plot that otherwise would have cost untold numbers of lives and millions of dollars in war production—a man who, instead of being rewarded for valor, had been duped by the G-men, railroaded into prison, and then banished.

Germany also became hostile toward him. German news-papers described him as a traitor who had saved his own skin by sending six comrades to the electric chair. Thereafter he was hounded from town to town, occasionally spat upon or threatened, unable to hold for long jobs as a waiter or bartender. Several times his life grew so uncomfortable that he took refuge in Switzerland. He kept writing plaintive letters to the American Civil Liberties Union, J. Edgar Hoover, Attorney General Tom Clark, and eventually to President Eisenhower, seeking permission to return to the United States. In 1959 he wrote a book published in this country, *Eight Spies Against America*, which he hoped would be sold to the movies and would justify what he described as his courageous anti-Nazi, pro-American adventure. One point he made was that he had voluntarily surrendered some eighty thousand dollars to the United States government instead of skipping off to the South Seas with it.

But one of the conditions of the suspension of Dasch's prison sentence and his deportation was that he would not be allowed to return. The ban was never lifted. Even the lost eighty thousand dollars seemed to gain him no sympathy. He could never win a particle of the esteem enjoyed by another man who had lost money—young coastguardsman Cullen. Cullen had turned in the $260 that Dasch gave him to his commanding officer. "I never thought to get a receipt for it," he recalls, "so it went to the government. I never really missed it."

—*April 1970*

"I'VE SERVED MY TIME IN HELL"

by GEORGE McMILLAN

So thought many a weary Marine after the bloody, interminable battle for Guadalcanal. It was only a dot in the ocean, but upon its possession turned the entire course of the Pacific war.

O n May 3, 1942, a small detachment of Japanese sailors, the 3rd Kure Special Landing Force, landed without opposition on Tulagi Island, then capital of the British Solomon Islands.

Their prize was a group of faded, tin-roofed wooden buildings, a cricket field, and one of those peculiarly British colonial institutions called "The Residency." The usual inhabitants of the little seat of government, the mixed group of missionaries, civil servants, and Chinese traders, had been forewarned and had left.

After making what shift they could for their own comfort, the Kure men settled down in the tropic heat. They were only an outpost. They had been landed on Tulagi as the flank of the New Guinea front the Japanese were trying to develop in the late spring of 1942.

After they had been there a month, the men of the Kure unit started laying out an airstrip. Because Tulagi was totally unsuited, they chose a location on the larger island across the bay: Guadalcanal.

No one needs to be told that a battle was fought at Guadalcanal. It was one of the few battles in World War II that the United States stood a real chance of losing. And the outcome hung in the balance, not for a day, but for three months. It often rested on life-and-death combat between individuals, between a handful of Americans and a much larger Japanese force, fighting hand to hand.

It is not surprising that the style and stereotypes of the entire Pacific war were drawn at Guadalcanal. The dungaree-clad Marine, his helmet covered with camouflage cloth, lunging forward at the enemy with his rifle at the ready, became the single, larger-than-life figure of the Pacific theater of operations. And when anybody in those days said, "the island," there was no doubt about which island he meant.

What is surprising is that the facts about Guadalcanal live up to the fictions. Guadalcanal was pivotal in a purely military sense, too. With years of hindsight and careful research behind them, military and naval historians agree that it was a turning point of the Pacific war. At Guadalcanal the United States moved from the defense to the offense. The only direction in which the Japanese moved after Guadalcanal was backward.

As early as February 1942 there had been talk in Washington about some kind of operation in the islands north of New Caledonia. But there was little or nothing in the way of men or matériel with which to carry out such an operation. Besides, the joint chiefs of staff had given the war in Europe clear priority.

There were only 291 land-based airplanes in the hundreds of thousands of square miles the United States still held west of Hawaii, and fewer than half of these were modern, first-line combat aircraft. Excepting a few Marine defense battalions and Army antiaircraft units, there was only one amphibiously trained major combat unit in the Pacific—the First Marine Division, which was in the process of moving from the States to New Zealand for further training. It had been told it would not be used until 1943.

But all this suddenly changed when the Kure force lit grass fires to clear away the underbrush for their airfield on Guadalcanal. Suddenly, every man, every plane, every ship, and every minute counted.

The Japanese could not be allowed to finish that airstrip. Their bombers would for the first time be within range of the vital American shipping lanes to Australia. The United States was going to have to try to retake Guadalcanal. And it would be just so much easier to do if the island could be retaken before the Japanese finished the strip and could add land-based airplanes to their defense.

The race to get there in time began. On June 26 the newly appointed South Pacific commander, Vice Admiral Robert Ghormley, held a conference at his headquarters at Auckland. Major General Archer Vandegrift, commander of the First Marine Division, was to work out a training schedule for his outfit. But Ghormley had just received a warning order from Admiral Chester Nimitz, Commander in Chief, Pacific Ocean Areas, calling for an operation in "the lower Solomons" with D-day set for August 1. Vandegrift was to be It.

Vandegrift was in a fix; he was going to have to have his division ready to fight in thirty-seven days. His advance echelon had been in Wellington only twelve days. His rear echelon was still at sea, not due to arrive until July 11. The rehearsal was to take place at Koro in the Fijis, six days' travel from Wellington. That left thirty-one days. Koro is seven days from Guadalcanal; that left twenty-four days.

In those twenty-four days Vandegrift had to reconnoiter his target, get information about it, plan his assault, issue orders, load thirty-one transports and cargo carriers, and embark nearly 20,000 men and sixty days' supplies.

On June 30 the entire division was organized into 300-man, eight-hour, three-shift working parties for around-the-clock stevedore duty. A command line-up was hastily put together. Ghormley was theater commander, number one in the South Pacific—and a new boundary was drawn between him and General Douglas MacArthur, commander of the Southwest Pacific. Commander of the task force that was to go to Guadalcanal was to be Vice Admiral Frank Jack Fletcher, who had commanded the carriers at the Battle of the Coral Sea in May. To command the amphibious force, Rear Admiral Richmond Kelly Turner was named. And Vandegrift's place, as commander of the landing force, was directly under Turner.

The line-up looked good on paper. If there was a weakness it was at the top. Instead of pulling his people together in the little time left, Ghormley shoved off for a powwow with MacArthur in Australia. The outcome was a joint message to Washington asking that the Guadalcanal operation be postponed; the two "found themselves in agreement as to the doubtful feasibility of this first offensive," as one official history puts it. In short, Ghormley, bearing the top responsibility for the operation, did not believe in it.

The request was disallowed. Then, on July 28, when the tactical commanders met at Koro for the rehearsal, they discovered that there were serious unresolved differences between them. Fletcher astonished the others by revealing for the first time that he had no intention of risking his carriers in the waters of Guadalcanal for more than four days. This was a blow to Vandegrift and was not happy news to Turner.

The task force, in the luck of the draw, was concealed by squalls and an overcast as it moved from Koro to Guadalcanal. The first notion the Japanese had of its presence was at daylight August 7. At 0647 the traditional signal, "Land the landing force," was sent by Turner, and the Marines went over the side—"paled by days of inactivity . . . dripping with sweat . . . their dungarees clinging to their bodies," a man who was there remembers.

The first flight of Zeros had been scheduled to land on the Guadalcanal airstrip later that morning! The Japanese had just completed a 3,600-foot, coral-surfaced runway. The race was won, and the landing was unopposed, a stroke of the best fortune. At Guadalcanal, the Japanese simply took off, leaving behind (another stroke of good fortune) all their food and road-building equipment, and even a batch of propaganda leaflets.

But there were two separate assaults, and the one directed at Tulagi and its adjoining islands, Gavutu and Tanambogo, ran into some nasty opposition from the Kure force, which was still there. In July the Japanese had brought a construction unit to Guadalcanal, relieving the Kure men. In a prophetic defense the Kure men burrowed into the faults of the coral-hillocked islands, and the Marines had to blast and burn them out. There were two days of hard fighting.

Meanwhile, unloading was not going well. Low-flying Bettys from Rabaul attacked the American transports on the first day, slowing down the flow of supplies. The second day, August 8, they came back again in broad daylight and set fire to the transport *George F. Elliott*.

By nightfall, when only a fraction of the Marine supplies were ashore, Admiral Fletcher sent a message to Admiral Ghormley: "In view of the large number of enemy torpedo planes and bombers in this area I recommend the immediate withdrawal of my carriers." He ordered his carriers to change course for the southeast, and sailed away from Guadalcanal.

This left Admiral Turner the ranking American officer on the scene, with his transports and a protecting force of cruisers and destroyers, only a few of which had ever worked together before, operating under an Australian, Admiral V. A. C. Crutchley.

At 2032 Turner summoned Vandegrift and Crutchley to his command ship, *McCawley.* Because it would take several hours to get there in his barge, Crutchley came in his flagship, the cruiser *Australia.*

Now Turner gave Vandegrift the really bad news. He was going to have to pull out and take the transports (and the supplies still unloaded aboard them) with him. He couldn't stay without Fletcher's air cover. He would stay through part of the next day, leave in time to be out of there before deep dark set in. It is recorded that Vandegrift had a few angry words to say before he went ashore. Before Crutchley left, he asked Turner about a report he had heard that a Japanese force was on the way down to Guadalcanal.

It was nearly midnight. Turner, like most American naval officers, had a traditional distaste for night action. He dismissed the report. It was probably nothing more than an escort force for tenders that would launch a seaplane raid the next day, Turner said.

But Turner was quite wrong. A Japanese task force especially trained in night surface fighting was almost upon the Americans at that moment. It had been steaming at top speed all day long down the "Slot" between the chain of islands, headed for Guadalcanal, looking for a night fight—that night.

Before he went off to meet Turner, Crutchley had given his cruisers and destroyers their assignments for the night. They were to patrol the entrance to the twenty-by-thirty-mile body of water (eventually to be called Iron Bottom Sound, for the number of ships sunk there) between Tulagi and Guadalcanal in which rode the vulnerable transports. A tiny island called Savo sits in the middle of the entrance, and Crutchley put half his force (the cruisers *Chicago* and *Canberra*, his own flagship *Australia*, and two destroyers) on the south of Savo and the other half (the cruisers *Vincennes, Astoria*, and *Quincy* and two more destroyers) on the north. The radar-equipped destroyers *Blue* and *Ralph Talbot* were assigned to patrol the western approaches to the sound and give early warning of enemy attack.

At 0130 on August 9 the Japanese force (five heavy cruisers and two light ones) was at the south entrance. They had sighted the U.S. picket destroyer *Blue* at 0054, had slowed down and trained their guns on her. But when she had shown no signs of knowing they were there, they had sped up and come on. They knew exactly the disposition of the American forces; their float planes had been snooping for an hour.

At 0145 the Japanese cruisers sighted the southern group (minus *Australia* because Crutchley had not yet returned from the conference with Turner). Within two minutes every Japanese ship had fired torpedoes. They hit both *Chicago* and *Canberra*, crippling the latter so badly she had to be sunk the next morning.

They then turned the corner around Savo, into the sound, toward the northern group, which was taken by surprise. The Japanese quickly sank *Quincy* and *Vincennes* and damaged *Astoria*, which went down the next morning.

In the first surface battle that the U.S. Navy had fought since Santiago it suffered one of the worst defeats it had ever suffered or, fortunately, would suffer again throughout World War II. When daylight came there was nothing left in the sound except crippled and burning or sinking warships, and the transports. The transports hurried to unload as much as possible before dark, and then departed.

The quality of that Marine unit ashore now became critical. Could it hold alone, without any help from the air or from the sea? Could it take the punishment the Japanese were almost certain to pour on?

If a professional tradition and a record of rugged duty meant anything, the First Marine Division was the best in the American armed forces in 1942. Its nucleus, the First Marine Brigade, was led by men who had done hard, dirty, and largely thankless duty in the banana wars of the 1920s and 1930s in Haiti and Nicaragua. They had stubbornly persisted (even after Gallipoli) in their belief that it was still possible to make an amphibious assault against a defended shore in modern war, and had formed the landing force for six fleet landing exercises between 1931 and 1941. The brigade tested and perfected many of the most important innovations in amphibious warfare. And when the reserves had been called up in 1941, wrote Marine historian Colonel John W. Thomason, "the Leathernecks, the old breed of American regular, regarding the service as home and war an occupation . . . transmitted their temper and character and viewpoint to the high-hearted volunteer mass . . ." They had done the same in World War I.

The essential position on Guadalcanal was defensive. General Vandegrift wanted only as much land as he could be sure of keeping. The perimeter was a toe-hold and nothing more: the lines were drawn like an arc around the airfield. It was as if Marines had landed on Long Island and taken only Jones Beach. At one end of the beach the line was put down along a small, sluggish tidal river, the Tenaru. At the other end there was no natural defensive position: the line hung in the jungle. Inland, some outposts were strung along a bald ridge which overlooked the airfield.

The Japanese threw something against this diminutive beachhead every day and every night, from August through November, but their major offensive moves fell into a pattern. There was one in August, one in September, one in October, and one in November. The time interval was dictated by logistics; each time it took the Japanese about a month to rebuild their forces.

The Japanese were also operating at the farthest extremity of their lines of supply. It is necessary to understand that Guadalcanal was just as much an improvisation for the Japanese as for the Americans.

First the Japanese would make a heroic effort to bring in enough men and supplies to drive the Americans off the island. Then the Americans would make an equally heroic effort to back up the Marine landing force with whatever reinforcements they could get to the island. Before the battle was over the Japanese had brought men to Guadalcanal from southeast Asia, from China, from the home islands of Japan itself; the Americans were bringing troops from the U.S. mainland.

This build-up would go on for three or four weeks, and then there would be a climactic test of strength. The Japanese would attack, would fail, and then would fall back into the jungle. Then the build-up would start again.

The Japanese were slightly irrational. Or at least they seemed to have nourished a conviction of superiority. An example of this came to hand several days after the Battle of Savo. A few days after Marines landed, the Japanese had occupied Mount Austen and set up a listening post there. A

Marine officer who later stood at the same point said that he could easily see from there the shape and size of the Marine landing force. From this it is obvious that the Japanese must have known exactly how large the American force was. But apparently their minds did not listen to the reports of their eyes. Knowing that something like a division of Americans was on Guadalcanal, they nevertheless decided to attack with something less than a battalion. This was to be their test of strength for August.

On August 12 the Japanese high command in Tokyo ordered Lieutenant General Haruyoshi Hyakutake's Seventeenth Army to take over the ground action on Guadalcanal, and Rear Admiral Raizo Tanaka's Eighth Fleet to take over at sea. The nearest thing at hand for Hyakutake's use was a 2,000-man force of infantry, artillery, and engineers under Colonel Kiyono Ichiki that had been put together as the landing force for Midway. Tanaka put the first echelon— some 900 men—of Ichiki's force ashore on Guadalcanal on August 18.

What happened now was a calamity for the Japanese. Without waiting for the rest of his men, cocky Colonel Ichiki sent those he had across the sandspit at the Tenaru River against the Marines on the night of August 21. He lost 600 men, accomplished nothing, and expressed his chagrin by committing suicide.

That was the August offensive, but it was no sooner over than the build-up started again. The Japanese moved almost at once to reinforce. On August 23 they sent down a large convoy that included several troop-carrying transports. This news caused Admiral Fletcher to set sail for Guadalcanal again, and the result was: (1) an inconclusive naval skirmish (the Battle of the Eastern Solomons) and (2) a lesson learned by the Japanese—that they could not bring troops all the way down to Guadalcanal on slow-moving transports. They took all their infantry to the Shortland Islands, reloaded them there on fast destroyers, and then brought them down the last leg at night, on what soon came to be called the Tokyo Express.

These troops—about 6,000 men—were the rest of Ichiki's force plus a new outfit General Hyakutake was sending down, the Kawaguchi Brigade, veterans of China, Borneo, and the Philippines. Their whereabouts on Guadalcanal was not a mystery to General Vandegrift; natives were soon coming through the lines with the news that the Japanese were moving up the Lunga, into the hills behind the airfield.

Aware of his weakness there, General Vandegrift had already brought his raider and parachute battalions over from Tulagi on August 31 and given them the mission of defending this rugged piece of terrain. By September 12 Lieutenant Colonel Merritt ("Red Mike") Edson, the raider commander, had set up a thin line of defense across a bald ridge, facing a blank wall of green jungle in front and on both sides.

At 2100 that night a Japanese float plane dropped a flare over the ridge, and a few minutes later a Japanese light cruiser and three destroyers standing offshore began to shell the area. They kept this up for about twenty minutes.

Then the men of Kawaguchi Brigade came out of the jungle at the Marines. They hit hardest at the extreme right flank of the American position—almost at the bank of the Lunga. But words like "flank" and "position" are misleading pieces of language at a moment like this. They make a battlefield sound more orderly than it ever really is. This one was a melee.

The Japanese cut a hole in the Marine line and pushed some of the flank men back and upward to the crest. There were minutes when the Japanese had it their way, with nothing much left between them and the airfield, at that moment the prize of the Pacific war.

But it was no easier for the Japanese to fight in the jungle than it was for the Marines. They couldn't mobilize enough men to exploit their advantage, and the attack for that night sputtered out with sporadic rifle fire.

There were Japanese planes over the perimeter nearly all the next day, in three major attacks, and the Marine raiders worked with last-minute energy to improve their foxholes and to clear, as best they could, fields of fire between themselves and the jungle. There were about 400 raiders and parachutists on the ridge, holding a line about 1,800 yards long. That's one man about every five yards. If estimates of Japanese strength are good, there were at least five, maybe six, Japanese for every Marine that second night.

At 2100 on September 13 a Japanese plane dropped a flare over the lines. Destroyers started firing immediately. Then a flare rose from the Kawaguchi lines, and the Japanese struck.

Edson at once called on the Eleventh Marines, the First Division's artillery regiment. As the Japanese advanced Edson called the fire closer and closer to his own lines. By 10 P.M., 105 mm. howitzer shells were falling within 200 yards of the Marine foxholes. By then, the Japanese had again cut through the lines on the side of the hill; the Marines began to fall back to the crest as they had the night before.

In all the Japanese struck twelve times through the night, "grinding themselves into the fire from Marine artillery, mortars, machine guns and rifles in vain attempts to dislodge Edson from his final knoll of Bloody Ridge," says the official Marine history.

Squads of a reserve battalion from the Fifth Marines began to filter into the thin raider and parachute lines at 0400. By dawn the Japanese had spent themselves.

That was the September battle, the famous "Battle of Bloody Ridge," for which both Edson and Major Kenneth Bailey were to get the Medal of Honor.

Almost as soon as the firing died away, men all along the perimeter turned to the simple routines of life, and found them, as fighting men always have, to be gratifying sources of quiet pleasure. By this time there was both a swimming-hole and a laundry-hole on the Lunga. A fallen, half-submerged tree nearly spanned the river at one point. This interval was the time of the great housing project on Guadalcanal. Everybody built himself a crude shack and lean-to, using whatever materials came to hand.

But this tropical pastoral quickly passed. Before the September battle was over, the Japanese held a powwow at Truk and decided to make an even greater effort to retake Guadalcanal in October.

For this one, General Hyakutake himself was coming down. No more battalions, no more brigades: this time there would be two divisions-the 2nd (Sendai) and the 38th (Nagoya)-and then some. No more reliance on mortars alone, either; this time there would be 150 mm. howitzers with which to knock out the airfield and keep it knocked out.

Only one fresh American unit, the 164th Infantry Regiment of the Army's Americal Division, was sent to Guadalcanal. This outfit left Noumea on October 9 in two transports under escort of a force of four cruisers, eight destroyers, and three mine-layers commanded by Rear Admiral Norman Scott.

Scott was a perfectionist who had his cruiser force drilling for weeks in night operations. He reached Guadalcanal on October 11 and defeated a Japanese naval force in the night battle of Cape Esperance. The American regiment moved in safely.

What Scott had hit was, however, nothing more than a slightly oversized version of the daily Tokyo Express. And the Japanese had bigger things in store: early in the morning of October 13 their big push began. Twenty-two Japanese fighter-bombers came in at 1202, and they had no real opposition. They were after the airfield, and they left thirteen bomb holes in the strip. A subsequent bombing attack caught the American planes refueling and hit the main gasoline storage tanks. Five thousand gallons of precious and almost irreplaceable airplane fuel went up in black smoke.

No sooner had that flight disappeared than fifteen 150 mm. enemy howitzers, newly arrived, opened with their first bombardment of the airfield. They kept this up all afternoon.

Just before dusk two of the largest Japanese ships that had ever entered these waters, the battleships *Haruna* and *Kungo*, came plowing in, loaded with 300 shells of a new type, with greater bursting radius. Float planes lit the field with flares and the big ships cut loose, firing over 900 shells. Night bombers continued their strikes until daylight.

By noon of October 14 Henderson Field was out. The Japanese had succeeded. But still their bombers and howitzers kept working over the field all day, and that night a cruiser force threw in 752 eight-inch shells. The next morning, in broad daylight and in plain sight of the helpless and punch-drunk Marines, six Japanese transports unloaded the Sendai Division.

The Marine airmen made desperate efforts to stop this piece of arrogance. They sent out scouts to scavenge for gas, did what they could to repair the airstrip, and enabled Brigadier General Roy S. Geiger, the Marine air commander, to get some American dive bombers into action. By the end of the day three Japanese transports were beached and burning. But Hyakutake had got ashore most of his men—3,000 to 4,000—and 80 percent of his supplies.

Altogether Hyakutake now had about 20,000 more or less fresh troops on the island. Except for the Army regiment that had just come ashore, the Marines had less than this number, on whom malaria, malnutrition, and constant tension had worked their inevitable debilitating effect. Except for marginal forays, the airfield was useless; and the Japanese had control of the sea. It was a critical moment.

The one good piece of good news was that a new man had been put in charge of the whole Guadalcanal operation. He was Vice Admiral William F. Halsey. He took over down at Noumea as COMSOPAC (Commander, South Pacific), relieving Admiral Ghormley on October 18.

But the Japanese were moving into position. They struck at the mouth of the Matanikau on October 20. This and another attack on October 23 were repulsed.

This affair did not have the appearance of being a major push, and it was not. It was one prong of a three-pronged attack. The big push was to be a strike at the ridge, Bloody Ridge. This time the Japanese were simply going to pour more on—more men and, particularly, more fire power. They were going to get artillery up there.

The story of how they did so, the heroic effort and blood they put into moving the heavy guns through the jungle, is and will probably remain one of the most awesome parts of the whole Guadalcanal epic.

Nightmare stories trickle through the captured documents and testimony of Japanese who cut out this "Maruyama Trail" through the steep abutments and tangle of jungle. Every soldier who wasn't actually manhandling the guns had to carry an artillery shell plus his regular gear, infantry rifle, and ammunition.

The Japanese suffered: it is only a legend that they got along better in the jungle than did the Americans. The Japanese soldier did not, it is true, expect the same degree of personal comfort as did the Americans. But if he complained less, he undoubtedly suffered more. His army's medical services were primitive; the Japanese say that they lost more men on Guadalcanal through sickness than they did from American bullets.

This time the ridge was to be defended by a little bantam of a Marine, Lieutenant Colonel Lewis B. ("Chesty") Puller. Puller got his nickname from his posture: he stuck his chest out so far he looked deformed. Chesty was the Patton of the Marine Corps, the most decorated and in some ways the most controversial Marine officer of World War II. Once when an

Army chemical warfare officer finished a demonstration of a new flamethrower, Puller was heard to ask: "Where do you put the bayonet on it?" He was suspicious of any refinement of war above the hand-to-hand struggle.

His men, the 1st Battalion, 7th Regiment, were to get some of that on the night of October 24.

Shortly after dark, a heavy, squelching tropical rain began to fall. A few minutes after midnight the Japanese came lunging out of the jungle toward the ridge, crying out their *banzais*, throwing grenades, firing rifles and light machine guns, striking Chesty's men on a narrow front.

Marine artillery and mortars turned on the Japanese assembly areas, pounded away, pulled their fire up forward toward Marine lines, threw it back again into the Japanese assembly areas. At one point the Marine positions were swamped. But only momentarily. That was near where Sergeant "Manila" John Basilone had his section. He recalled afterward: "When the first wave came at us the ground just rattled. A runner came in and told me that at the emplacements on the right Japs had broken through. With their knives they had killed two of the crew and wounded three, and the guns were jammed. I took off up the trail to see what happened. . . . We left six Japs on the trail.

"While I fixed the jams on the other two guns up there, we stayed to set up. Bullets were smacking into the sandbags. I rolled over from one gun to the other, firing them as fast as they could be loaded. The ammo belts were in awful shape. They had been dragged on the ground. I had to scrape mud out of the receiver.

"Some Japs would sneak through our lines and behind us. I'd have to stop firing every once in a while and shoot behind me with my pistol. By dawn, when the fighting was over, our guns were just burnt out. Somebody figured we got rid of 26,000 rounds."

For what he did, Basilone got the medal of honor. He was later killed at Iwo Jima.

It was obvious to Puller that his men were taking the brunt of the Japanese October attack, and he asked for help. Division headquarters sent him a battalion from the 164th Infantry. There was no use trying to put them in as a unit while the Japanese were attacking. Instead, Chesty ordered his NCO's to come out of the line and lead the reinforcements in by squads. Shoulder to shoulder, Marines and soldiers fought on together until the Japanese firing died away at 0330.

The next day, Sunday, October 25, is remembered in Marine annals as "Dugout Sunday." Japanese warships stood offshore in broad daylight and shelled Henderson Field and the Marine perimeter. Dodging in and out of their foxholes, Seabees worked away at the airfield, like ants. Soon Marine fighter planes were rising from the field, holding off some of the incoming enemy bombers.

At 2200 that night the Japanese struck again at the ridge near where they had struck the night before and the month before *that*. But they got no place this time.

At another point on the perimeter, upstream on the Mantanikau, along the front held by the 2nd and 3rd Battalions, Seventh Marines, it was a different story. The Japanese kept charging there, up the steep escarpment which the Marines were defending, until they made a penetration. But here, as at the ridge, individual bravery did much to save the position at the crucial moment. The hero was Marine Platoon Sergeant Mitchell Paige, who won the Medal of Honor for what he did; that was, in his own words: "I would fire a burst and move. Right off the nose, in the grass, thirty Japs stood up. One of them was looking at me through field glasses. I let them have it with a full burst and they peeled off like they had been mowed.

"After that, I was so wound up I couldn't stop. I rounded up the skirmish line, told them I was going to charge off the nose and I wanted them to be right behind me. I picked up the machine gun, and without hardly noticing the burning hot jacket, cradled it in my arms and threw two belts of ammo over my shoulder. Behind me the skirmish line came whooping like a bunch of wild Indians. We fired on until we reached the edge of the clearing and then there was nothing left to fire at.

"I was soaked and steam was rising from my gun. My hand felt funny. I looked down and saw a blister running from my fingertips to my forearm."

That was the end of the October battle.

To the men who had been there since August, Guadalcanal had begun to seem infinite, almost eternal—a tragic and wearisome existence so profoundly felt that any other was difficult to remember.

"The weight loss averaged about 20 pounds per man,"

said a medical report. "Examination revealed marked dehydration as shown by dry skin and sunken eyes. Many of these patients reported being buried in foxholes, blown out of trees, blown through the air, or knocked out."

The single most seriously debilitating factor was the anopheles mosquito. There were 173 new cases of malaria in the first week of October; in the second week, 273; in the third, 655; and in the fourth, 840—the October total was 1,941. Chills and fever had grown so common that men didn't bother to turn into the hospital: they simply sweated it out in their own bivouac areas.

The essential tactical truth about Guadalcanal was evident now: it was a battle of attrition. The point had come when both sides had to ask themselves just how much the pestilential island was worth.

For the Americans the decision was appropriately made by the commander in chief, President Franklin D. Roosevelt. On October 24 the President sent individual messages to each member of the joint chiefs of staff calling on them to do whatever needed to be done to insure the capture of Guadalcanal.

Indecision, hesitation about committing men and materials to the battle, disappeared. The campaign might—and still very well could—be lost. But if it was, it would not be because the U.S. high command did not send every man, gun, and plane it could get there.

History's insights into Japanese high-command thinking are cloudy, but apparently the Japanese now also decided to pour more into Guadalcanal.

They were going to follow the well-established pattern they had laid down in August, September, and October. With one difference: this time the Imperial Japanese Navy insisted on being overall boss. Its ships and planes were going to shell Henderson Field out of commission on the nights of November 12-13 and November 13-14. The troop transports were to arrive on the morning of the fifteenth.

The U.S. reinforcements got there first. One echelon arrived on November 11 under the escort of a convoy commanded by Admiral Scott. The other arrived November 12 in a convoy escorted by Admiral Daniel ("Uncle Dan") Callaghan.

These forces got word at 1317 on November 12 from the

coastwatcher at Buin that Japanese planes and ships were on the way. The American troop transports and the other non-combatant vessels continued unloading until dusk and then shoved off to leave the night's work for Callaghan, who was senior to Scott.

The *Helena* got the first radar fix on the approaching Japanese at 0124 November 13. From there on for forty-five minutes there took place "the wildest most desperate sea fight since Jutland," according to historian Samuel Eliot Morison. By 0200 the Japanese admiral had had enough, and ordered his battleships to turn north.

The price both sides had paid was apparent at dawn. There were eight crippled ships lying in the narrow waters between Savo and Guadalcanal—five American and three Japanese.

That night, as they had planned, the Japanese came in again. This time there was nothing left to oppose them but motor torpedo (PT) boats. Just after midnight the Japanese stood offshore and shelled Henderson Field for thirty-seven minutes.

But Henderson Field was in business again soon after daylight, and the American planes had a prime target: the approaching group of Japanese transports, whose location had now been discovered. As the day wore on, planes from the "Big E," the carrier *Enterprise*, arrived, and by the afternoon U.S. airmen were taking a terrific toll. Admiral Tanaka retained an "indelible picture" of the scene that day—"of carrier bombers roaring toward targets as though to plunge full into the water, releasing bombs and pulling out barely in time; each miss sending up towering columns of mist and spray; every hit raising clouds of smoke and fire as transports burst into flame and take the sickening list that spells their doom. Attacks depart, smoke screens lift and reveal the tragic scene of men jumping overboard from burning, sinking ships."

It got so bad that Admiral Tanaka transferred a good part of the army force to destroyers. It was a good thing he did. By dark, Marine, Navy, and Army airmen had sunk seven Japanese transports and one heavy cruiser while losing only five planes.

At this point Tanaka asked his higher echelon if he might simply beach the four transports that were still afloat. The answer was No! But he did so anyway.

For some days two of America's newest and biggest battleships had been floating in the roads at Noumea, held there because, as one history puts it, "Many [officers] at COMSOPAC doubted the wisdom of committing two 16-inch battleships to waters so restricted as those around Savo Island, but Admiral Halsey felt he must throw in everything at this crisis." And so *South Dakota* and *Washington* steamed off to Guadalcanal, arriving there under the command of Admiral Willis Lee on November 14—ready to take on that night's Tokyo Express.

The fighting started at 2317. Aside from its distinction as one of the few actions in World War II where battleships fought *each other* in surface actions, it was another somewhat mixed-up and inconclusive fight. Neither of the American battleships was lost, but Japan lost its *Kirishima*. By 0025, in the first minutes of November 15, Admiral Kondo, commanding the bombardment group that night, ordered a withdrawal.

That moment is just as good as any to fix the point at which the United States won the victory of Guadalcanal.

It was not so much that the Japanese had been thrashed as that they could not afford to go on. Those troops sent in by the Japanese in November (only 4,000 of the 10,000 got safely ashore) were never to fight a major offensive action. It simply was too expensive to supply them on a regular basis or to reinforce them. Just to keep them alive the Japanese had to put supplies in sealed steel drums and drop strings of them from destroyers, to float ashore.

The Americans, on the other hand, began to reinforce almost at will and continued until there was a corps-sized ground force on Guadalcanal. These men conducted an offensive under Army General A. M. Patch; finally on February 9 he was able to report to Admiral Halsey: "Total and complete defeat of Japanese forces on Guadalcanal . . ."

As for the weary men of the First Marine Division, they were no longer capable of offensive operations. In November, 3,213 new malaria cases were reported and with the disease went a form of secondary anemia.

"Weight loss in these muscular, toughened young adults ran as high as forty-five pounds," wrote a doctor who treated them. "Rain, heat, insects, dysentery, malaria, all contributed—but the end result was not a bloodstream infection nor gastrointestinal disease but a disturbance of the whole organism—a disorder of thinking and living, or even wanting to live."

They were relieved on December 9. Shortly before their departure they went to the cemeteries to clean up and mark the graves of their buddies. On one mound they laid out an inscription in broken bits of stick which read, in crude lettering, "A Great Guy." Others read: "Our buddy," "A Big Guy with a Bigger Heart," "The harder the going the more cheerful he was."

And there was some poetry:

And when he goes to Heaven
To St. Peter he'll tell:
Another Marine reporting, sir,
I've served my time in hell.

—February 1966

THE GALLANTRY OF AN "UGLY DUCKLING"

by ROBERT L. VARGAS

Outgunned by the Nazi raider, the Stephen Hopkins *could have struck her colors. Instead she elected to fight.*

Whenever an unescorted American freighter encountered strange ships in the South Atlantic in 1942, her master knew that within minutes he might face a bitter decision: to surrender and have his vessel captured—probably scuttled—or to fight and be sunk. This was the quandary of Paul Buck, captain of the Liberty Ship *Stephen Hopkins*, when two unidentified vessels appeared out of the morning mist at 9:35 on September 27 of that year. A smaller object, possibly a small boat, seemed to be moving in the water between them.

Within minutes, any hope that the two ships might be American or British vanished. German colors were raised on both, and gun flashes broke from the bow of the smaller, appearing simultaneously, as if aimed by a central gun director.

Buck quietly ordered the general alarm sounded and called for hard left rudder to bring his ship from her heading of 310° true to 260°, directly away from the danger. If he had to fight, he wanted to offer the smallest possible target, his stern.

Unluckily, Buck and the *Hopkins* had encountered the German auxiliary cruiser *Stier* and her escort, the blockade runner *Tannenfels*. Built as the Atlas Levante Line's 4,778-ton *Cairo*, the *Stier* had been fitted out in December 1941 as an armed commerce raider and placed under the command of Fregatten Kapitän Horst Gerlach. At the time of her encounter with the *Stephen Hopkins* she was known to American and British naval intelligence only as Raider "J."

Outwardly the *Stier* was a dirty-gray freighter, somewhat lighter than standard war color, with a clipper bow and cruiser stern. Red-lead splotches dotted the superstructure and sides of her 322-foot length. In the words of one of the *Hopkins*'s crew, "She appeared like a converted fruit ship which runs from the West Coast of the U.S.A. to Europe." But underneath the disguise lay a modern arsenal. The central gun director controlled six 5.9-inch guns located behind shields just forward of the bridge structure and in the after well deck. Her firepower also included smaller director-fired guns, a twin 37-mm. mount, and 20-mm. antiaircraft guns. She carried two torpedoes.

The second German ship, the *Tannenfels*, was a former Hansa Line freighter now operating out of occupied France through the Allied cordon to deliver supplies and to take off prisoners from surface raiders in the South Atlantic. At 7,840 tons she was larger than the *Stier*, but she was armed with only 20-mm. antiaircraft guns. The *Tannenfels* had evidently been keeping a scheduled rendezvous with the raider when they were suprised by the *Stephen Hopkins*. When the equally surprised Liberty Ship was recognized, both Germans turned to pursue her.

The *Stephen Hopkins* was one of the war's first mass-produced U.S. Emergency Cargo vessels, or EC-2's, popularly known as Liberty Ships. She was strictly a work horse with a work-horse ancestry, for the Maritime Commission designers had patterned her, with few significant alterations, on a prewar British freighter type, the "Sunderland tramp." They had replaced the traditional coal-burning plant with oil-burning boiler furnaces. Steam from these drove already obsolescent triple-expansion "up-and-down" engines, since the demand for more modern turbine and diesel equipment had already strained war production capacity to the limit. Further, in the race to launch cargo ships faster than Axis submarines could torpedo them, American yards had substituted welded for riveted hull construction.

Almost identical with each of her 2,700 sister ships, the *Stephen Hopkins* had a displacement of 7,181 tons; her 441-foot hull resembled, one critic said, "half a watermelon." President Franklin D. Roosevelt, announcing the emergency shipbuilding program in January 1941 had dubbed the standard ship "a dreadful-looking object," and *Time* magazine had reported it under the heading "Ugly Duckling."

The *Stephen Hopkins* was now sailing in ballast on a northwesterly course, en route from Capetown, South Africa, to Paramaribo, Dutch Guiana, to load a vital war cargo of bauxite. She carried a crew of forty, one passenger, and a fifteen-man naval armed guard. High on her stern, ringed by a waist-high circle of gray-painted steel plate, sat her main firepower, one 4-inch gun. Perched on the bow was a dual 37-mm. mount, while two .30-caliber and four .50-caliber machine guns were scattered about her superstructure. She was hardly a match for the heavily armed German raider and her escort. These guns, predicted the naval authorities who had them installed, might protect a merchantman from a German U-boat in the Atlantic, perhaps for a Stuka dive bomber along the freezing wartime lanes to Murmansk. Realistically, however, the greatest value of even the 4-inch gun was psychological: at least, if attacked, the naval armed guard and the crew could shoot back.

Sighting the unmistakable profile of a Liberty Ship must have elated the raider captain. The capture of a new American ship, at a time when German battleships were bottled up in Norwegian fjords by the British navy, was an opportunity not given many Nazi officers. The *Stier*'s battle-trained crew were at their gun stations as the *Stephen Hopkins* put her rudder over. To prevent his victim from radioing for help, Gerlach ordered his gunnery officer to fire at the bridge and wireless room. At this point, Paul Buck could have chosen to strike his colors, but with the German shells on their way he had already made his decision. He would fight. Thus began an engagement that at least one naval historian has found reminiscent of the ship-to-ship battles of the War of 1812. Not every captain would have made Buck's unhesitating choice. No stigma of cowardice could attach to any merchant shipmaster who surrendered to Kommandant Gerlach. In only four months since he had left Germany and audaciously moved south through the English Channel under the noses of the British, Gerlach had terrorized merchantmen in the South Atlantic, sinking or capturing almost 50,000 tons of British and American shipping.

Relying on his vessel's innocent appearance, Gerlach would approach a lightly armed merchantman closely enough to order her to heave to before revealing his identity. One of these, the 10,169-ton American tanker *Stanvac Calcutta*, ignored the command, and he ordered her decks swept clear with his 37- and 20-mm. guns. When she continued to fight, she was promptly sunk with a loss of fourteen of her merchant crew, including the captain, and two members of her naval armed guard. When her survivors were picked up by the *Stier*, they learned that though the raider had met and sunk nineteen other merchant vessels of various Allied nationalities, there had been no casualties: none of the other ships had put up the slightest resistance.

The *Stier*'s 5.9-inch guns could sink even a cruiser. Months earlier, a sister ship, the *Kormoran* ("Raider 'G' " to naval intelligence), had deceived the Australian cruiser *Sydney* by apparently consenting to come alongside to be boarded and searched. Then at point-blank range the *Kormoran* opened fire, and she and the *Sydney* shot each other out of the water. Not a man of the Australian crew of seven hundred survived.

Such was the adversary Captain Buck had decided to duel.

The first 5.9-inch salvo slammed into the *Stephen Hopkins*'s superstructure. Shrapnel whistled. Jagged holes opened in thin, unarmored bulkheads. Shorted electrical wires started fires. Shells from both German vessels churned the water alongside, seeking the range; then they hammered the ship herself.

As on any vessel under fire, individual crewmen knew only what was happening in their immediate vicinity. In the engine room Second Assistant Engineer George Cronk had donned a telephone headset to communicate with the bridge. His only knowledge of the shelling came over the headphones.

On the boat deck Ensign Kenneth M. Willett, U.S.N.R., commander of the naval armed guard, was running to his battle station at the stern gun when a high-explosive shell burst. He gasped in pain, struck in the stomach by a shell fragment.

On the bridge Captain Buck impatiently waited for his gun crews to shoot back. But down on the decks he saw only confusion. The bow 37-mm.'s were unmanned. Sailors milled about amidships, and he had to send Third Mate Walter Nyberg down to order men to put on their steel helmets and life jackets.

The small raider was now only 1,000 yards astern. A

solitary rainsquall off the starboard bow offered no shelter for Buck's ship. Determined not to surrender, he continued to give the helmsman orders to keep the stern toward the Germans. On the other side of the wheelhouse Chief Mate Richard Moczhowski stationed himself where he could watch the enemy ships and shout information to the captain.

Chief Steward Ford Stilson was in his room making out a menu when the first shots were struck. He later wrote: "At the end of this first minute or so word was passed to me that the Chief Mate had been wounded. I went back to my room, secured bandages and antiseptics and proceeded to the bridge deck, where I found the Chief Mate reclining on the deck in the thwartship passageway adjacent to the wheelhouse but very active in shouting orders and advising the Captain to keep her turning with her stern bearing on the enemy. The Mate was shot high in the chest and in the left forearm. I applied a tourniquet and bandaged both wounds. I started below to get more material ready for the next casualty, but returned up the ladder at the sound of severe groans.

"He [Moczhowski] had gotten to his feet with the aid of one of the ordinary seamen, Piercy, and had turned [to] the opposite passage where he was again struck, this time in the leg by a fragment. All this time shells had been riddling the superstructure. . . ."

The fire that the *Stier* and the *Tannenfels* were pouring into the *Stephen Hopkins* was now intense, but instead of producing the panic that Kommandant Gerlach presumably intended, it jarred the merchant seamen and armed guard into action. Second Mate Joseph Layman's 37-mm. guns on the bow fired first, their shells thumping into the *Stier*. Amidships a .50-caliber machine gun joined the battle. One by one, five other machine-gun crews fired their weapons, the scattered bursts growing into a steady roar as tracer bullets guided the aim of the inexperienced gunners. Soon a storm of machine-gun bullets was raking the *Stier* and the *Tannenfels.*

On the *Stephen Hopkins*'s stern Ensign Willett had reached his battle station at the 4-inch gun. With one hand clutched to his stomach wound, he rallied his young armed guard crew. His orders were short and crisp. Reacting, one seaman grabbed a shell from the ready magazine and shoved it into the breech. Another relayed the range, one thousand yards. Willett ordered his gunners to fire at the raider's waterline. The 4-inch gun roared. Seconds later the shell exploded inside the *Stier*.

Again and again the gun crew loaded and fired. A fourth, then a fifth shell hit the *Stier*. Very soon white smoke was pouring from holes near her waterline. Willett, straining to see his target through the smoke, yelled for the pointer and trainer to keep aiming at the hull.

Engineer Cronk no longer needed his headphones to hear the battle. Explosions echoed down the funnel into the engine room. Like every other man there, Cronk dreaded the shell that might explode a boiler. Then the deck shuddered and the lights went out. Cronk stood rigid, watching the boiler fires, until dim emergency lights flickered on, casting eerie shadows.

Topside, a high-explosive shell hit the freighter's bow. As the smoke drifted away, Captain Buck could see the 37-mm. gun platform wrecked and burning, the gun handlers killed or wounded. Another shell wrecked the radio room, ending the radioman's frantic SOS signals. Lifeboats along the port side dangled, splintered and torn, from their davits. The accurate German gunnery continued to rip gaping holes in the hull, and incendiaries started new fires.

But Buck still commanded a fighting ship. His machine-gun fire peppered both the *Stier* and the *Tannenfels*. When the raider tried to maneuver into position for a six-gun broadside, Buck saw to it that the helmsman kept his ship stern on. At regular intervals, above the din, he could hear the 4-inch gun crack.

At 1,000 yards' range Ensign Willett's crew furiously loaded and fired. In less than twenty minutes they had fired thirty-five 4-inch rounds, most of which had hit the *Stier* near the waterline. Between shots Willett praised his men or leaned down the ammunition hoist and shouted encouragement to the seamen passing powder and shells up from the magazine. Through the smoke he could clearly see the effects of his gunnery. The raider was listing slightly to port and settling by the stern. Fires burned from her bow to her stern.

On Gerlach's bridge, the hope of a quick, easy victory had vanished. A shell from the merchantman's lone gun had disabled his torpedo tubes, and a fire was threatening his magazine. Below decks his men struggled in waist-deep water to plug holes below the waterline. The *Stier* was fighting to stay afloat, but with his vastly superior firepower Gerlach had no intention of breaking off the battle. He ordered his gun director to silence the enemy's 4-inch gun.

Exploding shells seeking the gun tub immediately began to rock the *Stephen Hopkins*'s stern. One that missed its target smashed into the engine room. The starboard boiler burst. Steam billowed into every crevice of the darkened engine room, rolling up ladders, scalding men.

Her power plant crippled, the *Stephen Hopkins* lost headway until she was finally lumbering along at one knot. All Buck's signals for more speed remained unanswered. Instead, out of passageways and escape tunnels the burned and choking survivors of the engine-room inferno began to stumble onto the open decks. Among them was George Cronk.

With their target almost dead in the water, Gerlach's gun crews sent salvo after salvo into the *Stephen Hopkins*, turning the stern into twisted, burning wreckage. Still the 4-inch gun fired back. One by one, the armed guard crew were killed or wounded, until Willett manned the gun alone. He was struggling to load again when a shell hit the magazine below the gun tub.

The harried German captain, seeing the explosion, must have assumed that the gun was out of action and that he could at last finish off his adversary. His own ship was settling at the stern, and a telephone talker relayed a story of fires fore and aft, one dangerously near the magazine. Moreover, the sea was rising, a light, intermittent rain was falling, and visibility was deteriorating. Gerlach ordered his gun crews to hurry and sink the merchantman. But he barely had turned his attention to saving his ship when the *Hopkins*'s 4-inch gun fired again.

It must have seemed impossible. The Germans had seen the gun tub explode. But through the mist the 4-inch gun on the *Stephen Hopkins* now fired a second time. Aboard the shattered Liberty Ship, the concussion of the magazine explosion had hurled Willett to the deck of the gun tub, wounding him again. He was struggling to his feet when the youngest member of the *Stephen Hopkins*'s crew, eighteen-year-old Engineering Cadet Midshipman Edwin J. O'Hara, took over the gun.

O'Hara, who had escaped the blazing engine room, had learned the basics of naval gunnery at the United States Merchant Marine Academy at King's Point, New York, and from his friend Willett. Quickly examining the gun, he found it damaged but in firing condition. In the ready magazine lay five live rounds. O'Hara shoved one into the breech, pointed the gun, and yanked the firing lanyard. The barrel jumped and a 4-inch shell hit the *Stier*.

With the magazine below the gun tub in flames, O'Hara manned the gun alone, loading and firing the four remaining rounds at 900 yards' range, and scoring hits on the *Tannenfels* and the *Stier*. Only when the shells in the ready magazine were expended and no others were to be found did he leave the gun tub and help his friend look for a lifeboat.

The fight had lasted about twenty minutes. On the *Stephen Hopkins*'s bridge Paul Buck surveyed the blazing wreck. Besides exploding the starboard boiler and demolishing the radio shack and the mast, the *Stier*'s shells had wrecked the engine steering room and shattered the deckhouse and hull. With the superstructure afire and his command sinking beneath him, he reluctantly gave orders to abandon ship.

Buck, now joined by George Cronk, found only one lifeboat still serviceable. Together they struggled to lower it into the water as shellfire continued to demolish the *Stephen Hopkins*. They then separated and, except for a fleeting glimpse of him on a life raft, no more is known of Paul Buck, the freighter captain who had fought a warship to the death.

The rest of the story falls to Engineer George Cronk as senior American survivor and commander of the only *Stephen Hopkins* lifeboat to make it to land.

"The raider was using shrapnel and incendiary shells," he reported. "I lowered the after fall of boat Number One, which was about five feet from a roaring inferno of flames. A shell burst along the boat on the way down, killing two and wounding four men. The remaining crew was putting over rafts when I jumped overboard. I was later picked up by this boat, and with all the able men in it we got out the oars, and among the dying we got several men from the water and from rafts.

"Then the wind started rising and the sea running high, the visibility becoming very bad. All sighted the Third Mate in one of the smashed lifeboats that had been blown off the *Stephen Hopkins* by shellfire. He had it bolstered up at one end by a doughnut raft, but row as hard as we could, we could not get to him on account of the wind and seas.

"A doughnut raft went by with at least five men on it. We rowed for two hours until our hands were blisterd, and still we could not pick up the men. The wind and seas were getting higher all the time and at last poor visibility blotted out everything."

Cronk, hoping to rescue more survivors, put out his sea anchor and drifted in the vicinity until noon the next day, but he found only floating wreckage. He was in command of a lifeboat 1,000 miles from the nearest land. Ordering his able-bodied men to rig a sail, he headed northwest.

It was a brave decision. He and the eighteen other survivors faced the open Atlantic. In the lifeboat's lockers were twenty-four gallons of water, plus enough malted milk tablets, C rations, and chocolate to last for perhaps a month. That morning Cronk made the first entry in a terse log, from which the following are extracts:

"Attacked by enemy raiders . . . approx. lat. 31, long. 16, at 9:38 A.M. September 27th. Shelled by two armed merchant ships for about 29 minutes. . . . Ship went down in flames. . . .

"SEPTEMBER 28TH. Found two abandoned rafts but no sign of men on them. Took stores and water breaker . . . from two rafts and set sail for the coast of South America. . . .

"OCTOBER 1ST. . . . Cut water ration to 6 ounces per day per man, so as to give more to wounded men.

"OCTOBER 2ND. Strong winds from southeast. Sailing due west. Have no idea of position of ocean currents or prevailing winds as there is no South Atlantic chart in boat. . . .

"OCTOBER 6TH. . . . Rainwater caught has bad taste due to chemical in sail cloth.

"OCTOBER 7TH. . . . McDaniels, 2nd cook, died at 6:30 P.M. Stopped ship for five minutes and buried him. . . .

"OCTOBER 8TH. . . . Gun crewman Brock has infected shoulder from shrapnel. . . . [Messman] Romero died at 2:30. Buried at sunset. . . .

"OCTOBER 11TH. Good breeze until 9 A.M., ran into rain squall, caught 1 gallon of water. Becalmed. Something sent up a green rocket right over our mast from a very short distance. Apparently from a submarine. We answered with 2 flares from Very pistol. All this at about 3:15 A.M. . . .

"OCTOBER 12TH. George Gelogotes, fireman, died this morning. . . .

"OCTOBER 16TH. . . . Wiper Demetrades died at 7 A.M. . . .

"OCTOBER 17TH. Took in sea anchor at 6 A.M. Steering northwest. Fill all water casks and empty ration tins with water. . . .

"OCTOBER 19TH. High winds and seas, shipping lots of water, bailing all night, everybody wet from rain and spray. Most everyone has sores that won't heal. Violent squalls. Steering northwest. Hove-to all night. High seas. . . .

"OCTOBER 23RD. Poor breeze, just steering way. Sun hot, everyone kind of weak. Cut food ration in half 4 days ago. Now getting 1 oz. of pammicon [pemmican], 1 oz. of chocolate, ½ oz. of malted milk tablets, 1 type C ration biscuit per man per day, water ration 20 oz. per man per day due to rain water caught. . . .

"OCTOBER 24TH. Been becalmed for 24 hours. Very hot, everyone very weak. Seen some kind of sediment floating in water. Saw a butterfly and 2 moths. . . . Very poor visibility. . . . Fair breeze at sunset. Steering west.

"OCTOBER 25TH. . . . Seen a yellow moth. Makes us think we are near land. . . .

"OCTOBER 27TH. Hurrah, sighted land 4 A.M. Landed at the small Brazilian village of Barra do Itabopoana. . . .

The survivors—fifteen men of the *Hopkins*'s total complement of fifty-seven—were reported to be "in wonderful condition, considering what they'd gone through," according to Lieutenant Joseph E. Rich, who traveled from Vitória, Brazil, by taxi, Piper Cub, and locomotive to meet them. "One could not help but feel the deepest admiration for these men who had faced such odds and were never for one moment beaten. After thirty days of being battered together on a cramped lifeboat, they were still lavishing praise on one another, helping one another."

George Cronk modestly refused credit for his epic thirty-day voyage in an open boat. Instead he paid tribute to Ensign Willett and Cadet O'Hara.

Although the *Stephen Hopkins*'s battle with the *Stier* and the *Tannenfels* was but a brief episode in a very big war, it was memorable in the annals of the Navy and the Merchant Marine. Not until the war's end was it definitely known that the *Stier* followed the *Stephen Hopkins* to the bottom in the 2,200-fathom deep above which they had duelled. The *Tannenfels*, although damaged, made Bordeaux, carrying Kommandant Gerlach and his officers, men, and prisoners who had abandoned the *Stier*.

Comparing their battle experiences, the survivors gradually determined the fate of each missing man on the *Stephen Hopkins*. Captain Buck had vanished on a doughnut raft in the rising sea. Chief Mate Moczhowski was last seen on the starboard side of the boat deck badly wounded. Cadet Midshipman O'Hara was killed by shrapnel after he left the gun tub. Ensign Willett, covered with blood, was last seen cutting life rafts loose for his naval armed guard and the merchant crew.

The nation bestowed a whole cluster of posthumous honors on the ship and her heroic company. The *Stephen Hopkins* herself was awarded a "Gallant Ship" citation, and two later Liberty Ships were christened the *Stephen Hopkins* and the *Paul Buck*. A destroyer escort (DE-354) was named for Ensign Willett. On the campus of the United States Merchant Marine Academy a major building was named O'Hara Hall. For extraordinary heroism and conspicuous courage, Willett was posthumously awarded the Navy Cross. Merchant Marine Distinguished Service Medals were posthumously bestowed on Captain Buck and Cadet Midshipman O'Hara.

Final, comprehensive tribute to all who served on the *Stephen Hopkins* during her great fight was paid in the words of a spokesman for the Office of the Chief of Naval Operations: "The extraordinary heroism and outstanding devotion to duty of the officers and crew of the Armed Guard and the ship's company were in keeping with the highest tradition of American seamanship. Their fearless determination to fight their ship, and perseverance to engage the enemy to the utmost until their ship was rendered useless, aflame and in a sinking condition, demonstrated conduct beyond the call of duty."

—December 1969

SORRY, NO GAS

by STEPHEN W. SEARS

How Americans on the home front met the Great Gasoline Crisis.

Accoring to the members of the blue-ribbon committee, the situation was desperate. Their report, released to the Washington press corps, had been blunt, unsparing, and apocalyptic. "We find the existing situation to be so dangerous," it warned, "that unless corrective measures are taken immediately this country will face both a military and civilian collapse." The committee proposed to counter the dire threat by the imposition of nationwide gasoline rationing.

It is easy to imagine such a report issuing from a latter-day, OPEC-inspired energy crisis. In fact, however, it was issued on September 10, 1942, with the United States nine months into World War II, and it triggered the nation's first—and, thus far, only—encounter with the full-fledged rationing of gasoline. How the American people coped with so traumatic an experience may be instructive.

To be sure, the lessons of history need to be used with caution. We were then at war, united against a common enemy. We were then not hostage to foreign sources for petroleum. Indeed, in 1942, for much of the country at least, there was not even a gasoline shortage. Yet if the origins of wartime gas rationing have little in common with the energy crisis of a new age, the actual rationing experiences of 1942 to 1945 may offer certain lessons worth a second look.

The blue-ribbon committee that issued its outspoken report in September 1942 had been assigned the task of bringing order out of confusion. It was a distinguished panel, including the educator James B. Conant, president of Harvard, and physicist Karl T. Compton, president of the Massachusetts Institute of Technology; at its head was Bernard Baruch, Wall Street wizard, director of industrial mobilization during World War I, and confidant of Presidents. Franklin Roosevelt had turned to him almost in desperation. "Because you're 'an ever present help in time of trouble,' " the President pleaded in a handwritten note, "will you 'do it again'?" The time of trouble in this instance was what the press called the "rubber mess."

When the Japanese bombed Pearl Harbor, rubber instantly became the most critical strategic material for making war. Nine-tenths of the nation's rubber came from the Far East, and it was painfully evident that nothing would now stop Japan from cutting off that source. Stockpiles on hand, enough for about a year of peacetime demand, were grossly inadequate for the growing war machine. Synthetic rubber eventually would provide the answer, but the American synthetic-rubber industry was in its infancy. Just four days after Pearl Harbor a freeze was put on the sale of new passenger-car tires, and on December 27 tire rationing was authorized, to go into effect early in January 1942. Sales of new cars also were halted, leaving America's motorists to contemplate an uncertain driving future with their present cars and tires.

There was much complaint on Capitol Hill at the administration's lack of foresight in not undertaking a synthetic-rubber program earlier, as well as much heated debate over which manufacturing process should receive priority; the oil bloc promoted the petroleum-derivatives process, while the farm bloc trumpeted the virtues of the grain-alcohol method. Finally this was straightened out and the synthetic-rubber program put in train, but not before the issue of gasoline rationing was injected into the whole business, complicating it infernally.

At this point, in the early months of 1942, gas rationing was an issue plaguing only the Eastern seaboard. Observant Eastern motorists, however, could have detected the handwriting on their gasoline pumps as early as the previous summer, six months before Pearl Harbor. Fully 95 percent of the coastal states' petroleum needs were supplied by tankers from the Gulf Coast. In the late spring of 1941 the administration made and emergency loan of one-fifth of these vessels to the British to shorten the voyage time of their war-ravaged tanker fleet: oil exports from Caribbean and Gulf Coast refineries were shipped in the American tankers to New York and Halifax, then transshipped across the Atlantic in British tankers. Shortages soon appeared at Eastern filling stations, and the administration's petroleum coordinator, Harold L. Ickes, veteran New Dealer and self-styled curmudgeon, lectured the public on voluntary cuts in nonessential driving and called for early station closings. He was largely ignored, although the New Jersey legislature took enough notice to pass a resolution condemning the requested cuts as a threat to the state's tourist industry. After some dislocations as oil companies reduced their allotments to meet the shortfall, the minicrisis passed when the British returned the borrowed tankers. In any future fuel crisis, Ickes remarked pointedly, "I suspect that it is going to require something more than persuasion. . . ."

Ickes put his finger squarely on the problem: human nature. To ask the average American motorist to cut his use of gasoline voluntarily in a time of peace and prosperity was to ask him to cut his standard of living voluntarily, which was a lot to ask, particularly if his next-door neighbor was doing nothing of the kind. The automobile culture was perceived as very much a part of the good life, a fact recently and vividly confirmed during the Great Depression. Americans somehow managed to drive straight through the worst economic upheaval in their history. After the slightest of dips in 1932-33, when the economy sounded the depths, gasoline consumption climbed steadily, and in 1941, despite the gasoline minicrisis in the East, passenger cars used over 10 percent more fuel than in 1940.

To all appearances, the future was secure as far as gasoline stocks were concerned. The United States was entirely self-sufficient in oil, and indeed was a major exporter of petroleum products. At the outbreak of World War II in 1939, North America accounted for 64 percent of the world's crude-oil production. (The Near and Middle East's share, by contrast, was a mere 5.7 percent.) Dr. Robert E. Wilson, a government consultant on oil production, said in mid-1940 that the outlook for the American petroleum industry was such that "even satisfying the enormous demands of a mechanized army presents no serious problems."

While Wilson's forecast would prove essentially accurate, war's cold realities made short work of any feelings of complacency. It was the Eastern seaboard that felt the pinch first. Beginning in mid-January 1942 German U-boats opened a fearsomely effective campaign against American coastal shipping. In just two weeks they torpedoed nine tankers. By May, daily deliveries of gasoline to the East Coast had been slashed 80 percent. It would be months before the U.S. Navy could make inroads against the submarine offensive. Ickes was candid about the crisis: "Storage on the Gulf Coast and in the Southwest is brimming," he acknowledged, but there was simply no way for railroads and barges to compensate fully for the tanker losses. Washington announced that on May 15 gas rationing would go into effect in seventeen Eastern states. That same month the national speed limit was reduced to 40 miles an hour to conserve fuel and tires.

The emergency rationing program was put in the hands of Leon Henderson, head of the Office of Price Administration. Henderson—an economist, a warrior in a hundred New Deal battles whom conservatives regarded as a wild-eyed radical—occupied a decidedly prominent post. "For this job I need the toughest damned bastard in town," Roosevelt had told him, "and Leon, you are it." Henderson had to be all of that to survive as OPA head, for he was responsible for imposing a myriad of controls on the people and the economy. The hastily contrived Eastern rationing plan, with its basic allotment of three gallons a week, was something of a ramshackle affair, full of inequities, especially for motorists living on the fringes of the rationed areas who had to endure the sight of those from neighboring towns driving to their heart's content. It also had loopholes, the most notorious being the X-ration card that permitted unlimited gas for supposedly essential use. When two hundred members of Congress applied for and received X rations, editorial writers across the land raised a derisive shout.

By the fifth month of war, then, no American could buy a new car, tires were tightly rationed, and some 50,000,000 citizens in the East were trying to get by on drastically reduced gasoline supplies. The Petroleum Industry War Council was on record as warning of far worse to come. It pointed to the critical rubber situation and predicted that unless something was done promptly, the number of road-worthy automobiles, currently standing at 29,600,000 would be slashed to 9,000,000 by the end of 1943 and to 1,000,000 by the end of 1944. One million cars! That was something last seen in 1913 and would surely mark Judgment Day for the American way of life. The only way to prevent this, said the Petroleum Council, was to accelerate synthetic-rubber production—and to ration gasoline nationwide.

Such prophecy heated the political atmosphere in Washington. Bruce Catton, the future historian who observed it all from a ringside seat in one of the war-mobilization agencies, wrote sardonically that "there was a confusion of tongues and a blowing of great winds." Certainly it was an odd situation. The means of closing the critical rubber gap was the subject of intense debate. Almost nightly, in Caribbean and Atlantic coastal waters, oil tankers were ablaze, forcing millions of Americans to make do with only a few gallons of gas a week, while millions more could still "fill 'er up" whenever they felt like it, and storage tanks along the Gulf Coast were still full of gasoline. Experts said Draconian action must be taken immediately. Congressman Leland M. Ford rose on the House floor to exclaim, "What is the whole program? Why are not our people told the plain, honest-to-God truth?"

The truth may have been plain, but it was also unpalatable. Unless *all* civilians were force by edict to cut their driving to a minimum by means of gasoline rationing, they would run their tires down to the rims, and there was no possible way to replace all those tires. And without automobiles to get workers to their jobs, the Arsenal of Democracy would grind to a dead stop.

While the nation's industrial plant in the war years was nowhere near as decentralized as it is today, it clearly was tending in that direction. All across the country new arms factories were springing up in cornfields and meadowlands far from public transportation. This was particularly true in California, center of the burgeoning aircraft industry. Seven out of ten war workers in the Los Angeles area depended on their automobiles to get to work; at some plants the ratio was as high as nine out of ten. A survey in Michigan disclosed that 635,000 of 850,000 war workers had to drive to work. Investigators at two hundred key industrial sites in fourteen states found 69 percent of the employees had no alternative to commuting by car. For the duration the private automobile was going to be as vital a cog in the war machine as steel or copper or machine tools.

Roosevelt knew this truth better than anyone, but he could not bring himself to say it out loud and face the supposed wrath of a nation of gasoline-rationed car owners— and one out of five of the 132,000,000 Americans now owned a car. He knew, too, that the midterm congressional elections were due in the fall; so did the nervous congressmen up for re-election, particularly those from the wide-open Western states. In answer to a press-conference question about the rubber mess, the President admitted, "I don't know who is right. Now here is the greatest expert on it in the United States," he said pointing to himself, "and he doesn't know!" Urged by his aides to impose gas rationing, he called instead for a massive scrap-rubber drive, and thousands of tons of old tires, hot-water bottles, garden hoses, overshoes, and floor mats (including one snatched from the White House by Harold Ickes) poured into collection centers. Little of this scrap proved to be reusable, however, and the rubber shortage persisted. When he was asked about gasoline rationing, Roosevelt did not have an answer either, except to remark that he could understand why someone with a good car, four good tires, and an oil well next door might want to continue driving as he pleased. Predictably, none of this added to the public's understanding of the real issues.

In the summer of 1942 Congress took it upon itself to untangle the rubber mess (and by extension, the gasoline mess) by passing Iowa Senator Guy Gillette's bill to establish a "rubber czar" at the head of a special agency independent of the War Production Board then overseeing the war economy. Roosevelt knew he must veto the Gillette bill or risk serious damage to the mobilization machinery, and to make his veto stick he hit upon one of these brilliant political strokes for which he was famous. In his veto message he announced the formation of the blue-ribbon Baruch committee to examine thoroughly the whole business of rubber, gasoline, and civilian automotive transportation and to make recommendations. In one neat maneuver, he had side-stepped, gotten out from under, and passed the buck.

Baruch's panel delivered its forceful conclusions, and

with that weighty backing the President bit the bullet and announced that on December 1, 1942, nationwide gasoline rationing would take effect. A national "victory speed" was set at thirty-five miles an hour. William M. Jeffers, head of the rubber program, put the business in a nutshell: "This is not a gasoline rationing program," he said, "but a rubber conservation program; the object is not to take cars off the road, but to keep them on the road." The people accepted the verdict with apparent equanimity, for the turnout at the polls in November was low and Republican gains were regarded as normal for an off-year election.

Perhaps there was a certain degree of resignation in all this, for by the time gas rationing went on the books, the American people were well on their way to coming under government edict in virtually every aspect of their daily lives. Prices, wages, and rents were tightly controlled to fight inflationary pressures. At one time or another during the war years there was rationing of (among other things) meat, butter, kitchen stoves, fuel oil, fats, sugar, shoes, liquor, cheese, dried peas, canned goods, coffee, and typewriters, in addition to tires and gasoline. The citizenry found itself coping with ration stamps and coupons and red points and blue points and inspection records and stickers and booklets and leaflets and charts and certificates and regulations and applications and authorizations—a headache of red tape and paperwork unparalleled in the national experience.

Presiding over all this, and squarely in everyone's field of fire, was Leon Henderson and the Office of Price Administration. In size the OPA was second only to the Post Office Department; in bureaucratic complexity it was unmatched. It was, said one observer, "born in strife and lived in turmoil." Yet no one could complain that it was a distant bureaucracy, out of sight and out of reach. There was a total of fifty-six hundred local OPA boards to administer the various programs and controls, staffed largely by unpaid volunteers from every walk of life and generally bipartisan in political persuasion, for neither party wanted to shoulder the blame.

The gasoline rationing plan devised by Henderson's OPA differed fundamentally from most other wartime rationing programs. Since petroleum was a key strategic weapon of war, and since a major goal was to save tires, gas for civilians was rationed according to individual need rather than parceled out on the equitable one-to-a-customer principle followed with such items as meat or sugar or canned corn. Every car owner received a basic so-called A ration, initially four gallons a week, good for perhaps sixty miles of driving. If he could persuade the local rationing board that he simply had to have more fuel, he would be eligible for a supplementary B or C ration. The B allotment generally went to those who could prove they had farther to drive than A-ration gallonage permitted. The key test for a C ration was "relation to the war effort or the public welfare," as the OPA put it. War-plant workers fell into this category, as did doctors and others involved in "public welfare." There was an unlimited "emergency" category for police, volunteer firemen, civil defense personnel, and the like, and a special T ration for truckers. Tied to the system was a compulsory tire-inspection plan whose web of regulations had to be followed religiously in order for a vehicle to be eligible for a recapped or new tire.

All the world would know how well anyone had done at their local ration board, for lettered windshield stickers were handed out along with gas-coupon booklets in each category. At the gas pump, the attendant would remove the appropriate number of coupons, on which the car's license number had to be written, from the customer's ration booklet. Coupons were valid only for a specified period, to prevent saving up for a sunny day.

Motorists by the millions promptly descended on their local boards to seek supplementary gas rations. Processing war workers was simplified by plant transportation committees that approved mileage claims and organized car pools, whose members countersigned the applications. Both the virtues and the faults of the decentralized ration-board system soon were evident. Exaggerated claims of need could more easily be deflated by those who knew the local situation, and car owners found it hard to fool a neighbor sitting on an OPA board. On the other hand, there were many instances of neighborly favoritism and string pulling. (There were also small human dramas. A woman in Dunkirk, New York, wrote a letter pleading to her local board asking it *not* to grant her husband the B sticker he sought, for he only wanted it "to go out with other women.") Under the circumstances, it was probably about as fair a system as could be devised, and patriotic support of the war effort played a very real part in these across-the-counter negotiations. About half the nation's car owners obtained B or C classifications, and in the vast majority of cases they were legitimately awarded.

Along with the millions of windshield stickers and ration books came a flood of admonitory posters and leaflets and advertisements. Posters bluntly asking "Is This Trip Necessary?" were everywhere. Another poster warned, "When you ride ALONE you ride with Hitler! Join a Car-Sharing Club TODAY!"—a theme given emphasis by a picture of a joy rider breezing along in an open convertible, oblivious of the ghostly figure of the Führer on the seat beside him. A typical magazine ad depicted a slacker dozing on a couch above a copy that read, ". . . Sure, you out-smarted the ration board on gas all right . . . and kept a certain Army plane in Africa out of the war." The OPA's leaflet explaining the rationing program was embellished with a drawing of a satanic-looking Japanese soldier guarding a great pile of tires, with the caption "*This* is why your mileage is rationed."

So the American car culture settled gingerly into its new, poor-relation status. Since the mid-twenties the automobile had been seen as a necessity of life; now it was just that and nothing more. There was little gas for anything beyond getting to work and accomplishing other spartan tasks the OPA labled "general utility." "It takes practically the whole day, every day, to figure out how to get certain things done without using any gas," observed *The New Yorker*'s E. B. White.

Pleasure-seeking habits changed radically. The Sunday driver was gone from the land. Dr. Benjamin Spock (C ration) would remember with amazement "how easy it was to drive around New York City and to park the car." Resorts reported dramatic declines in customers, and many shut down for the duration. Thousands of roadhouses and restaurants and the other paraphernalia of the highway culture also closed their doors. In 1943, visits to national parks fell 68 percent below prewar levels. Emily Post unbent etiquette's rules enough to decree that it was no longer necessary to drive to the station to pick up one's weekend guests. Lovers' lane was replaced by those stand-bys of an earlier generation, the front parlor and the porch swing. Neighborhood bars and movie houses were jammed, as were any race tracks that could be reached by bus or trolley. But most of the time the average citizen simply stayed at home, marooned "on his front porch," *Time* reported, "with a well-stuffed wallet." It was the fat wallets that caused particular frustration, for personal income was rising at an astronomical rate. Although wages were controlled, there was full employment for the first time since the 1929 crash and all the overtime pay anyone could want, yet there was little to buy and, thanks to gas and tire rationing, nowhere to go.

In the emergency the gasoline engine's old rival enjoyed a brief renaissance. Here and there a rejuvenated Stanley or Doble steamer could be seen, and elegant tall black electrics glided silently along city streets otherwise empty of traffic. Bicycling was encouraged by publicity photographs of the OPA's portly Leon Henderson puffing a cigar as he pedaled his "victory bicycle." Soon bicycles by the thousands could be found in factory parking lots—although most were old ones, for bicycle manufacture was on the wartime proscribed list. And horses were back, too, pressed into service to pull delivery wagons.

This is not to say that America's car owners ever stopped trying to change the rationing rules. Pressure groups and lobbyists and politicians laid siege to OPA headquarters in Washington, where a "gasoline eligibility committee" met regularly to contend with their petitions and to set policy guidelines for the local boards. The committee would have welcomed Solomon and his wisdom to its sessions.

The American Bar Association, for example, maintained that all lawyers were upholders of the public welfare and thus entitled to C-ration stickers, but the OPA ruled only in favor of country lawyers, leaving city attorneys to make do with A or B allocations. The medical field, too, needed definition, leaving such practitioners as chiropodists, naturopathic healers, and masseurs out in the cold as far as extra gasoline was concerned. However, healers of ailing cars, such as used-car brokers, won C allotments. B stickers might be granted for church volunteer work, but pleas for C stickers to attend church services fell on deaf OPA ears. Attending a funeral was not excuse enough for additional coupons. Boy Scout executives were praised for contributing to the morale of the nation's youth, but were denied extra allotments. The pleas of hunters and fishermen that with C rations they could add to the country's food supply were rejected. And while the administration urged everyone to plant a "victory garden" to relieve the strains of food rationing, the OPA ruled that unless those gardens were larger than fifteen hundred square feet, even the most patriotic yeoman was not entitled to extra gas to reach his plot.

The job of overseeing all this proved too much for even Leon Henderson: worn out, ill, and "bleeding from his political wounds," he resigned in December 1942 and was replaced by Prentiss M. Brown, a former Michigan senator. It was during Brown's tenure that the gas-rationing program took a new, tough, and highly unpopular turn. On January 7, 1943, a fiat was issued banning all pleasure driving on the Eastern seaboard, regardless of a motorist's windshield sticker. This was necessary, the OPA explained, because of continuing fuel-transportation problems.

Easterners were indeed plagued by spot shortages, which sometimes left motorists, even those with full ration books, woefully contemplating "Out of Gas" signs at filling stations. Any tank truck making a delivery run was customarily trailed by a long line of cars. But to ban what little driving pleasure was left to a law-abiding A-card holder struck many people as petty and unfair. The New York Automobile Club charged OPA inspectors with "Gestapo methods" in harassing motorists embarked on innocent errands. Those attending a concert or a wedding reception or a ball game (even though major-league baseball had Washington's blessing as a booster of civilian morale) risked the loss of their rations. Grumbling increased in June when, under orders from Harold Ickes, who was in charge of overall petroleum priorities, the weekly A ration was cut to three gallons and the B and C allotments to two and a half gallons apiece. The OPA did not help its case with such puritanical rulings as one that banned all trips to summer homes, but allowed a single journey to close up a summer place—provided that the driver came straight back and did not tarry one extra minute to enjoy himself.

Chester Bowles, the advertising executive who was then head of rationing in Connecticut and who would replace Prentiss Brown as OPA head in October, called 1943's pleasure-driving ban a "fiasco." "From the beginning," Bowles recalled, "it was clear to us that this edict was totally unenforceable, and the public soon came to realize it." The completion of the "Big Inch" oil pipeline (and the near completion of the "Little Big Inch") from Texas to the East

Coast gave the OPA a face-saving excuse to lift the ban in September. In all probability it had saved very little gasoline, succeeding only in souring the public's view of those in charge of rationing.

In any event, gas rationing was proving to be startlingly effective. During 1942, largely because of the emergency rationing in the East, civilian consumption fell from 18.0 billion gallons to 14.4 billion, a drop of 20 percent. In 1943, the first full year of nationwide rationing, consumption fell another 20 percent. Car owners in 1941 had driven an average of 9,663 miles; in 1943 the figure was down to 6,366. (A portion of the dramatic drop was due to the fact that there were 3,700,000 fewer cars on the road, as vehicles wore out or were put up on blocks for the duration.) And thanks to rationing and the lowered speed limit, it was far safer to drive during World War II than it ever had been before; there were over sixteen thousand fewer traffic deaths in 1943 than in the last year of peace.

Gasoline rationing, in short, was accomplishing exactly what was intended of it: keeping Americans on the road in spite of themselves; keeping the Arsenal of Democracy racing along in high gear; and keeping the huge military machine fully supplied with rubber and gasoline. The driving public, however, began to reveal an ambivalent attitude toward the rationing as the war dragged on. Part of this was simply the result of war weariness. Part was a general resentment of the tangle of red tape involved in war rationing and contols. OPA rulings such as the pleasure-driving ban certainly irritated public opinion. Finally, even the most patriotic citizen could not always resist sampling a touch of freedom so long taken for granted in the car culture.

Consequently, beating the system became a common pastime. Initially at least it was a system fairly easy to beat. The lowest caliber violation was the use of a friend or relative's unneeded gas coupons, a practice winked at by most gas-station attendants, for it was relatively harmless and produced no actual net change in the amount of fuel allocated for civilian use. More serious was the patronage of the black market. Chester Bowles stated the case nicely when he wrote that "gasoline rationing presented a dangerously ripe field for black market operations." There were black marketeers dealing in every imaginable scarce or rationed wartime commodity, but nowhere were they more commonly found than around the nation's 225,000 filling stations.

The criminally inclined found the gasoline black market irresistibly attractive because of the ease of operation, the high profits, and the low risks. All that was needed was a supply of "hot" gas coupons and a complaisant station owner. The easiest way to obtain hot coupons was to steal them, and the OPA's rationing system offered numerous opportunities for the resourceful thief. The coupon chain began at the printing plant, from which coupon booklets were shipped to local OPA boards, where they were doled out to car owners. The coupons were collected from customers by the filling-station operator, who periodically turned them in to his wholesaler; the gallonage the coupons represented was the basis for the dealer's next gasoline delivery. From the wholesaler the coupons went to the supplier, and from there to a collection point, usually a bank, where they were logged in and destroyed.

Thieves operated all along the coupon chain, but they found the easiest pickings at local ration boards. Security tended to be lax, occasionally a bribe bought an "insider," and the supply of coupons was sizable. Bureaucratic excess sometimes contributed significantly to this supply; OPA investigators found some boards stocked with five or ten or even twenty years worth of gas coupons, and one board was found to have enough coupons on hand for a 137-year war. During the first eighteen months of rationing, coupons worth 300,000,000 gallons of gasoline were taken in 650 robberies of OPA boards.

A second source of hot coupons was counterfeiting. The appeal the inch-square gas coupons held for veteran counterfeiters is suggested by the fact that the amount of phony currency seized in 1944 was only one-tenth of that picked up in 1939. Late in 1944 the OPA reported that fake coupons worth an average of 1,500,000 gallons a week were being discovered, no doubt only a fraction of what was being passed. Organized crime was deeply involved. In March 1944, for example, the Boston police picked up members of Detroit's notorious Purple Gang who were found to have twenty-six thousand phony A coupons sewn in the linings of their overcoats.

Hot coupons might be sold to individual car owners in bar or back-alley transactions, but most black-market operators preferred working with filling-station owners, where the deals—and the profits—were larger. A dealer usually was charged between eight and fifteen cents apiece for hot coupons. Favored couponless customers were then treated to extra gas at whatever markup above the controlled price the market could bear, with the dealer making up the shortfall in his coupon records from his black-market stock. The profits in this business were considerable for all concerned; in the spring of 1944 *Newsweek* quoted Bowles's estimate that transactions in hot coupons were totaling one billion dollars a month.

In addition to the gasoline siphoned out of the allotments for legitimate needs, the black market posed a threat to the very rationale of the rationing program. If there was such a flourishing black-market, reasoned the motoring public, then perhaps there was plenty of gasoline to go around after all—which, as military needs multiplied late in the war, was quite the opposite of the actual situation. The OPA's vigorous crackdown on the black market began to take effect by the winter of 1944-45. The coupon chain was tightened up, more sophisticated methods were used to detect counterfeits, and OPA-run monitoring centers were inserted into the system. From there hot coupons were traced back to the dealers, who were fined or had their gas deliveries debited or, in the most serious cases, were shut down.

At its peak, about a year earlier, the gasoline black market was estimated to account for some 5 percent of the daily civilian allocation of 50,400,000 gallons. Sociologist Marshall Clinard, studying the black market as a symptom of white-collar crime, concluded that between one in two and one in five gas-station operators succumbed to temptation at one time or another. There is no way of knowing how many motorists patronized the black market, or what proportion of those who did made it a regular habit. Newspapers played up a tourist rush to Florida during the winter of 1943 that was fueled largely by hot coupons. OPA inspectors told of an A-sticker driver caught at a watering spot six hundred miles from home; when questioned, he piously claimed to be visiting his ninety-seven-year-old mother on her birthday, and was it his fault that she still liked to hang around summer resorts? Some commentators on the period have compared the level of black-market lawlessness to Prohibition, but that is a considerable exaggeration.

Chester Bowles, whose three years at the helm of the OPA gave him some perspective on the black market, concluded that 2 to 5 percent of the population was "inherently dishonest"; another 20 percent obeyed the regulations without questioning; and the remaining 75 percent "genuinely *want* to be honest" but disliked being proof of Barnum's assertion about suckers. When and where wartime gas rationing was fairly and equitably administered according to actual need, it seems clear that the vast majority of the people complied out of patriotic motives. When the system bumbled or took turns perceived as repressive, such as the pleasure-driving ban, the black market flourished. It should be remembered just how large a slice gasoline rationing took out of the car culture's accustomed way of life—a consumption cut of 40 percent in 1943 and 1944—which makes the overall record of compliance rather remarkable.

On V-J Day, August 15, 1945, as the nation joyously celebrated the war's end, motorists found their tanks running over. Bowles went on the radio that evening to announce the immediate end of gasoline rationing. "Now," he promised, "you can take your gasoline and fuel oil coupons and paste them in your memory book." America's love affair with the automobile could resume at last. Never again—or so everyone believed—would a frustrated motorist feel compelled to pray:

And when I die, please bury me
'Neath a ton of sugar, by a rubber tree.
Lay me to rest in an auto machine,
And water my grave with gasoline.

—*October 1979*

A FATEFUL FRIENDSHIP

by STEPHEN E. AMBROSE

Eisenhower dreamed of serving under Patton, but history reversed their roles. Their stormy association dramatically shaped the Allied assault on the Third Reich.

They never had much in common. George Patton was a conceited, spoiled child from an extremely wealthy, snobbish family. He dressed as he pleased, said what he liked, and did as he wished. He cursed like a trooper and told off his inferiors—and sometimes his superiors—with profane eloquence. Although he moved easily in America's highest society, many people, soldiers included, thought Patton vulgar. Dwight Eisenhower came from the wrong side of the tracks in a tiny midwestern town. He had to support himself while in high school by working nights in a creamery; he wanted to be well liked, and he obeyed his superiors. The only thing he did to attract attention was to do his duty quietly and efficiently.

Patton was an erratic genius, given to great outbursts of energy and flashes of brilliant insight. He was capable of sustained action, but not of systematic thought. A superstitious man, he was much taken by his own *déjà vu*, and his sensation of having been somewhere before; he devoutly believed that he had fought with Alexander the Great and with Napoleon, among others. Eisenhower had a steady, orderly mind. When he looked at a problem he would take everything into account, weigh possible alternatives, and deliberately decide on a course of action. Patton seldom arrived at a solution through an intellectual process; rather, he *felt* that this or that was what he should do, and he did it.

Patton strutted while Eisenhower walked. Both were trim, athletic, outdoor types; but Eisenhower was usually grinning, Patton frowning. Patton indulged his moods, while Eisenhower kept a grip on his temper.

Despite the differences, the two soldiers shared a friendship that survived two decades and (according to Eisenhower) "heated, sometimes almost screaming arguments. . . ." Their common West Point training—Patton graduated in 1909, Eisenhower in 1915—helped hold them together; other factors were, however, more important. Both had a deep interest in tanks and armored warfare. Patton, five years Eisenhower's senior, had led tanks in battle during World War I; Eisenhower had trained tank crews in Pennsylvania. After 1918, when the War Department almost ignored the new weapon, Patton and Eisenhower, like those junior officers in England, France, and Germany who believed that the tank would dominate the battlefield in the next war, naturally drew together. But beyond this mutual interest, they respected each other. Patton's dash, courage, and recklessness complemented Eisenhower's stubborn, straightforward caution. Each admired the other and benefited from the relationship.

The two young majors met in 1919, and almost immediately they began an argument that would last until Patton's death. Patton thought the chief ingredient in modern warfare was inspired leadership on the battlefield. Eisenhower felt that leadership was just one factor. He believed that Patton was inclined to indulge his romantic nature, neglecting such matters as logistics, a proper worldwide strategy, and getting along with allies.

A letter Patton wrote to Eisenhower in July 1926 illustrated the difference between the two men. "Ike" had just spent a year at the Command and General Staff School at Fort Leavenworth. He had applied himself with almost monastic diligence to his studies, and had graduated first in his class. Patton, fearful that his friend had concentrated too hard on such subjects as transportation, staff functioning, and how to draft a memo, decided to set him straight. After congratulating Eisenhower on his achievement, Patton declared, "We talk a hell of a lot about tactics and stuff and we never get to brass tacks. Namely what is it that makes the poor S.O.B. who constitutes the casualty list fight." Leadership was Patton's answer. Officers had to get out and inspire the men, keep them moving. One or two superheroes would not do; Patton thought any such notion was "bull." Finally, he concisely summed up the difference between his and Eisenhower's approach to battle. "Victory in the next war will depend on EXECUTION not PLANS." By execution, Patton said, he meant keeping the infantry advancing under fire.

Eisenhower disagreed. Plans, he said, meant that food and ammunition and gasoline would continue to reach the men at the front lines, the pressure would be applied where it hurt the enemy the most, that supreme effort would not be wasted. The most difficult tasks in the next war, Eisenhower believed, would be raising, training, arming, and transporting the men; getting them ashore in the right places; maintaining good liaison with allied forces. Execution would matter, of course, but it was only one part of the total picture.

During the thirties their Army assignments kept the two men apart, but they stayed in touch. It was a bad time for armor advocates: the Army had practically no tanks. Patton, disgusted, joined the cavalry, where he could at least play polo, while Eisenhower worked patiently through a series of staff jobs. Patton lived expensively—entertaining, racing around in sports cars, keeping his own string of polo ponies, and traveling by private yacht and private plane. This was in an army that was, for most practical purposes, poverty-stricken. During the Depression, Congress cut officers' salaries and introduced annoying economy measures on Army posts. Most career men tightened their belts, entertained frugally, and associated only with their fellows. Patton's ostentatious display of his wealth was offensive to most of his colleagues, especially his superiors; they could not begin to compete with him.

Eisenhower, meanwhile, kept begging for assignments with the troops, but his superiors, most notably General Douglas MacArthur, liked to have the hard-working, efficient major around. He lived according to the accepted pattern and was one of the best-liked officers in the Army. While Patton disported himself outside the system, Eisenhower worked from within. In 1940, for example, Patton—who had finally become a colonel in 1938—took command of a tank brigade of the 2d Armored Division. He found that most of his tanks were not working because of an absence of spare parts. When a mechanic pointed out that many usable parts were available from Sears Roebuck, Patton ordered them and paid out of his own pocket. He kept the bill a secret, but it probably ran into many thousands of dollars. As chief of staff of a division, Eisenhower often faced similar problems. His solution was to write a friend in the War Department and, with this extra prodding, get the material he needed through the proper channels.

When World War II began in Europe, Patton quickly forgot about polo and his active social life. Eisenhower was certain that Patton would go straight to the top when America got into the war, and in September 1940 he wrote his friend: "I suppose it's too much to hope that I could have a regiment in your division, because I'm still almost three years away from my colonelcy." Still, he thought he could do the job.

Patton may have had his doubts, and in any case he had a better idea about what Eisenhower could do for him. Apply for armor, Patton advised, and join up with me as my chief of staff. "He needs a brake to slow him down," General George C. Marshall once said of Patton, "because he is apt to coast at breakneck speed, propelled by his enthusiasm and exuberance." Patton himself understood this, and he thought Eisenhower would be the perfect brake.

They did not get together, however, until two years later. Eisenhower, by 1941, had become a temporary colonel and was chief of staff for the Third Army. His son, John, was considering whether to go to West Point or to study law, and he asked his father's advise. Eisenhower said that the Army had been good to him, although he expected to retire as a colonel and admitted that his hopes had once been higher. Still, he had to be realistic; he warned John that he would never get rich or famous in the Army. He could get instead the satisfaction of knowing he had made a contribution to his country. John took West Point.

Patton, meanwhile, continued to move ahead in armor. He did so because of his abilities, of course, but more to the point because the Army Chief of Staff, General Marshall, was a remarkable man, able to overlook idiosyncrasy and to judge by performance. A rigid soldier and old-fashioned gentleman himself, Marshall had seen the impetuous Patton in action at Saint-Mihiel in World War I. He had marked him favorably in his famous little black book, a book he used ruthlessly after he became chief of staff to weed out the unfit and to jump men like Patton over their superiors. Marshall moved Patton up to temporary brigadier general in 1940 and, in April 1941, to major general.

When America entered the war in December 1941 Marshall called Eisenhower to Washington; he did not know Eisenhower, but he had read his efficiency reports and observed his brilliant staff work in maneuvers in Louisiana in 1941. Within three months Eisenhower was head of the Operations Division of the War Department. Marshall was so favorably impressed that three months later he sent Major General Eisenhower to London to take command of the European Theatre of Operations. In July 1942 Great Britain and America decided that their first joint offensive of the war would be an invasion of French North Africa. Eisenhower had pleased the British as much as he had Marshall, and they agreed that he was the ideal Supreme Commander for the invasion. He could choose his own assault commanders; the first man he picked was Patton. It was an ironic reversal of what Eisenhower had hoped for two years earlier.

Eisenhower gave his old acquaintance the potentially toughest assignment, that of hitting the beach at Casablanca. Shortly after Patton arrived, however, the French quit fighting, as a result of Eisenhower's deal with Admiral Jean Louis Darlan, Vichy's chief of state in French Africa. This brought the North African French into the Allied camp, and Patton lost his chance for glory. He compensated by competing with the local sultans in lavish living during three months as head of United States occupation forces in Morocco, and by hobnobbing with upper-echelon Vichy Frenchmen so convivially that it struck some Americans as aid and comfort to the enemy.

In March 1943, following the Battle of Kasserine Pass, Eisenhower brought Patton to Tunisia to take command of the II Corps, which had been badly battered. He told Patton to restore morale, raise the image of American troops in British eyes by winning a victory or two, and take care of himself. Patton, Eisenhower said, did not have to prove to him that he was courageous.

Patton had always been a martinet when it came to morale. He himself indulged in gaudy uniforms, but he insisted that his enlisted men dress meticulously according to regulations, even in the front lines. He worked them hard, subjecting them to twice as many drills and training exercises as most generals. His insistence on spit and polish was so great that he once tried to get Bill Mauldin's famous "Stars and Stripes" cartoons banned from his area because Mauldin's G.I.'s always looked like the sloppiest soldiers in the world. (Eisenhower, incidentally, overruled Patton on the issue, after Patton called Sergeant Mauldin into his headquarters and raked him over.) It is doubtful that Patton's men ever loved him—that notion was mainly journalists' copy—but they did respect him, and they respected themselves as a result. He used his techniques with the II Corps, and they worked. He made the men shave regularly and stand straight, and then scored a tactical victory over the great German tank commander, Erwin Rommel. A grateful Eisenhower gave Patton the most coveted combat position in the Army—command of the invasion of Sicily.

Patton did well. His Seventh Army sent the German and Italian opposition reeling across Sicily past Palermo. It was a campaign that left the British, especially General Bernard Montgomery, awe-struck. Patton had proved himself to be a master of pursuit, a general who could keep the troops going under all conditions. He was not so good at a set-piece battle. When he turned his army east for the drive to Messina, across from the Italian toe, the Germans were waiting. Progress was exasperatingly slow. The narrow roads, winding through the mountains, gave the Germans every advantage. Patton was almost beside himself.

On August 3, while he was in this mood, he tried to make himself feel better in a way that had often worked well before: visiting an evacuation hospital near the front and talking to brave soldiers who had recently been wounded in action. This time it backfired. The general had gone around the tent and chatted with a number of bandaged men, asking them how they got hit, where they were from, and so on, when he came to Private C. H. Kuhl, a young infantryman from Mishawaka, Indiana. Kuhl was sitting on a box, and he had no visible sign of wounds. To Patton's query, the soldier said simply, "I guess I can't take it."

As Patton admitted later, he "flew off the handle." In his opinion, most cases of "shell shock" or "battle fatigue" were just plain cowardice, and he proceeded to say so to Kuhl in a high, excited voice and with an appropriate selection from his rich selection of profanity. Then he slapped Kuhl across the face with his gloves and turned to the medical officer in charge, shouting: "Don't admit this son of a bitch. I don't want yellow-bellied bastards like him hiding their lousy cowardice around here, stinking up this place of honor!" Patton then stalked out. Kuhl, who had indeed been admitted to the hospital on a diagnosis of psychoneurotic anxiety, was found upon examination to have a chronic diarrhea, malaria, and a temperature of 102.2°F.

This slapping incident, although it shocked those who witnessed it, was not widely reported. Patton felt that he had done the right thing; he dictated a brief account of the episode for inclusion in his diary, and added in his own hand: "One sometimes slaps a baby to bring it to." He then issued a memorandum to the officers of his command directing that any soldiers pretending to be "nervously incapable of combat" should not be sent to hospitals but, if they refused to fight, should be "tried by court-martial for cowardice in the face of the enemy."

Having rehearsed his hospital scene with Private Kuhl, Patton repeated it a week later with added flourishes. Early on the hot Monday afternoon of August 10, while on his way to a military conference with General Omar Bradley (who was then Patton's subordinate), his command car passed a sign pointing the way to the 93rd Evacuation Hospital. Patton told his driver to turn in. A few minutes later he was going from litter to litter, talking to the battle casualties and commending them for doing a good job against the Germans. Then he came to a man who, like Privat Kuhl, was fully dressed, unbandaged, and apparently in good health. "What's the matter with you?" the general asked.

When the soldier said the trouble was "my nerves" and began to sob, Patton exploded. "Your nerves, hell, you are just a goddamn coward, you yellow son of a bitch," he screamed. He then struck the soldier twice, knocking his helmet liner off so hard that it rolled into the next tent; Patton even pulled out one of his famous pearl-handled revolvers and waved it in the man's face. "You ought to be lined up against a wall and shot," one witness reported the general as shouting. "In fact, I ought to shoot you myself right now, goddamn you!"

The commanding officer of the hospital was incensed. Private Paul Bennett, the victim of Patton's outburst, was a regular-army soldier with a good fighting record; he had begun to show signs of unusual nervous tension only after receiving from his young wife a picture of their newborn baby. Moreover, he had gone to the hospital reluctantly, insisting that he did not want to leave his unit. Within a week a detailed report of the incident had worked its way from the hospital through channels to Eisenhower's headquarters in Algiers.

It was 10:30 A.M., August 17, and Patton's men had just triumphantly entered Messina. Eisenhower was feeling friendly toward Patton, and after reading the report he said mildly, "I guess I'll have to give General Patton a jacking up." He then praised Patton for the "swell job" he had done in Sicily. Eisenhower did order Brigadier General Frederick Blessé, his surgeon general, to go to Sicily and conduct a full investigation, but he warned him to keep it quiet. "If this thing ever gets out," Eisenhower told Blessé, "they'll be howling for Patton's scalp, and that will be the end of Georgie's service in this war. I simply cannot let that happen. Patton is *indispensable* to the war effort."

Eisenhower then sat down and wrote a personal letter to Patton. By now he was beginning to feel the seriousness of Patton's offense and to realize that more than a "jacking up" was required. "I clearly understand that firm and drastic measures are at times necessary in order to secure desired objectives," Eisenhower wrote, "but this does not excuse brutality, abuse of the sick, not exhibition of uncontrollable temper in front of subordinates." Eisenhower said he did not intend to institute any formal investigation, or put anything in Patton's official file; but he did warn that if the reports proved true he would have to "seriously question your good judgment and your self-discipline." This would "raise serious doubts . . . as to your future usefulness."

In conclusion Eisenhower declared, "No letter that I have been called upon to write in my military career has caused me the mental anguish of this one, not only because of my long and deep personal friendship for you but because of my admiration for your military qualities." But, Eisenhower warned, "I assure you that conduct such as described in the accompanying report will *not* be tolerated in this theater no matter who the offender may be."

But by this point the press corps in Sicily had got hold of the story. The reporters had conducted their own investigation and were prepared to make it public. "If I am correctly informed," one reporter noted, "General Patton has sub-jected himself to general court-martial by striking an enlisted man under his command." They wanted to know, a commit-tee of correspondents told Eisenhower's chief of staff, what Eisenhower was going to do to punish Patton.

All of Eisenhower's famous abilities as a mediator were needed now. He called the reporters into his office and frankly confessed that he was doing all he could to hold on to Patton. He asked them to keep the story quiet so that Patton could "be saved for the great battles facing us in Europe." The effort worked. The correspondents entered into a gentleman's agreement to sit on the story.

Patton, meanwhile, tried to make amends. He apolo-gized, although somewhat curtly, to Private Bennett and to the nurses and doctors of the 93rd Evacuation Hospital. He wrote Eisenhower, "I am at a loss to find the words with which to express my chagrin and grief at having given you, a man to whom I owe everything and for whom I would gladly lay down my life, cause for displeasure with me." The incident was closed, or so Eisenhower hoped.

Three months later Drew Pearson learned of the Patton slapping incident and gave it full treatment in a radio broad-cast. Eisenhower's chief of staff made matters worse when, in a press conference, he admitted that Eisenhower had not offi-cially reprimanded Patton. Since there was a shortage of battlefront news at the time, the story received front-page treatment everywhere. Eisenhower, the War Department, and the White House each received hundreds of letters, most of them demanding that any general who would strike a private in a hospital be summarily dismissed from the service. The letter writers were especially upset because Eisenhower appar-ently had done nothing to censure Patton.

Eisenhower made no public defense of his actions. Nor was he willing to throw Patton to the wolves. He did answer a number of the incoming letters of criticism, carefully pointing out that Patton was too important to lose. In each case he asked that the letter be regarded as strictly personal. He advised Patton to keep quiet, since "it is my judgment that this storm will blow over." In the end, it did.

In the late fall of 1943 Eisenhower received his appoint-ment as Supreme Commander for OVERLORD, the invasion of France. One major factor in his selection was his ability to get

British and American officers to work together, something that would be even more important in OVERLORD than it had been in the Mediterranean. For this reason he was tempted to leave Patton behind. "Georgie" was something of an Anglophobe and loved to tweak sensitive English noses, especially Montgomery's; and Montgomery would be one of the chief commanders in OVERLORD. But despite this, and despite the slapping incident, Eisenhower decided to bring Patton along. He told Marshall, who had doubts, that he thought Patton was cured of his temper tantrums, partly because of his personal loyalty to you and to me," but mainly because "he is so avid for recognition as a great military commander that he will ruthlessly suppress any habit of his own that will tend to jeopardize it." Marshall, remembering his own earlier admiration for Patton, and bending to Eisenhower's insistence, agreed.

Eisenhower's most important responsibility as Supreme Commander was the defeat of the German armies. He felt that whatever trouble Patton caused him in other ways, he would make a tremendous combat contribution to victory. Without accepting Patton's contention that execution was more important than planning, Eisenhower recognized that "the first thing that usually slows up operations is an element of caution, fatigue or doubt on the part of a higher commander." Patton was never affected by these.

So Patton, who had been in the doghouse without a real command since Sicily, went to England to prepare for the great invasion. On April 25, 1944, he went to the opening of a Welcome Club that the people of Knutsford had organized for the growing number of American troops in the town. About sixty people were there, sitting on hard-backed chairs in a cold, damp, depressing room, listening to insipid speeches on Allied unity. Patton was thoroughly bored. When asked to speak, he ad-libbed: he thought Anglo-American unity important "since it is the evident destiny of the British and Americans to rule the world, [and] the better we know each other the better job we will do."

Patton thought the meeting was private; but a reporter was present. The statement went out over the British wire services, and the next morning the British press indignantly featured it. Some editorial writers were angry because Patton had omitted Russia from the list of ruling powers; others cited the implicit insult to the smaller nations. The next day Patton's remarks were widely circulated in the United States, where he was denounced by both liberal and conservative congressmen. All agreed that generals ought to stay out of politics.

Patton, in short, had put his foot in his mouth. Eisenhower was disgusted. In his small office at SHAEF headquarters in Bushey Park, on the Thames River near London, he dictated a letter to Patton. "I have warned you time and again against your impulsiveness in action and speech and have flatly instructed you to say nothing that could possibly be misinterpreted. . . ." Then he sent General Marshall a cable expressing his disgust over the incident. He added, "I have grown so weary of the trouble he constantly causes you and the War Department to say nothing of myself, that I am seriously contemplating the most drastic action"—namely, sending Patton home.

Marshall told Eisenhower to do what he thought best, and on April 30 Eisenhower replied: "I will relieve him unless some new and unforeseen information should be developed in the case." Eisenhower felt Lieutenant General Courtney H. Hodges would be satisfactory as Patton's replacement—and Hodges had no record of getting his superiors in trouble. Eisenhower admitted that he had about given up on Patton: "After a year and a half of working with him it appears hopeless to expect that he will ever completely overcome his lifelong habit of posing and self-dramatization which causes him to break out in these extraordinary ways."

At 11 A.M. on May 1, Eisenhower met with Patton at Bushey Park. An old hand at getting out of a fix, Patton let out all the stops. He told Eisenhower that he felt miserable, but he would fight for his country if "they" would let him. Alternatively, he dramatically offered to resign his commission to save his old friend from embarrassment. He seemed on the verge of tears. The outpouring of emotion made Eisenhower slightly uncomfortable; he did not really want Patton on his knees begging. He ended the interview by dismissing Patton without having made a decision.

For the next two days Eisenhower mulled it over. He finally decided that Patton was too valuable to lose, and sent a wire informing him that he would stay on. Patton celebrated with a drink, then sent a sentimental letter to Eisenhower expressing eternal loyalty and gratitude. To his diary, however, he confessed that his retention "is not the result of an accident" but rather "the work of God."

Eisenhower's aide, Harry Butcher, noted that Patton "is a master of flattery and succeeds in turning any difference of views with Ike into a deferential acquiescence to the views of the Supreme Commander." But if Butcher saw something that Eisenhower missed, there was a reverse side to the coin. Patton bragged that he was tolerated as an erratic genius because he was considered indispensable, and he was right. The very qualities that made him a great actor also made him a great commander, and Eisenhower knew it. "You owe us some victories," Eisenhower told Patton when the incident was closed. "Pay off and the world will deem me a wise man."

Patton paid off. On July 30, 1944, eight weeks after the invasion of Normandy, his Third Army began to tear across France in a blitzkreig in reverse. Eisenhower used Patton's talents with the skill of a concert master, giving him leeway, holding him back when necessary, keeping him away from Montgomery's throat (and vice versa), and making sure that Bradley kept a close watch on his movements. It must be added that Patton showed small appreciation of Eisenhower's peculiar responsibilities. To hold the alliance together, Eisenhower had to humor Montgomery on a number of occasions. When he learned that Eisenhower had given more supplies to Montgomery than to the Third Army, Patton is said to have mumbled, "Ike's the best damn general the British have got."

Patton had something of the boy in him. He liked to believe that he was putting something over on his superiors, that he was getting away with mischief. On a number of occasions Patton thought he was fooling both Bradley and Eisenhower. When he received orders to carry out a reconnaissance in force at the German border, for example, he turned it into a full offensive. He thought neither Bradley nor Eisenhower realized what he was up to; but of course they did, and had counted on it.

Aside from his drive through France, Patton's two great moments came during the Battle of the Bulge and when he crossed the Rhine River. On December 19, three days after Hitler's last offensive began, Eisenhower and his chief subordinates at SHAEF met at Verdun with Bradley, Patton, and other field commanders. The Germans had caught the Allies by surprise and were making significant gains. Sitting around a potbellied stove in a damp, chilly squad room, Eisenhower opened the meeting by announcing that he only wanted to see cheerful faces at the table. "The present situation is to be regarded as one of opportunity for us and not of disaster," he said. Patton grinned and declared, "Hell, let's have the guts to let the ------ ------ ------ go all the way to Paris. Then we'll really cut 'em off and chew 'em up." Eisenhower grinned back, but said that the Germans would never get across the Meuse River.

When the Germans struck, Patton had been preparing an offensive of his own, headed east. Eisenhower ordered him to switch directions, attack north, and hit the Germans in the Bulge on their left flank. In three days Patton got all his divisions turned and was on the road. By December 26 he had battered his way through to Bastogne and, along with Montgomery's forces on the German right flank, had stopped the German thrust.

In March 1945 Patton's Third Army reached the Rhine. A few American troops had already made a surprise crossing at Remagen, where they had found a bridge intact, but the main crossings were yet to come. The big effort was to be made in the north, near the Ruhr industrial concentration, by Montgomery's British and Canadian troops. Ever since Sicily, Patton had been in keen competition with Montgomery, and he was determined to get his men across the historic river first. The British general's preparations were detailed and meticulous. On March 24, after a massive artillery barrage, Montgomery started to cross. To his astonishment, he learned that Patton and his men were already over. Patton had been carrying bridging equipment and a Navy detachment with landing craft close up behind his infantry ever since the liberation of Paris, for just this moment. With less than half Montgomery's strength, he beat the British to the east bank. While he himself was going over one of the Third Army's pontoon bridges, Patton paused and deliberately undid his fly. "I have been looking forward to this for a long time," he said.

Six weeks later the war was over. Peace highlighted the contrasting personalities of Eisenhower and Patton. Eisenhower moved smoothly into his new job as head of the occupation. He faithfully and without question carried out his superiors' orders. Patton chafed. He talked about driving the

Russians back to the Volga River. He got chummy with German generals. As military governor in Bavaria, he kept former Nazis and even some SS officials in the local administration because, he argued, no one else was available. Actually, there were others available, men of Konrad Adenauer's stamp; but it was easier for Patton to work with the old hands. In any case Patton's policy ran exactly counter to national policy, and Eisenhower ordered him to get rid of the Nazis. But except for a few prominent officials, Patton did nothing. He was sure that, before long, German and American generals would be fighting side by side against the Russians.

His area soon gained a dubious reputation, and the press waited for a chance to bait Patton into damning the de-Nazification policy. It came on September 22, when he called a press conference and asserted that the military government "would get better results if it employed more former members of the Nazi party in administrative jobs." A reporter, trying to appear casual, asked, "After all, General, didn't most ordinary Nazis join their party in about the same way that Americans become Republicans or Democrats?"

"Yes," Patton agreed. "That's about it."

The headlines the next day screamed that Patton had said the Nazis were just like Republicans and Democrats back home.

Eisenhower phoned Patton and told him to get over to headquarters in Frankfurt right away. Patton arrived wearing a simple jacket and plain trousers rather than his fancy riding breeches, and he left behind the pearl-handled pistols he usually wore. The generals were together for two hours. When Patton walked out he was pale: Ike had taken the Third Army away from him.

Eisenhower gave Patton a meaningless paper army to command. He stayed in Germany, spending most of his time hunting. In December, on a hunting expedition, his neck was broken in an automobile accident. Eisenhower, who had returned to Washington to become chief of staff, wrote him on December 10. "You can imagine what a shock it was to me to hear of your serious accident," the letter began. "At first I heard it on the basis of rumor and simply did not believe it, thinking it only a story . . . I immediately wired Frankfurt and learned to my great distress that it was true."

Eisenhower told Patton he had notified Mrs. Patton and

had given orders that everything possible should be arranged, including the fastest transportation available to fly Mrs. Patton to his bedside. "By coincidence, only the day before yesterday," Eisenhower continued, "I had directed that you be contacted to determine whether you wanted a particular job that appeared to be opening up here in the States. The real purpose of this note is simply to assure to assure you that you will always have a job and not to worry about this accident closing out any of them for your selection."

Eisenhower confessed that "it is always difficult for me to express my true sentiments when I am deeply moved," but he wanted Patton to know "that you are never out of my thoughts and that my hopes and prayers are tied up in your speedy recovery. If anything at all occurs to you where I might be of some real help, don't hesitate a second to let an aide forward the message to me."

Mrs. Patton arrived at her husband's bedside the next day, and she read Eisenhower's letter to him. When she reached the end, he asked her to read the part about the job again.

Nine days later, George Patton died.

—April 1969

THE BOMBING
OF MONTE CASSINO

by MARTIN BLUMENSON

The Allied drive toward Rome had stalled. Was the destruction of a historic monastery justified in an effort to break the German line and get the campaign moving again?

Halfway between Naples and Rome, on a mountaintop and visible for miles, stands the Benedictine abbey of Monte Cassino, serene and benign, apparently indestructible. Of cream-colored stone, its longest side extending 200 yards, four stories tall, with a thick, battlemented base and rows of cell windows, the abbey resembles a fortress. Not particularly beautiful, it is impressive because of its massive size and commanding location. Crowning Monte Cassino, which rises abruptly 1,700 feet above the plain, the abbey overlooks the town of Cassino and the Rapido River, at its foot; to the northwest it superbly dominates the Liri Valley, stretching off toward Rome. It is built around five cloistered courtyards and includes a large church, a seminary, an observatory, a school for 250 boys, a vast library of priceless archives, and various workshops and outbuildings. Since 1866, when Italy dissolved the monasteries, the abbey has been a national monument, the monks remaining as custodians of the structure and its treasures.

The abbey was founded by Saint Benedict himself around 529 A.D. It was ravaged by Lombards in the sixth century, pillaged by Saracens in the ninth, knocked down by an earthquake in the fourteenth, sacked by the French in the eighteenth, and reduced to rubble by bombs and shells in the twentieth.

To many, the last act of destruction seemed as senseless and wanton as the others. Yet as the men who leveled the sanctified walls believed they had compelling reasons. In order to save soldiers' lives, they felt they had to sacrifice an edifice representing one of the great traditions of a civilization they sought to preserve.

The setting was World War II, the stage the Italian campaign, and the destruction an apparent departure from a consistent policy scrupulously observed.

The Combined Chiefs of Staff, the highest Anglo-American military command, had made that policy very clear. Religious, historical, and cultural properties, they said, were to be spared from damage, together with "local archives . . . classical monuments and objects of art." But only if their preservation was "consistent with military necessity."

Although no one ventured to define military necessity precisely, the commanders in the field had made every effort to respect the injunction in the campaigns of North Africa, Sicily, and southern Italy. General Dwight D. Eisenhower, the Supreme Allied Commander in the Mediterranean theater, assured his superiors that "all precautions to safeguard works of art and monuments are being taken. Naval, ground, and air commanders have been so instructed and understand fully [the] importance of preventing unnecessary or unavoidable damage." General Mark Clark, who commanded the Fifth Army in Italy, directed his subordinates "to protect these properties, and intentional attacks will therefore be carefully avoided. . . . If, however, military necessity should so dictate, there should be no hesitation in taking whatever action the situation warrants."

In the fall of 1943, although the fighting front was far from Monte Cassino, Italian museum officials reminded the Allied command of the historic and artistic importace of the abbey. Word went out to air units at once: "All posssible precautions to be taken to avoid bombing abbey on Monte Cassino."

"Let me see pictures of this place," ordered General Alfred Gruenther, Clark's chief of staff. "Will our ground troops have occasion to demolish it by artillery fire?"

The question was academic until early January 1944 when Vatican authorities complained that the abbey had been "seriously damaged" by artillery. An immediate investigation revealed what had happened. The town of Cassino had been heavily bombed and shelled for some time and was still under fire because it was occupied by German troops. Since there were "many gun positions and enemy installations in the vicinity of the town," the investigating officer reported, "it is possible that . . . an erratic round hit the Abbey. Any damage caused by our artillery fire would be purely unintentional. . . ."

Despite the clear comprehension reflected in this report, General Clark repeated his instructions. Even though the abbey occupied a commanding terrain that "might well serve as an excellent observation post for the enemy," this artistic, historical, and ecclesiatical shrine was to be immune from attack. Except, of course, that this immunity "will not be allowed to interfere with military necessity."

That was the basic issue, and this the essential question: From a military point of view, was it necessary to bomb the abbey?

Having entered southern Italy in September 1943, Anglo-American forces took Naples and headed for Rome, moving into increasingly difficult ground and meeting stiffening resistance. By mid-autumn the Germans had been in retreat for over a year—driven back from Egypt, expelled from Libya and Tunisia, forced out of Sicily, pushed out of southern Italy toward Rome. Now they intended to stop. In the steep-sided mountains around Cassino, they would stand and fight. It was not a hastily prepared position, but a series of formidable strong points known as the Gustav line.

Incorporated into their defense positions was the hill of Monte Cassino. Inside the abbey, at its summit, were seventy resident monks, about two hundred schoolchildren, nuns, and orphans normally housed there, and several hundred people who had fled the battlefield and sought refuge and sanctuary.

Both warring armies recognized the sanctity of the monastery, but neither had control over accidents. When a German pilot inadvertently flew his plane into the cables of a funicular tramway connecting the abbey and the town at the foot of the mountain, he smashed not only his aircraft but also the tramway. Several days later, when Allied planes dropped bombs on the town of Cassino, they unintentionally released several loads over the abbey. Minor damage resulted. But the monks remained steadfast and calm. They were confident that the Allied and German military forces would respect the building and its grounds.

In mid-October, two German officers drove up the steep hill from the town of Cassino, carefully negotiating the seven hairpin turns over a distance of almost six miles, and reached the gate of the abbey. They asked to see the abbot. Ushered into his presence, they explained that the Ministry of National Education in Mussolini's government had expressed concern over the possible destruction of the abbey's works of art. It would be desirable, they suggested, to remove these treasures to a safe place in Rome, and they offered their assistance.

The abbot, Bishop Gregorio Diamare, was a small and alert man of seventy-eight years who wore his age and title with ineffable dignity. He found the idea of carrying out the art treasures rather ridiculous. Both adversaries in the war had publicly proclaimed their intention to conserve cultural and religious properties. What harm could come to this holy place?

The German officers bowed and withdrew.

Two days later they returned. This time they insisted that the abbey was in danger because of the military importance of the hill on which it was located. Although the Germans preferred to fight elsewhere, the officers explained, they had no choice. The hill of Monte Cassino was far too valuable to be excluded from the fortifications being constructed. A battle was sure to take place, and the abbey was certain to incur damage.

The abbot accepted their offer. On the following day the German military truck arrived, was loaded with art treasures, and made the first of several trips to transport the most venerable relics and objects to Rome. Almost all of the monks also departed for Rome, along with nuns, orphans, schoolchildren, and many of the refugees. The abbot, five monks, five lay brothers, and about 150 civilians remained. Life on the hill was quiet and somewhat lonely. The sounds of cannon were occasional and distant.

Early in December, the commander of the German Tenth Army in Italy, General Heinrich von Vietinghoff, requested help in solving a problem. How could he use the hill of Monte Cassino in his defenses, he asked his superior, without harming the abbey? "Preserving the extraterritoriality of the monastery," he warned, "is not possible: of necessity it lies directly in the main line of resistance." To fight on Monte Cassino would endanger the monastery. To give up Monte Cassino without a fight would definitely impair the usefulness of the defensive line. For "along with the renunciation of good observation posts and good positions of concealment on our part, the Anglo-Americans almost certainly would not bother about any sort of agreement at the decisive moment [of battle] but would without scruple place themselves in occupation of this point [the abbey itself] which in certain circumstances might be decisive [for the outcome]."

Field Marshal Albert Kesselring, the commander in chief of the German forces in Italy, gave Vietinghoff an unequivocal answer. He had assured representatives of the Roman Catholic Church in Rome that German troops would refrain from entering the abbey. "This means," Vietinghoff specified when he passed the word along to his subordinates, "only that the building alone is to be spared."

Placing the abbey off limits and drawing a circle with its circumference about 200 yards from the walls, he forbade all troops to cross the line, stationed several military policemen at the abbey entrance to enforce the order, and assured the abbot that no military installations of any sort would be constructed within the confines of the abbey—that is, within the circle he had traced.

But the slopes of Monte Cassino outside the circle were not off limits. German troops demolished the abbey's outlying buildings to create fields of fire for their weapons, and set up observation posts and emplacements for crew-served guns. There is evidence that they established at least one position inside the circle, an ammunition supply dump in a cave probably no more than 50 yards from the monastery wall.

In January 1944, as Allied troops approached, the Germans were ready. They evacuated all the refugees still in the monastery except a handful too sick or infirm to be moved. They said they would continue to respect the abbey, but they asked the abbot to leave. Despite the bustle of Germans digging on the hill and the more frequent and louder sounds of gunfire, the abbot refused. He had faith in the promises made by both sides.

Recognizing how difficult it would be to batter down and go through the solid defenses around Cassino, the Allied leaders decided to bypass them. They would send a sizable contingent of troops up the west coast of Italy in ships. These men would come ashore at Anzio, about seventy-five miles ahead of the main Allied forces and only thirty miles below Rome. At Anzio they would pose a direct threat to the capital and menace the rear of the Germans holding the Cassino line. Taken by surprise, the Germans would probably have to divert strength from Cassino to defend Rome. And this, the Allies hoped, would enable Allied troops to move forward through Cassino, rush overland, and join the soldiers at Anzio. There they would gather strength for a final surge into Rome.

The plan involved a grave risk. Until the Allied body of troops could move from Cassino to Anzio, the units holding the beachhead there would be isolated, exposed, and highly vulnerable. But the prize was too tempting. The prospect of quickly capturing the Eternal City persuaded the Allied leaders to accept the hazard.

The importance of Rome was undeniable. Above all, it had symbolic and psychological value to both contestants; and in this connection there was a time factor. The Allies wanted Rome by a certain date—before the cross-Channel attack into Normandy, which was then scheduled for May 1944. Taking Rome, they believed, would lower the enemy's will to resist and facilitate the Normandy invasion. Thus, a sense of urgency was imparted to the Allied activities in Italy.

In January, General Sir Harold Alexander, the British officer who commanded the two Allied armies in Italy, gave the signal to start the "Rome Operation." General Clark, as commander of the U.S. Fifth Army, thereupon opened a massive attack at Cassino. Designed to divert German attention, it culminated on January 20—two days before the Anzio landing—with an attempt to cross the Rapido River and push up the Liri Valley. The river assault, which took place in the shadow of Monte Cassino, failed for a variety of reasons to crack the strong Cassino defenses. The Anzio landing on January 22 succeeded; but, contrary to Allied expectations, the Germans moved quickly to contain the beachhead there. At the same time they managed to retain enough troops at Cassino to keep their defenses intact and solid.

Now the urgency felt by the Allies underwent a change in emphasis. No longer was Rome the overriding objective. Far more important was an overland advance from Cassino to link up with the American soldiers cruelly exposed on the Anzio plain. And this depended on getting across the Rapido River. Since Monte Cassino dominated the Rapido, giving the Germans excellent observation posts from which to direct artillery and mortar fire, the Allied leaders moved against the mountain. American infantrymen fought a battle marked by extreme exertion and heroism. They got part way up the mountain, but were unable to wrest it from German control. The defenses were simply too strong, the defenders too tenacious. After twenty days of effort, and heavy casualties, the Americans were exhausted and had to admit failure.

Had the ruling that exempted the monastery from direct fire affected the outcome of the struggle? Some who looked with longing eyes to the high ground that would open the way to Anzio found themselves staring at the abbey. Aloof and indifferent, crowning the mountaintop that represented victory, the building seemed to have taken on a sinister appearance.

Now General Alexander brought in two fresh divisions—one of New Zealanders, the other of Indians—for a renewed assault. According to a new plan that envisaged stretching the German defenses, the Indians would attack Monte Cassino while the New Zealanders crossed the Rapido. The double blow, it was felt, would certainly open up a path to Anzio.

Mark Clark was responsible for operations at both Anzio and Cassino. Under Clark, and in direct command of the two-division attack at Cassino, was General Sir Bernard Freyberg.

A New Zealander of imposing physical appearance and impressive reputation, Freyberg was a legendary hero of World War I. He had already sustained his image in World War II by a magnificent record in North Africa and in Crete. Not only was he the commander of New Zealand's military forces in the European theater; he was also the chief political representative of his government. His dual function was an oddity that sometimes embarrassed his colleagues. For though his military rank subordinated him in the command structure, his political status placed him above his military superiors.

When Clark met Freyberg early in February, he was taken with the New Zealander's commanding presence; his heavy-set figure exuded authority and evoked instant respect. Clark was pleased, too, with Freyberg's energy and aggressiveness. But he also felt a brief twinge of discomfort. Freyberg's dominion troops, he noted, were "very jealous of their prerogatives. The British have found them difficult to handle. They have always been given special considerations which we would not give to our own troops."

Several days later, when the two officers conferred on the new attack, Clark learned that Freyberg was concerned about the abbey of Monte Cassino. Freyberg, as Clark reported the conversation, "expressed some apprehension that the monastery buildings were being used by the Germans and stated that in his opinion, if necessary, they should be blown down by artillery or bombardment."

Clark disagreed. The subject had been thoroughly discussed several weeks earlier, and American commanders felt that firing against the abbey was unwarranted. Civilians from the surrounding countryside were known to be taking shelter there. And the Americans doubted that enemy troops were using the building in any way. The Germans had no need of the abbey—the hill itself offered excellent sites for individual foxholes and for weapons emplacements, while higher hills nearby gave even better observation over the approaching Allied troops. What the Americans suspected was that the Germans would be glad to entice the Allies into bombing or shelling the building for the propaganda benefit to be gained. Moreover, the policy forbidding destruction of historical, religious, and cultural monuments was still in effect.

Yet the commander of the Indian division, General F. S. Tuker, a British officer, felt sure the monastery was a very real obstacle to progress. He had closely studied the problem of taking Monte Cassino, and he had no illusions that the task would be easy. The strength of the enemy forces, the rugged terrain, and the freezing weather would make success extremely difficult. Symbolizing the advantages held by the Germans, and seeming to mock Allied efforts, was the Benedictine monastery. Tuker felt that the abbey was exerting a baleful psychological influence on the Allied troops. He decided it would have to be destroyed in order to insure a successful attack with a minimum of losses. He therefore asked Freyberg for an air bombardment of the abbey.

Freyberg found himself in agreement with Tuker. He telephoned Clark. Clark was visiting the Anzio beachhead, and his chief of staff, General Gruenther, took the call. The time was 7 P.M., February 12.

"I desire that I be given air support tomorrow," Freyberg said, "in order to soften the enemy position in the Cassino area. I want three missions of twelve planes each; the planes to be Kitty Bombers carrying thousand-pound bombs."

The request was hardly excessive—thirty-six planes to drop eighteen tons of high explosive. Unfortunately, most of the planes in the theater were scheduled to fly missions in support of the Anzio beachhead. Gruenther doubted that he could obtain thirty-six aircraft for the thirteenth, but said he would "go into the matter at once." After checking with his staff officers, he phoned the New Zealander and told him he could have twelve A-36 fighter-bombers carrying 500-pound bombs for a single mission. Which target would he prefer the aircraft to attack?

"I want the convent attacked," Freyberg replied.

Did he mean the abbey of Monte Cassino?

"Yes," Freyberg said. "I want it bombed. The other targets are unimportant, but this one is vital. The division commander who is making the attack feels that it is an essential target, and I thoroughly agree."

The restrictions on that particular target, Gruenther said, made it impossible for him to approve the request. He would have to take the matter up with General Clark, and he promised to do so.

Unable to reach Clark for the moment, Gruenther telephoned General Alexander's chief of staff and explained the situation. He asked for Alexander's opinion as to "the advisability of authorizing the bombing." The chief of staff said he would talk with the general, and let Gruenther know.

Before the return call came, Gruenther reached General Clark, who said he saw no military necessity to destroy the monastery. Would Gruenther pass along his opinion to Alexander? Clark added that he felt somewhat embarrassed because of Freyberg's extremely strong views. If Clark refused an air bombardment and the Indian attack failed, he supposed he would be blamed for the failure.

Trying to marshal support for Clark's position, Gruenther next phoned General Geoffrey Keyes, the corps commander who was responsible for the American effort in the Cassino area. Keyes expressed his belief that there was no military necessity to destroy the monastery. He said further that bombing the monastery would "probably enhance its value as a military obstacle, because the Germans would then feel free to use it as a barricade."

Several minutes later—it was now 9:30 P.M.—Gruenther heard from Alexander's chief of staff. General Alexander had decided that the monastery should be bombed if Freyberg considered its reduction a military necessity. Alexander regretted "that the building should be destroyed, but he has faith in General Freyberg's judgment."

The announcement seemed final, but Gruenther tried to argue. He said that he had talked with General Clark since his earlier phone call. Clark's view was clear—he was against a bombing, so much so that if Freyberg were American, Clark would turn him down. But "in view of General Freyberg's position in the British Empire forces, the situation was a delicate one, and General Clark hesitated to give him such an order without first referring the matter to General Alexander." Clark emphasized that a bombardment would endanger the lives of civilian refugees in the building, and that it very probably would enhance the value of the monastery as a defensive fortification.

The response was quite cold. "General Alexander," his chief of staff said, "has made his position quite clear. . . . He regrets very much that the monastery should be destroyed, but he sees no other choice."

Gruenther now phoned Clark again and reported Alexander's position. Somewhat upset, Clark asked Gruenther to tell Freyberg that he, Clark, "was willing to defer to General Freyberg's judgment." At the same time, he wanted Gruenther to tell Alexander that Clark would speak personally with him in the morning in order to state fully his conviction that bombing the monastery would be an error. Meanwhile, Gruenther was to go ahead and set up the bombing mission— but to schedule it for no earlier than 10 A.M. By that time, Clark hoped to have spoken with Alexander; if Alexander changed his mind, the bombardment could still be canceled.

Gruenther first passed Clark's message on to Alexander's chief of staff; then—at 10 P.M.—he telephoned Freyberg once more to say that he was "reluctant to authorize [the abbey's] bombing unless you are certain that its destruction is necessary."

Freyberg refused to budge. It was not "sound," he said, "to give an order to capture Monastery Hill [Monte Cassino] and at the same time deny the commander the right to remove an important obstacle to the success of this mission." A higher commander who refused to authorize the bombing, he warned, would have to be held responsible if the attack failed.

Gruenther repeated that Clark was ready to authorize the bombing if Freyberg considered it a military necessity.

Yes, Freyberg said; in his "considered opinion," the bombardment was "a military necessity."

The magic formula having been categorically stated, Gruenther informed him that the air mission was authorized. Would he please arrange to move any Allied troops who might be endangered by the bombing to a safe place?

Around midnight, Freyberg called back. Would Gruenther temporarily defer the bombardment? There was not time to move the Allied troops to safety.

On the morning of February 13, Clark talked on the telephone with Alexander and told him that he was "greatly concerned." Despite Freyberg's conviction that the Germans were using the abbey for military purposes, there was no firm proof. But they would certainly have no compunctions about using it after a bombing. Humanitarian, religious, and sentimental reasons, Clark said, also argued against bombing. There was in addition a practical problem—the number of aircraft available to attack the building would be unable to destroy the value of the structure as a defensive work. These considerations, he felt, were more valid than the slim chance of facilitating the capture of the mountain.

All this was so, Alexander admitted. But if Freyberg wanted the monastery bombed, the monastery would have to be bombed.

Yet despite his apparent assurance, Alexander referred the matter to his immediate superior, Field Marshal Sir Henry Maitland Wilson, a British officer who had succeeded Eisenhower in command of the Mediterranean theater. Wilson approved Alexander's view—what Freyberg wanted he would have to have.

Facing the massive force of Freyberg's personality and prestige, all his superiors were uncomfortable. It seemed unlikely that the Germans had violated the sanctity of the abbey. Yet it was true that some of their positions were so close that it was scarcely possible to fire on them without striking the religious structure.

It was true also that many soldiers sincerely believed that the Germans *were* using the building for military purposes.

One regimental commander thought he had seen the flash of field glasses within the monastery. An Italian civilian declared that he had counted eighty Germans manning thirty machine guns inside the building. An American artillery battalion reported that "our observers had noted a great deal of enemy activity in the vicinity of the famous monastery, and it became ever clearer that they were using the abbey as an observation post and also had gun emplacements installed." A rifleman had been seriously wounded "by a sniper," he said, "hiding in the monastery." And frequent reports verified "much small arms fire seen and heard coming from the vicinity of the abbey."

To settle the question of whether German troops were actually inside the abbey, General Jacob Devers, Wilson's American deputy, and General Ira Eaker, the American in command of the Mediterranean theater air forces, flew over German lines in two small observation planes. Because the Germans rarely fired on light aircraft, which they suspected were sometimes decoys sent up to draw fire and pinpoint the location of their guns, Generals Devers and Eaker were able to pass directly above the abbey. Both believed they saw radio masts inside the monastery walls, and other convincing proof of the presence of enemy soldiers.

This confirmed the military necessity of a bombardment. In a report later made to explain his approval of the act, Field Marshal Wilson said he had what he called "irrefutable evidence" that the abbey was part of the German main line of defense, that observers were directing artillery fire from within the building, that snipers fired from the structure, and that gun emplacements, pillboxes, and ammunition dumps were located within the shadow of the walls. Thus, when General Freyberg insisted that destroying the abbey was a necessary preliminary for taking Monte Cassino, his argument, Wilson said, outweighed "historical and sentimental considerations."

The ground attack of the New Zealand and Indian divisions having been postponed to February 15, a bombardment was scheduled for the same day. But this bombing was to be far different from Freyberg's original request. No longer was he talking of a few planes attacking to soften the defenses. He was now saying that the abbey would have to be flattened before the Indians could take the mountain.

What had caused the escalation? There was a growing

concern over the security of the Anzio beachhead, where the precarious equilibrium between Allied and German forces seemed about to tip in favor of the Germans—who, as it turned out, actually launched a massive attack on the sixteenth. There was an uneasy feeling that time was slipping by—that the cross-Channel attack was fast approaching while Rome remained as distant and elusive as ever. There was an increasing realization that some extraordinary measure was needed to blast through the Cassino defenses. And there was an idea novel to the doctrine of warfare, and as yet untried: that the power of massed strategic bombers, normally used for long-range missions, might contribute to a tactical victory—which would give the employment of heavy bombers at Monte Cassino the additional dimension of an experiment.

Still, the military debate was not over. The ranking French commander in Italy, General Alphonse Juin, made a special trip to see Clark on the fourteenth to urge that the abbey not be destroyed. Christendom, he said, would be shocked. Clark agreed with that judgment; but unfortunately, he said, the decision was irrevocable.

That evening, Allied planes dropped leaflets on Monte Cassino to warn civilians of the impending bombardement. Apparently none fell within the walls of the abbey. A refugee—at some danger to himself, for there was firing all around—emerged from the building and retrieved one. He took it to the abbot.

"Italian friends," the leaflet read. "Until this day we have done everything to avoid bombing the abbey. But the Germans have taken advantage. Now that the battle has come close to your sacred walls we shall, despite our wish, have to direct our arms against the monastery. Abandon it at once. Put yourselves in a safe place. Our warning is urgent." The message was signed "Fifth Army."

The abbot sent his secretary to a nearby German headquarters to make arrangements for the occupants to leave. By the time he arrived, it was late; too late, the Germans said, for the inhabitants of the abbey to depart that night. They could guarantee the safety of the civilians only during the hours of darkness. Since the daylight of the fifteenth would soon come, they recommended deferring evacuation until the following night. The abbot agreed, promising to have everyone ready to leave just before dawn of the sixteenth.

On the morning of February 15, 250 Allied bombers attacked the monastery. According to one observer, they "soon reduced the entire top of Monte Cassino to a smoking mass of rubble." The planes attacked in waves, dropping about 600 tons of high explosive. Soldiers on a neighboring slope watched in awe. Between the waves of bombers, Allied artillery fired on the target, adding to the destruction.

The attack seemed to confirm the presence of Germans in the abbey. "Over 150 enemy were seen wildly trying to get away from the Abbey as the first planes dropped their loads," one observer reported. "Artillery and small arms fire took a heavy toll of these men as they exposed themselves across the open terrain." Other witnesses thought they saw German troops make repeated attempts to dash from the abbey to safer positions, "conclusive proof," one said, "that Germans had used the monastery for military purposes."

Brigadier General Frank Allen, head of the 1st Armored Division's Combat Command B, found the sight inspiring. "Our air," he wrote, "thoroughly demolished the monastery above Cassino. Reports indicate that a great number of Germans were driven out of the building and surrounding area. It was a tremendous spectacle to see all the Flying Fortresses come over and drop their bombs."

But Major General Fred L. Walker, who commanded the 36th Division, felt quite otherwise. "This was a valuable historical monument," he wrote, "which should have been preserved. The Germans were not trying to use it and I can see no advantage in destroying it. No tactical advance will result since the Germans can make as much use of the rubble for observation posts and gun positions as the building itself. Whether the Germans used the building for an observation post or for emplacements makes little difference since the mountain top on which the building stands can serve the same purpose. If I had had the decision to make I would have prevented its destruction. I have directed my artillery not to fire on it to date."

Yet to many Americans who had unsuccessfully assaulted Monte Cassino without the benefit of this kind of air support, and who had suffered a psychological malaise from the hypnotic effect of the building, the immediate reaction was merely one of bitterness. Why had *they* been denied this assistance?

The assistance, however, proved futile. Though airplanes returned on the afternoon of the fifteenth to hammer again at the ruined abbey, though 150 aircraft struck on the following day, and fifty-nine on the seventeenth, though artillery expended an enormous number of shells directly against the abbey, the Indians failed to take the hill and the New Zealanders failed to force a passage across the Rapido. For the time being, the military situation at Cassino remained unchanged. The beachhead at Anzio was still isolated.

Aside from the destruction of the abbey, the bombardment blasted and burned off much of the vegetation on Monte Cassino. Stripped of its cover, the hill revealed a surprising complex of dugouts and trenches, thus confirming, in the words of one report, its "extensive organization . . . by the enemy."

Around noon of February 15, the German corps commander in the Cassino sector, General Frido von Senger und Etterlin, had informed Vietinghoff of the bombardment. Senger was calm and confident. "Field police," he reported, "have maintained steady watch that no German soldier entered the building. Therefore, the enemy measures lack any legal basis."

Ten years after the war, Senger firmly repeated that no German troops were inside the abbey before the bombardment. He confirmed Clark's view: there was no need to use the abbey as an observation post, because other sites on the mountain offered better locations. Anxious to keep from alienating the good will of the Vatican and of Catholics throughout the world, the Germans were scrupulous in respecting the neutrality of the monastery; so scrupulous, in fact, Senger said, that when he visited the monastery on the eve of 1943 and dined with the abbot, he was careful not to abuse the privilege. He refrained from looking out of the windows. Yet he admitted that observation posts and weapons were "as close as 200 yards" from the abbey walls.

A civilian who had been in the abbey during the bombardment and who came into the American lines on the following day confirmed that the Germans had never had weapons inside the abbey and had never used it as an observation post. Numerous emplacements, he added, were no more than 200 yards from the outside wall, and one position was about 50 yards away.

Ten days after the bombardment, Fifth Army counterintelligence agents verified the fact that no German troops had occupied the abbey before the bombardment. But the information was given no dissemination. The Allied forces never officially announced whether German troops had been in the monastery.

One thing became self-evident: the Germans had little hesitation about moving in afterward. They waited exactly two days. Then, when the abbot departed, German paratroopers installed themselves and their weapons in the ruins. The rubble provided excellent protection against the attacks on the mountain by the Indians.

On the day after the bombardment, German photographers took pictures of the destroyed monastery. That evening an officer flew the films to Berlin for processing. They would receive wide showing and have great propaganda effect. This, the Nazi Ministry of Information would proclaim, was how the Allies were liberating Europe.

Abbot Diamare left the ruined monastery at dawn on February 17. He and most of the other occupants had huddled in the deep crypt of the abbey during the bombardment. Now, accompanied by those who could walk, he wended his way down a mule path until he was picked up by Senger's automobile, which had been solicitously dispatched to bring him to the German's headquarters. Brokenhearted, dazed by the shock of the bombs, hardly believing what had happened, the abbot accepted Senger's hospitality.

After letting him rest a day, Senger interviewed the abbot in front of microphones. The production started with a statement read by a lieutenant:

The Abbey Monte Cassino is completely destroyed. A senseless act of force of the Anglo-American Air Force has robbed civilized mankind of one of its most valued cultural monuments. Abbot Bishop Gregario Diamare has been brought out of the ruins of his abbey under the protection of the German Armed Forces. He voluntarily placed himself in their protection and was brought by them through a ring of fire of Allied artillery . . . and into the Command Post of the Commanding General. The aged Abbot . . . found here a place of refuge and recovery after the days of horror which he, his monks, and numerous refugees, women, children, old men, crippled, sick and wounded civilians had to undergo because of the order of the Allied Supreme Commander.

We find the General . . . and the Abbot . . . in a voluntary discussion to which we now cut in:

The General: ". . . and everything was done on the part of the German Armed Forces, definitely everything, in order to give the opponent no military ground for attacking the monastery."

The Abbot: "General, I . . . can only confirm this. You declared the Abbey Monte Cassino a protected zone, you forbade German soldiers to step within the area of the abbey, you ordered that within a specified perimeter around the abbey there be neither weapons, nor observation posts, nor billeting of troops. You have tirelessly taken care that these orders were most strictly observed . . . Until the moment of the destruction . . . there was within the area of the abbey neither any German soldier, nor any German weapon, nor any German military installation."

The General: "It came to my attention much too late that leaflets which gave notice of the bombing were dropped over the area of the monastery. I first learned this after the bombing. No leaflets were dropped over our German positions."

The Abbot: "I have the feeling that the leaflets were intentionally dropped so late in order to give us no possibility to notify the German commander, or, on the other hand to bring the some eight hundred guests of the monastery out of the danger zone. . . . We simply did not believe that the English and Americans would attack the abbey. And when they came with their bombs, we laid out white cloths in order to say to them, do nothing to us, we are certainly without arms, we are no military objective, here is a holy place. It did not help, they have destroyed the monastery and killed hundreds of innocent people."

The General: "Can I do anything more?"

The Abbot: "No, General, you have done everything—even today the German Armed Forces provides for us and for the refugees in model fashion. But I have something still to do, namely to thank you and the German Armed Forces for all the consideration given the original abode of the Benedictine Order both before and after the bombardment. I thank you."

Senger must have thanked the abbot, although this was

not recorded. He sent him under escort to Rome.

The Vatican protested the bombardment in strong terms, and President Roosevelt replied that he had issued instructions to prevent the destruction of historic monuments except in cases of military necessity—not merely military convenience, he emphasized, but military necessity. The bombardment, he said, had been unfortunate but necessary for the prosecution of the war.

In the Allied camp, a profound disappointment took hold. Who had been at fault? The Army troops who had failed to take advantage of the bombing? Or the airmen who had failed to eradicate the enemy defenses? Was heavy bombing useless for giving direct support to troops on the ground?

No one seemed to know. General Eaker, the air forces commander, summed up the feeling: General Clark, he wrote, "did not want a single bomb on Cassino Abbey, but ... General Freyberg ... went over his head or around him and asked ... [Alexander] to have it bombed. We bomb it and it causes an uproar from the churchmen. You ask us then why we bombed; we make an investigation and discover a difference of view."

Exactly a month later, on March 15, the Allies launched another bombardment. This one employed twice as many planes as before, and the target was the town of Cassino. Although nearly all of its homes and buildings were destroyed, German paratroopers fought stubbornly amidst the ruins, and Allied ground attacks were only partly successful. Meanwhile, the wreckage of the monastery, high above the battle, remained in German hands.

At Anzio, the isolated Allied troops withstood German pressure by sheer determination, a scant seven miles from the water's edge. A virtual stalemate then characterized the military situation in Italy until early in May, when the Allies launched an overwhelming attack along the Cassino line. Clark's Fifth Army, spearheaded by Juin's French forces, broke the Cassino defenses at the Garigliano River, outflanked Monte Cassino, and forced the Germans to give way. Polish troops then captured what was left of the abbey. Toward the end of May, after moving forward relentlessly, American forces made contact with the troops at Anzio, who then broke out of their confined beachhead. A subsequent drive resulted in the capture of Rome on June 4, two days before the Normandy invasion.

Almost immediately after the battlefront had swept past Monte Cassino, plans were made to rebuild the abbey. And soon after the end of World War II, sufficient funds were raised throughout the world, with a large part coming from the United States, to start the laborious process of restoration.

Today Saint Benedict's structure again occupies its mountaintop serenely, a landmark visible from afar. Tourists speeding along the new superhighway between Naples and Rome can look across the fields and see it plainly in all its glory. There are no scars. Who can imagine that anything happened to the abbey during the war?

—August 1968

RETURN TO EAST ANGLIA

by JOHN McDONOUGH

It is to the U.S. Air Force what Normandy is to the U.S. Army. The monuments are harder to find, but away from the main roads is a countryside still eloquent of one of the greatest military efforts in history.

From 1941 to 1945 the biggest aircraft carrier in the North Atlantic was England. Once the U.S. 8th Air Force arrived in 1942, a new field was started every three days. By war's end there were more than 700 airfields spread across the country; the 8th had built 130 of them. Enough concrete had been slathered across cornfields and cow pastures to pave four thousand miles of highway—all in an area about the size of Vermont. "There were so many airfields," one pilot, Ray Galceran, recalls, "you could cut your engines at ten thousand feet and take your choice. Land anywhere." Most of the bases were concentrated in the rural countryside of East Anglia, that broad peninsula of Suffolk, Norfolk, Essex, and Cambridgeshire that presses into the North Sea like a thumb.

Today this bucolic land, still green with the memories of the men who served on it, is to the U.S. Air Force what Normandy, Midway, and Iwo Jima are to the lore of the Army, Navy, and Marines. This may be why an East Anglian from Lavenham or Bury St. Edmunds might first draw a deep breath before he talks about the men of the 8th, and speak with emotion when he does. Every one of these American fliers is honored as a hero, even if he never did another decent thing in his life. It was enough that these men once went to Germany in the frigid bellies of B-17s and that some came back and some didn't.

"I was five or six years old in 1944," says Ian Hawkins, who lives near Framlingham and has written a couple of books about those days. "We were used to the sound of American bombers. Paid no more mind to them than we did to the sound of a tractor engine. But I remember one day hearing an unearthly roar so loud I could feel floorboards jump under my feet. I ran outside and looked up. I'd never seen anything like it. More than a thousand B-17s were rendezvousing in a black cloud that kept coming and coming. Imagine! Four thousand engines, five million horsepower. It's something the world will never see again."

No American or East Anglian can think seriously about B-17s today without feeling the tug of their great purpose and density. They were the two-fisted tin cans that tore the roof off a deranged empire. When they swarmed over occupied Europe, people blessed them. One day several hundred roared across Holland, according to Rex Alan Smith in his book *One Last Look*, and a little girl cried in fear. Her father put his arm around her, took her hand, and looked up. "Listen to it, Helene," he told her. "It's the music of angels."

So you throw your imagination up into the silent skies of East Anglia, and sure enough, there they are—five million white horses galloping across the winds of England to the rescue of a kidnaped civilization. "We would come into these small communities in huge numbers," says Dan O'Dell, a pilot in the 390th now living in Houston. "We were different from the English. Noisy, a little rowdy. But after they'd see our planes go out in the morning and come back at night— always more going out than coming back—they started calling us 'our boys.'" Any American who travels to England in search of the 8th must understand this sense of pride. Otherwise the derelict old hangars, towers, and Nissen huts that spot the land will have no meaning.

E ast Anglia is much the same open landscape today it was when Roman legions first arrived two thousand-odd years ago. Outside Ipswich, Norwich, or Cambridge there is nothing even remotely urban about this loosely populated farm country. Roads ramble over the soft rolls of the country from one little town to another. A pub is never far away, and its floorboards creak when you enter; ancient wood beams sag overhead.

Little you see today suggests what once went on here. The clues are subtle and may be overlooked from the ground. The air bases are not always apparent. Signs rarely announce their presence, and usually no main road will lead you to them. But then, they weren't intended to stand out. And now accumulations of time and neglect have further camouflaged their remains. You may spot a patch of bleached concrete, for instance, lying disembodied on the edge of a bean field. If wedges of grass and weeds push up between its slabs, if weather has eroded its veneer of bituminous binding and chipped away at its edges, if only a packed undersurface of gravel and stones remains, you may be looking at the remains of a bomber runway.

Or you may spot a neglected storage shed with some farm equipment inside. Look carefully. If it's a Quonset hut, half swallowed up in underbrush, its corrugated metal skin rusted through, you may have come upon the remains of an 8th Air Force barracks hut or station office.

B y June 1944 East Anglia held forty-four 8th Air Force heavy bomber bases for B-17 Flying Fortresses and B-24 Liberators and another fifteen for P-47 and P-51 fighters. (The 9th Air Force, also based in East Anglia, was a smaller tactical force with separate fields.) A few bases were inherited from the Royal Air Force (RAF). Most were built on private land owned by local farmers, who were compensated by the government.

Each base was known by the name of the nearest town with a train station. Today's maps can take you to the towns but rarely onto the service roads that lead to the bases' remains. For these you must ask locally. And when you find someone who knows, you may get a few stories too. At Kimbolton you might hear that Jimmy Doolittle, who led the first American bombing raid over Tokyo in 1942, was nearly killed when a B-17 almost demolished the control tower. At Polebrook you might hear that Maj. Clark Gable once filmed *Combat America* here for the Air Force. Or at Molesworth, which is now an active NATO base a few miles north of Kimbolton, you may learn that one of the first journalists to fly a mission with the 8th took off from here. He was a young UP man named Walter Cronkite. Three people at Tibenham told me that the actor James Stewart was based here with the 445th

Bomb Group (BG).

The buildings that made up a heavy bomber base—workshops, barracks, huts, latrines, hospital, fusing buildings—were not just slapped onto the topography. They were built into it, and for good reason. East Anglia is no White Sands outback. By some primeval snafu of geography, the most strategically located strike points to the Continent in 1942 also happened to occupy the richest, greenest, most productive farmland in England. So bomber bases and croplands coexisted, even intermingled. Each base had three 150-foot-wide runways that formed a triangle. A perimeter road encircled them, although its path was anything but a circle; it rambled around barns, trees, houses, roads, slopes, even an occasional castle. Each base took only the land it needed. Farmers often worked adjacent to active runways.

Beyond the perimeter were the support buildings. They were usually widely dispersed to deny enemy planes a good target. The hangars stood only thirty-nine feet high; control towers were about half that height. They were bland and standardized, with a balcony off the second floor and sometimes a glass watch office on the roof. Barracks were organized by squadron and woven almost invisibly into the landscape. There were ten men to a crew, as many as eighteen planes to a squadron, and four squadrons to a group, plus spares and support personnel. At any given time almost thirty-two hundred men and a few women lived in these self-contained villages.

In June of 1989 I joined the members of the 390th Bomb Group when they returned to their old field outside Framlingham. Before I reached Framlingham, though, I undertook my own private search for the 8th.

Because the first two bases I visited were thoroughly adapted to new uses, they were definitely not typical. Stansted, once home of the 344th BG, is now a commercial airport thirty miles north of London just off the M11. The old control tower is still in place and active, although several awkward add-ons partly conceal its original core. A memorial plaque had been installed in the main terminal, but during a recent revamping it was mislaid. No one knew where it was. Stansted is too busy with its present to think about its past.

Another twenty miles up the M11 is the magnificent

Imperial War Museum at Duxford. An airfield during the First World War and used as a fighter base by the RAF and the 8th in the Second, in 1971 it became a museum that houses one of the largest collections of Second World War aircraft in Europe.

Ten miles north of Duxford on a broad thirty-acre slope along Madingley Road lies the American Military Cemetery at Madingley, a tiny village just west of Cambridge. There are 3,8111 Americans buried here, 24 of them unknown. An occasional rose lies at the base of a marble marker, though fewer now than a generation ago, as the personal links between living and dead dwindle. A 472-foot Wall of Remembrance bears the names of 5,125 men, all missing in action.

East from Cambridge on the A45 about three miles past Bury St. Edmunds is Rougham, where the 94th BG was based. Here scraps of the field remain, scattered around like ancient ruins. The base gym sits just south of the highway in a small clearing. "A bunch of hippies live there now," a farmer told me with little pleasure. The main part of the base—or what's left of it—is on the north side of the A45. I pulled into the parking lot of the BOCM-Silcock Company, which processes and makes building materials, and asked if anyone knew about the old 94th base.

"Sure," said Terry Bray, the company's administrative manager. "I used to come up after school and watch the aircraft. Saw a couple of disasters too."

"Do a lot of people come by asking about the base?"

"Not as many as you'd think. It's nice to see people who are interested. This field is near to my heart. Actually, a lot of people in this area are rather sentimental about the field," he said, pointing to several rotting huts. Parachutes had been dried in one; another had held dead bodies. Both are on the verge of collapse. A dilapidated strip of the perimeter road heads north, crosses what's left of the original main runway, then turns west and peters out in back of the Wallow farm. A runway, once 150 feet wide, has been cut to the width of a suburban driveway and is used as a service road for farm equipment. The control tower was home to an elderly widow until her death a year or so ago. Hidden by trees at the end of a narrow road, it sits abandoned across from a Cash 'n Carry store.

With its narrow streets and half-timbered houses, Lavenham, ten miles southeast of Bury on A1141, is a superbly intact medieval town. At the foot of High Street is the Swan Inn. Its cozy pub would look familiar to veterans of the 487th BG, whose base a couple of miles northwest of town occupied the old Davis Alston farm. But then, the Swan would look familiar to veterans of the Hundred Years War. It's been here since the fourteenth century. The proprietor will give you directions to the old base and even phone young John Pawsey, David Alston's grandson, to let him know you're coming.

Though there hasn't been a military aircraft on the Alston field since August 1945, its runways and tower, like Miss Havisham's lonely manor house and wedding cake, are virtually intact, though shabby. Pheasants and rabbits scamper across the idle runways of one of the most perfectly preserved wartime bases in England. Lt. Col. Beirne Lay once commanded this field, pacing the same balcony of the same tower on which I stood. After the war he went to Hollywood and wrote a great motion picture based on his time here, *Twelve O'Clock High*.

A s the sun set, six thousand feet of main runway lay before me. On Christmas Eve 1944 Brig. Gen. Frederick Castle lifted off from this very concrete to lead the climax of the air war against Germany. More than two thousand bombers and seven hundred fighters took part in the largest air armada ever assembled by the 8th Air Force. General Castle, who never returned from that sortie, became the highest-ranking officer to win the Congressional Medal of Honor. His portrait hangs in the Swann Inn.

"I run this farm with my uncle," John Pawsey told me. Pawsey's probably not much over thirty, but he has a sense of the history over which he has custody. "Did you know that the concrete on the runways is worth six thousand pounds an acre now?"

"No, I didn't. Then why not sell it?"

"Well, it's a lot of work," he said, "and crops don't grow well for several years."

"Then your reasons are practical, not sentimental."

"Not really," he admitted. "My grandfather loves the field and tower and what they represent. I love them too. I wouldn't want to wipe it away. We've done some patchwork on the runways to keep them in shape, but no restoration. We may do a full restoration on the tower one day. But we'll never destroy it."

The first 8th Air Force field I reached that had actually been turned into a museum was Thorpe Abbotts, five miles east of Diss, where the 100th BG was based. Part of the service road leading through Sir Rupert Mann's farm to the tower is the actual perimeter track and crosses a fragment of the original runway. The tower itself is superbly restored and houses one of the few tower museums in East Anglia. It's flanked by several large Nissen huts, including a former officers' bar or PX, which is open on Saturday and Sunday afternoons.

About seven miles north of Thorpe Abbotts the runways of the old 445th BG at Tibenham, where James Stewart commanded the 703d Squadron of B-24 Liberators in 1944, are still in place—even active. The Norfolk Glider Club paid 250,000 pounds for the field, uses it often, and maintains it well. Piper Cubs now fly gliders like kites off the runways.

"Did you know the old tower was haunted?" said the flying instructor John Ayers. "A lot of people saw them—you know, American fliers walking around the tower at night. There were people who wouldn't go near the place." He didn't say whether they were friendly ghosts or not. No matter; the tower was torn down in 1978. Today an unghostly orange windsock waves in its place. About two hundred feet east a black marble memorial plaque stands on a concrete island.

The Railway Pub is about two miles from the base. Only freight trains rattle past now. The last passenger service ended fifteen years ago, and the station across the street is long gone. But it was in this pub, not the station, where the London-bound men of the 445th waited for their leaves to begin. "If you were a flier," the pilot Dan Coonan told me later, "all you ever saw of the local town was the train station."

At Ipswich I finally met up with the eighty-one members (plus wives) of the 390th BG at the Ipswich Moat House. This was the third reunion in East Anglia for the 390th, and they all happened because of John Quinn, a stocky Arizonan whose knack for storytelling is surpassed only by his fierce determination to locate lost members of the group. Quinn, who had been a sergeant with the 390th during the war, handled the stateside arrangements for this tour. Roy Handworth, an East Anglian friend of the 8th, managed the local logistics.

After dinner there was a pub crawl that ended appropriately at the Flying Fortress Pub and Free House. Once a private home, its front yard became part of the perimeter track for the Bury St. Edmunds field during the war. A fragment of the perimeter is now the parking lot, and the pub sign hanging out on Mount Road is made from the aluminum skin of a B-17. Inside, the owner Keith Allchin has filled his walls with photos and 8th Air Force memorabilia.

There is something astonishing about this congenial reunion that no outsider would ever guess. It is this: With a couple of exceptions, none of these men actually knew each other—or even met—during the war. Men in different squadrons had little contact. Men within a squadron may have served at different times. But it made no difference. These were members of an intimate secret society, founded at Framlingham in July 1943. Something like seventy-eight hundred men passed through the 390th by the time the war ended in August 1945. Its book of common prayer was the group memory. Each one here was a proxy for those who weren't. When a man shook hands with a fellow member of the 390th, he was face-to-face with the great adventure of his life.

"You can't imagine how close I feel to these guys," said Dutch Biel, a former combat photographer who was in East Anglia for the first time since 1945. "I don't think anyone could conceive how great that is."

"The whole experience is something you feel like sharing only with someone who was there," said Dan Coonan, "regardless of whether you knew him or not. When you're in a plane getting shot at, you become very close to your associates. You worry about them, though you try not to show it. We tried to hide the fear then."

The next morning two busloads of men and their wives traveled the thirty or so miles from Ipswich to Percy Kindred's farm between Framlingham and Parham, where the heart of their old field still lies. This includes the original control tower, now a remarkable museum. (Open Sundays from Easter through the first Sunday in October, on bank holidays from 1:00 to 6:00 P.M. and other times by arrangement with Mr. Kindred.) And just south of the tower on the other side of the perimeter is the hangar where the Glenn Miller band played on August 23, 1944. It was the 390th's two-hundredth mission against Germany. Two days later Paris was liberated.

As the buses approached the field, men pointed out vaguely familiar sights to their wives, who seemed to be trying hard to grasp what it was their husbands once did here. When the tower came into view, the men seemed more oriented in this once-familiar landscape. Lt. Rolland Webber said later he wept when he stepped off the bus. A wreath was laid at the west wall of the tower, and someone played recordings of the British and American anthems.

A surge of patriotism swept the little crowd. It was the kind of pride that made Americans shiver with emotion in the early forties—and cringe with embarrassment during Vietnam. Vietnam was discussed here. These men of the 8th couldn't imagine their later counterparts ever meeting in Saigon or Da Nang thirty years from now. "It wasn't a war history will honor," said one. "It makes me sad for the brave men who died."

The *Sally B*, one of only twelve airworthy B-17s left in the world, was supposed to fly over the Framlingham field this day. But it was being prepped for its role in a new movie, *Southern Belle*, being shot at Duxford. (One of the movie's producers is Catherine Wyler, whose father, William Wyler, shot the Academy Award-winning *The Memphis Belle* for the Air Force in 1943.)

For the next two hours people mingled, talked, and remembered. The pilot Dan MacGregor was startled to find photographs taken when his Pathfinder clipped a cluster of trees and crash-landed. It was the night of April 12, 1945—coincidentally, the day Franklin Roosevelt died. "I was coming in with a full bombload and twenty-eight hundred gallons of gas to lead a mission the next day," he said. "At about two hundred feet from the runway, a Messerschmitt comes out of nowhere and opens up. It took out three and four engines and shot up a wing. I cut the power, pulled up the landing gear, and did a belly landing just past those trees."

Three of MacGregor's crew were killed, and his navigator broke his back. "You have to write an official transcript," he said, "but I had such a tremendous sense of guilt over those three guys it took me forty-three years to do it. Finally, last year, I completed it. Now I can talk about it."

There was no pattern to these stories that afternoon. The gunner Rawlin O'Leary went down on August 1, 1944, in France on his very first mission; George Arnold, on his third.

Both became POWs. In September 1944 Al Ball stayed behind the day the rest of his crew was lost. He found three of them years later in a cemetery in the Ardennes. Yet Otto Kramer flew thirty-four missions and never aborted or lost a man or got a scratch.

Many of the men who were here had the disturbing sense that they had lived on time borrowed from the ones who were not. "As a POW I had a lot of time to think about fate," said Rolland Webber, who was liberated at Danzig and joined the American lines on a Russian tank. "As an engineer I tried to look at fate as a machine and find the combination of factors that made it favor some and not others. You know—character, education, habits, ethics, everything. I never found it."

He never found it because fate works outside character, in league with hidden allies. For example, the crew of the 379th BG that returned to its base at Kimbolton one evening with eleven unexploded shells in its tank no doubt congratulated itself on some great luck. But was it fate? Or was it the fact that those shells had been made by forced labor in occupied Czechoslovakia? When the tech crew broke them open, ten were as empty as a football. And the eleventh contained a note of apology—in Czech: "This is all we can do for you now."

L ater in the afternoon the men of the 390th explored the rest of the base by bus. About a mile west of the tower, remnants of the original headquarters were still visible. Projector windows on the back wall are all that identify what was the camp movie theater. White plastic sheets that had patched the roof hung from the ceiling of the dilapidated mess hut and moved in the wind like lazy ghosts.

Someone peered across the mud and stench of pigsty and spotted the vestige of a blackboard with a few chalk markings still visible. This pigsty was the command briefing room, where mission orders were once received from the 8th Air Force headquarters at High Wycombe. After tea on the neighboring Moat Farm we walked through the remains of the 571st Squadron barracks. Most of the buildings remain. The words ORDERLY ROOM and MAIL ROOM are still faintly embossed in the doors. The shower is about three hundred feet from the barracks, a long walk on a winter morning in East Anglia. "The floors were so cold," said the navigator Bob Hensen, "you'd get dressed standing on your bed."

On Friday the buses pulled up to hangar number three at the Imperial War Museum at Duxford. Inside is the *Mary Alice*, a B-17G that was built in 1944 but never saw combat. It's on permanent exhibit, and that day it was opened up to the men of the 390th. Jim Horan and Henry Perez took turns squeezing into their old places in the ball turret. Others walked the plank over the bomb-bay doors. "How did we ever fit in here?" someone asked. "Yeah," said another, "it's shrunk."

More than anything else, this tough old khaki bucket (and the 12,730 other B-17s built from 1935 to 1945) lies at the heart of what the war was about for a flier. The B-17 could do incredible things. In 1944 one took off from Bassingbourn and landed in Belgium—with no crew. After a direct hit the crew had bailed out. Still, the plane not only continued to fly when the fuel ran out but actually landed itself intact—all on automatic pilot. Ray Galceran said his B-17 once landed with more than 480 holes in it; it was patched and flew the next day.

The B-17 had no jet walk to coddle you aboard. You grabbed the handles at the forward hatch and pulled yourself up into the fuselage. A half-century ago these men slid gracefully through the motions in seconds. Today they tried one more time. But neither the plane nor their own bodies showed them mercy. They are, as the Brits like to say, a bit long in the tooth. But they can laugh at themselves, too, because when it counted, they could do it, and that's all that matters. The next day the 390th left for London and the flight back to America.

Maybe they'll be back. Other reunion groups are coming to East Anglia. So are their sons and daughters—more every year, before it's too late. Because the 8th Air Force didn't build these fields to be monuments. They built them because a homicidal maniac was loose in the world and had to be stopped. And when the job was done, that was that. Today the Mighty 8th is headquartered near Shreveport, Louisiana, at Barksdale Air Force Base. As for the airfields it left behind, they are at war with nature, time, and commerce, as they sink into the earth or are ripped up for salvage. One way or the other, East Anglia will reclaim its ancient title over these lands. But it won't soon forget the 8th or the 390th.

—April 1990

THE LONGEST WAIT

by JOHN LORD

The G.I.'s were far more numerous than any army that ever occupied Britain; none left so little visible trace, none so touching a legacy.

Acold coming awaited Melburn Henke in all respects but one. A leaden Irish sky, damp air that mortified the flesh, a mournful horizon of rusting cranes and dilapidated warehouses, channels of gray water and drab groups of longshoremen—these made up Henke's landscape. He was wearing a steel helmet with a shallow crown and a flat brim cocked somewhat rakishly over one eye; on his back a regulation pack sat trim and heavy, a bayonet as long as a sword strapped to it, and from his right shoulder hung an M-1 rifle no longer new. His expression was confident and, considering the climate, happy. Those old enough to recall it might have thought him every inch a doughboy en route for the Argonne or Belleau Wood. Certainly there was something of repetition about Pfc. Henke's appearance that wintry morning, for he was the first American soldier officially to set foot on the soil of Great Britain in World War II, and the term "G.I." was not yet in common use for his species.

It was January 26, 1942, and the United States was entering the eighth week of war with Germany and Japan. When he actually stepped ashore, as flash guns popped and a band played, Henke achieved immortality of a sort: the spot was later marked with a plaque. Henke himself described the experience as "one I won't easily forget" and marched smartly out of the limelight. No one could have seen in Private First

Class Henke that dank morning the first physical indication that the United States of America was about to assume the leadership of the Western world.

Two million Americans, most of them very young, followed Henke into the European Theater of Operations. They razed cities with high explosives and fire; they leveled hills and built temporary towns with their great machines; they killed the innocent in their assault; and with their allies they broke the armed power of Nazi Germany. But in Britain, the greatest change they effected was not in executing policies hatched by Roosevelt, Churchill, and Stalin, but simply by being there. The ordinary commerce of day-to-day living rubbed away illusions and antipathies, introduced new attitudes and modified old ones; and familiarity bred not contempt but a deep and lasting understanding. Britain already bore many marks of former armies, beginning with the forts of the Romans garrisoned; none had been so numerous or so massively equipped as the divisions that now poured in. None left so little visible trace, none so touching a legacy.

Today the memorials of D-day have to be sought out. When found they are no more than bronze tablets listing statistics, stone columns, or fountains filled with rocks from Arkansas or Maine. A few English pastures that are too meager to be farmed are still crossed with runways that once shook under the wheels of Flying Fortresses and Mustangs, concrete that once men kissed, tumbling deliriously from their planes, out of joy at having survived one more mission. There were afternoons when those airstrips, so small in this jet age, ran pink as ground crews hosed out from shattered turrets what was left of gunners caught by machine guns or the jagged shards of flak. Now, gray and anonymous, softened in summer by buttercups or the proud lavender of rosebay willow herb, they speak of nothing.

On the edges of beech woods or in clearings among the pines there are still oblongs of brick and concrete where the quonset huts, black and echoing, were home or hospital, workshop, bar, church, or prison for a community of men. They carry no echoes now. The pubs are still there, as they were after Cromwell's troopers had clattered by, a few with insignia torn from a uniformed shoulder and pinned to a beam, or with scribbled alien signatures fading on the ceiling. The names are still the same—the Queen's Head, the St.

George & Dragon, the Star and Garter, the Royal Steamer, the Eagle and Child—but the signs above their bars that warned of careless talk or exhorted everybody to dig for victory have been replaced by arch verses refusing credit, or announcements of bingo nights at what was once the village hall. Beside a hawthorn hedge here and there deep ruts still record the tracks of tanks or howitzers moving into their parks; but they might have been made by long-forgotten harvest carts. Of the tarpaulined dumps of shells and bombs that lined mile after mile of English lanes; of the acres of cannon, wheel to wheel, their muzzles pointing dumbly to the sky and aligned as if with millimeter gauges; of the pyramids of rations looming in open fields, the drums of gas and oil; the coffins prudently stacked by the hundreds on hangars; of all the impedimenta of a civilized and mechanized army there remains hardly a trace.

And yet, what was left behind was more enduring. For in the memory of a generation of Britons and Americans there are responses that spring to instant life at the mention of a name—Rainbow Corner, Spam, Glen Miller, Omaha—and being reborn they bring the legacy back to consciousness. It is, in a sense, a folk legacy, unwritten and mostly unarticulated, in which the collective memory has glossed over what was brutal. But it is all there, an invisible memorial to what was then called without any sense of bathos The Great Crusade.

The men who followed Private Henke when it all began did not think of themselves as knights in shining armor, however. They were too bewildered. When Europe had first gone to war, the standing army of the United States could not muster two hundred thousand men; for more than two years it had slowly grown, and now it was about to mushroom into millions. Its organization was not designed to promote the welfare of the individual, and its schedules did not allocate much time to self-contemplation anyway. Life in the army was concentrated on the immediate—on what was for the next meal, on who got weekend passes when, on the name of the smallest part of the Browning automatic rifle, on how to avoid crawling through the stinking puddle in front of your nose, and above all, on who was lucky at mail call. Men seized eagerly on such trivia to anchor their logic in a crazy world. That world opened for John B. Thomas of Gallatin, Tennessee, as it would for thousands of others, one midnight in the staging area at Indiantown Gap, Pennsylvania, when he was given a rifle clotted with black grease and told to clean it. He had never in his life seen such a repulsive object, and it never occurred to him that the last hands to touch it must have been those of a doughboy of his father's generation. Busy all night with old newspapers and interrupted several times to accumulate dozens of articles of equipment, including gasproof underclothing, by dawn Private Thomas was ready, as ordered, to move out with his comrades. A month later they did so, having learned the first lesson of war—that the waiting around greatly exceeds the fighting.

The British had been waiting for a long time, though they would have been taxed to explain for what, exactly. They had seen defeats and had triumphed in a few battles, but as yet they saw no end to the war. They had fought in France, in Norway, in the Meditteranean, and in Africa; in the clear, sweet summer of 1940 they had won an unimaginable victory over the Luftwaffe. They had stood without arms to await an invasion that miraculously never came. They had suffered, rallied, and endured. And yet they were still being bombed, their finest army was surging back and forth across the African desert without being able to reach a conclusion, and the whole spreading continent of Europe was still a fiefdom of Germany. Being stubborn and romantic, they expected to win the war; but in 1942 none of them could see just how to start the last battle. It was then that the answer came, in the shape of John B. Thomas, all innocence, not yet a soldier by any standard but full of enthusiasm, willing and able. To the grim British he seemed an unlikely sort of savior.

The first big contingent of American troops, 10,368 officers and men, arrived in the *Queen Elizabeth* at Gourock, Scotland, on June 9, 1942. The troops' last parade before embarking had been a "short-arm" inspection, and their first on disembarking would be the same; but the indignity did not diminish their pleasure at arriving on dry land, which they accomplished through lines of Scots waving and cheering in welcome. Though convivial, it was a confrontation of total strangers. To the British the Americans seemed fresh and full of energy, bright as new paint, the bodily expression of what Sir Edward Grey had noted about their country a generation before, comparing it with "a gigantic boiler. Once the fire is lighted under it there is no limit to the power it can generate."

They also looked soft.

To the Americans the British looked pitiful. They had known that Britain was at war, but there had been little reality until now. They had been aware of far-off battles; they had lost ships themselves even before war was declared. But nothing of this had hit with the shocking impact of what they now saw. Their reaction was natural: they gave away what they had.

Before his induction, George W. Marshall had been a delivery boy in Los Angeles. Now an acting corporal, he was under orders to deliver twenty-seven G.I.'s to some place he had never heard of. He figured the train ride would be brief since the country, according to the army orientation lectures, was hardly bigger than Minnesota. The ride took nine days. They were in a baggage car with no lights, no liquor, and nothing but K rations to eat; and after spending their first night immobile in a tunnel taking shelter from an air raid, they began to feel oppressed. Then they saw the kids, standing silently on a station platform watching the trains go by, looking with solemn awe at the young, healthy strangers smiling back at them. There were some cherries in Marshall's freight car, packed much the way California grapes might be back home. The cherries were disbursed. But at other stations there were more kids and some adults. Cigarettes, soap, razor blades were handed out. When they were gone there were still more stations. One man broke out his gasproof clothing and disposed of it; then finally others began dropping out their duffel bags just as they were. When the train reached Waterloo station in London, there was a lot more room in the baggage car. Marshall decided to take a stroll. Outside the station it was pitch black and the streets were empty. He could see search-lights playing and he heard the quick *whump-whump-whump* of antiaircrfat guns and the faint, warbling drone of aircraft engines. There was a sudden descending whistling noise, and a man running toward Marshall yelled at him what sounded like "It is, matey!" When Marshall stood still in surprise the man charged into him and knocked him flat. In the same instant a bomb crashed into some houses a little way up the block.

By now the Londoners had a routine for air raids. Some slept in the subways. Some with their own little houses had brick shelters at the end of the back yard, equipped and decorated according to taste, the more luxurious with bunks and stoves for making tea. Some put their faith in interior shelters built like steel tables, under which they could crawl when the bombs began to fall too close. Still others merely huddled into their broom closet underneath the stairs until the worst was over. Private Joseph Veto of Manchester, New York, found himself in this predicament one winter night in a house in Argyll Street, London. His knees were touching his chin and he was trembling with fear, though he said it was the cold. He heard a far bigger noise than the rumble of the bombs; it was a tearing, anguished noise as though the sky was tumbling down. A plane was falling. It hit a house farther along the street, its dead pilot landing on the owner's bed. His skin was crisp, like roast pork.

London offered other diversions than the bombing, which in any case was past its worst. One handsome young American lieutenant could often be seen standing on Shaftesbury Avenue, far enough removed from Rainbow Corner to avoid the heaviest competition, staring in a puzzled fashion at a shilling in his open palm. When he saw an attractive girl he would scratch his head and inquire politely of the young lady if she could tell him how many sixpences there might be in his shilling. He never failed to bear off a conquest to the movies, where she would weep a sentimental tear over Greer Garson keeping her upper lip exquisitely stiff as Walter Pidgeon, in a battered raincoat, came back from Dunkirk, or moon over Bing Crosby dreaming of a White Christmas just the way Irving Berlin intended him to. Martha Raye, the soldier's soldier, was playing to acres of olive drab at the Palladium; Beatrice Lillie (who had just lost a son in action) was at His Majesty's Theatre in *Big Top*; and Vivian Leigh was at the Haymarket in *The Doctor's Dilemma*. At the Windmill, as always, there was the chorus line, the bravest and barest in the world.

In the country, pleasures were simpler if not necessarily quieter. Most places could boast what Staff Sergeant Edward J. Twohig describes as "the surprisingly interesting stock met at some of the church parties." Conversely, the British were favorably impressed with the newcomers. Few of them withstood for long the ebullience of American spirits. The roster of Twohig's outfit carried nicknames like Silent Rapp, Skin Walbourne, Macadoo Machado, and Lightning Ruhberg, which startled the ears of the British, who confined themselves to time-hallowed familiarities no more daring than Dusty

Miller or Chalky White. Herbert D. Bidgett and a buddy called Bowers from the 81st Seabee Battalion were standing around when they were greeted by a gentleman who looked "very English." He was wearing a stylish dark suit and a bowler hat and carried a slim umbrella. He invited the husky young men to join him for a drink at his club. Stifling their worst suspicions, they went along. "It was strictly male and strictly for drinking men," Bidgett recalled. "We were introduced all around and after a time Bowers wound up playing the piano, and that guy was one hot number. He could play boogie-woogie like you never heard, and all the Limeys really lapped it up, requesting songs they'd heard of and all. First thing you know old Bowers is just sweating and playing and all I have to do is accept drinks. He didn't even stop to drink. I'd just tip it up and he'd swallow. After a couple of weeks of this we were asked to join the club and did."

Many American units found themselves in British barracks, even, ironically, in the old red-brick quarters in Winchester normally occupied buy the King's Royal Rifle Corps, which sometimes called itself (in memory of its foundation on Governors Island, New York, to deal with the rebel colonists) the 60th (Royal American) Rifles. Others, in villages and towns not garrisoned, trailed about with a sergeant and a policeman, being allotted in ones and twos to private homes. When Pfc. John J. Kenney of Wilmington, Minnesota, got to his billet the rain was dripping from his cap and his duffel bag was sodden black. The policeman knocked politely on the door and a gaunt woman opened it. She looked at Kenney and said "Oh, dear!" Not one to miss a nuance, John Kenney resolved that his behavior would be impeccable as long as he stayed in that house. It was. Before long Kenney joined the thousands of soldiers who, as members of the family, sat in front of the fire to listen to the B.B.C.'s nine o'clock news and explain why there was no ham in a hamburger, or to pop corn sent from home while their adopted mothers bustled about with tea and cookies.

There was not much food. An Englishman got two chops a week for his meat ration, two eggs if he was lucky, and a piece of cheese half the size of a pack of Lucky Strikes. Onions were as rare as pineapples. But many an American woke up on a Sunday morning with a plate of bacon and eggs on his bedside and toast made out of what was called "beetle bread." The bread was made from whole grain to save shipping space, and contained pieces of chaff from the wheat, which the G.I.'s darkly imagined, having been raised on the pure white blandness of store-bought loaves, were the wings of insects. The more imaginative soon homed in on the fish-and-chips shops whenever they were open and carried off greasy packages of newspaper smelling strongly of vinegar. Others made occasional attempts to live off the country: George Marshall and some friends were recruited by the village kids to shoot rabbits, the children offering to act as beaters. "We took a chance," Marshall recalled. "They did scare up two of them and we blasted away with our M1's at them, but no luck. I wish you could see the looks on those kids' faces when we missed."

The children were not the only ones to be dubious of the martial expertise of their allies. Winston Churchill had watched the first field exercises of the new divisions in North Carolina and asked the opinion of one of his aides, a general. "To put these troops against continental troops would be murder," the general said. Churchill, nevertheless, sensed the power of this raw material and guessed how quickly they would learn. Later, his judgment justified, he wrote: "Certainly two years later the troops we saw in Carolina bore themselves like veterans." But it took time to make a soldier. *As Time Goes By*, a slow, dreamy melody written eleven years before, was resurrected and seemed oddly appropriate. As Private Albert A. Turner put it, "The uncertain days stretched into uncertain weeks." Elsewhere, the plans to end the uncertainty had already been made.

The plans were given the code name Overlord. They were based on an American concept, and everything that happened in England was directed toward their execution. Overlord was the reason why the southwest of the island seemed to be sinking under the weight of foreign troops and foreign supplies; it was held up, people said, only by the barrage balloons. Though no one mentioned the name, Overlord caused hundreds of English families to leave their homes without knowing they would never see them again—by the time they were allowed to return, the walls had been pounded to rubble by American shells. Men like Colonel Robert T. Finn of La Jolla, California, moved in, building at Slapton Sands, three miles from the little port whence the *Mayflower* sailed, replies of

Omaha and Utah beaches so exact that later in Normandy a soldier could say to Finn: "Colonel, do you remember the damaged rowboat on the beach at the assault center? Well, I fell over the same damn boat last week during the real landing."

By May, Overlord had ground almost to its consummation. Opposite the French beaches the units were drawn up from east to west along the south coast of England in their order of battle, British on the left, Americans on the right. The assault troops had been funneled into special camps called "sausages," a macabre term in connection with an operation some said would be like a meat grinder. Churchill himself was doubtful, remembering Passchendaele and the Somme and Gallipoli. "It still seemed to me, after a quarter of a century," he revealed later, "that fortifications of concrete and steel armed with modern fire-power, and fully manned by trained, resolute men, could only be overcome by surprise in time or place, by turning their flank, or by some new mechanical device like the tank." The British had in fact offered some of their new devices (armored bridge layers, flame throwers, and flails for the mine field—collectively known as "the Funnies") to the Americans; but the latter to their cost used only amphibious tanks, which in the event mostly foundered in deep water.

When the Americans left their familiar villages for these camps, there had been weeping—more, one young medic thought, than when his draft contingent had left its home town in Iowa. Long afterward, Mrs. Betty Hinde described what the British felt: "Somehow or other in the morning the whole place seemed quiet and eerie as if all the life had gone out of it. It really was quite uncanny." There was an awareness, everywhere. This was the last spin of the coin and everything depended on it. Mrs. Barbara Boyd heard soft boots stepping through the night and thought, "There were all our friends, all the people that we knew, going away to the real war, to the fighting war. We never knew if we'd see them again." Marching to his ship, Sergeant Harold E. Williams passed an old woman whose face was a mask of tears. She was repeating over and over, "Thank you, lads, for helping us out."

As the Stag's Head in Chilton Foliat the dart game was desultory. The locals drank their warm beer thoughtfully, missing their friends of the 101st Airborne Division who on most nights had accounted for most of the beer and nearly all of what little whisky there was. As the light faded in the long summer evening of June 5, they heard the planes. Sergeant Ivan T. Nielsen of Superior, Wisconsin, watched the para-troopers board. Years later he could still remember their expressions: even the young ones, the noisy ones who had shaved their hair into a single central brush in the Iroquois fashion, were not talking very much.

Over Normandy, they dropped in silence in utter dark-ness toward something they could not imagine. Suddenly they were in another world in which everything that had been familiar was immediately, terrifyingly and mortally hostile. A hedgerow, they had always believed, was a place of ease, a molding of warm dirt and dry grass fitting the small of your back aching after harvest, giving off the slightly sour, faintly aromatic smell of sap from a broken leaf or a twig idly stripped of green. A hedgerow was a sanctuary; it was supposed to comfort you, not kill you. But these Norman hedgerows were monstrous, hiding the enemy so completely that you were close enough to feel the heat of his machine guns' firing before you saw him. General Maxwell D. Taylor landed quite alone and made his suspicious way toward one of those hedgerows. It was silent. He moved on. He began to wonder if he would ever find a single member of the division he commanded. He carried a cricket, as did each of his men, as a recognition signal, but it was a while before he decided to use it. After a long time he heard a faint sound, as of cattle grazing. He hazarded a click. It was answered. A figure rustled toward him, fully armed and confident, but helmetless. General Taylor's relief was so enormous that he found himself at a loss for words. Then he assumed command. "Soldier," he demanded, "where's your hat?"

Offshore, Lieutenant John E. Coleman, U.S.N.R., was catching a little sleep after being at sea in his tank-landing-craft for twenty-seven hours. A messenger woke him with "Mr. Coleman, the skipper says there's something you might like to see." Coleman joined his captain (who a few hours later would step out of his steel pilot house into a bursting shell) and watched the planes flying over. The sea was gray and misty, and chopped at the flat bottoms of the landing craft in a most uncomfortable manner. When Coleman began his run into the beach not a shot had yet been fired, though he could see warships with their great guns trained. One of the infantry officers he was about to land was uneasy. "It's too quiet," he muttered. The fleet opened up, slamming the air in great hot walls of sound over the boats slapping toward the sand. The Germans did not answer. Coleman was four hundred yards from the shore when they did. What he remembered after that was dying men.

There is no coherent picture of what happened on Omaha Beach during the first hours of June 6, 1944, because it was not a coherent battle. The men who were there remember incidents only, so the true picture recollected is as if lit by flashes. At low tide it was a flat, wide stretch of sand crossed by shallow channels. This was spread with ranks of explosive devices of various kinds. At about highwater mark a bank of pebbles, in places nine feet high, ran the length of the beach. Beyond this shingle there was flat, marshy ground two or three hundred yards across at its widest, much of it sown with mines. Now the shingle bank is gone, bulldozed away in the week after D-day to make way for the thousands of tons of supplies that were to come. There are patches in the sand still heavy with metal, shell fragments mixed with rusty rivets from ships sunk in the bay, all smoothed now by the action of the sea and oxidized a bright and symbolic red. Occasionally a mine is still discovered and placed nonchalantly on display by a dispenser of *vins-liqueurs* near the beach. The French have built little summer villas at the foot of the bluffs beyond the mine fields, not seeming to mind the ugly blockhouse ruins that still yawn toward the beach.

At first, that morning, it seemed impossible. There were blobs in the water like sacks glistening wet, dead men drowned or shot, bobbing gently in the making tide. There was the flat, shrieking *zip* of 88 mm. shells coming in too fast to dodge, and a tearing, cracking detonation when they hit and opened armor and flesh like paper. There was a lot of smoke, gray and acrid, but the color men noticed was red. "There was blood all over the sand, on the rocks," Leo Heroux said. He was an assault engineer at the tail end of the first wave. The waves lapping up the beach were being kicked into spray by machine guns playing on them but still men were lying in inches of water pretending, though they knew it did not, that it gave them protection. All along the beach the landing craft hesitated, plunged forward and dropped their ramps, and instantaneously the openings were tangles of dead men.

Private Philip Guarassi of Brooklyn, New York, had made the trip with infantry of the 1st Division. His ordnance company went in minutes after H-Hour. "There was no gaiety among us," he recalled. "The craft slid a little on the sand and the ramp was quickly let down. We immediately removed ourselves and waded waist deep in water to the shore. Soldiers were falling all around us. All types of equipment was being blown up before we could use it. It began to look more and more like a gigantic junkyard." Guarassi found the officer in charge of his combat team crouching behind a rock and asked him what his plans might be. "Beats the hell out of me," said the officer. Guarassi "immediately notified him that I was getting my dead ass out of there."

Most of the initial assault waves had got as far as the shingle. Lieutentant James Drew lay next to his sergeant, waiting for a chance to get his beach party into operation. A few yards to their right some Rangers were firing grapnels onto the top of the cliffs of the Pointe de la Percée, trying to secure scaling ladders. The Germans kept cutting the ropes and lobbing grenades down. After several failures Drew's sergeant called over to the Rangers, not without a touch of impatience, "Why the hell don't you get up the cliff?" A Sergeant of the Rangers turned around. "Why the hell don't you?" he asked reasonably. Slowly men with the cool courage of Guarassi began to inch forward and take a few comrades with them. Others were rallied by their officers. Colonel George A. Taylor, in command of the 16th Infantry, stood up and suggested, as Private Jean R. Bernard of Lawrence, Massachusetts, heard it behind the shingle bank, "Hell, we're dying here on this beach. Let's move *inland* and die." At that moment the battle was as good as won.

By the official estimate, the day's fighting cost 1,465 American lives for sure. Amother 1,928 men were missing. The bodies of some of those who died that day still lie not far from the beach, most of them under white crosses marked "Known But To God." The American military cemetery at St.-Laurent-sur-Mer in Calvados lies atop the bluffs within view of the beach and nowadays is a picnic spot much favored by the French. It is green and beautiful and immaculate, and about it broods the terrible, useless decorum of death. But it is not the only or the most touching memorial.

All over England mature men and women remember how when they were children the big relaxed strangers tossed oranges at them, or gave them ice cream for the first time, or came to tea and called everything by the wrong name. Old people remember their vicarious fears for boys they had grown fond of, catching at premonitions, real or imagined, when a name is mentioned. "He was killed," a man says. "Yes," his wife adds, "we thought he might be. He *looked* like it." Mothers of families remember without rancor how as lissome girls they clung closer in dark parks or on the banks of placid streams and whispered, knowing already the answer, "Will you *really* take me to the States?" What was there and what is left are after all parts of a dream. But the dream has not yet faded. It is peopled with perilous, rangy young men who brought with them from the New World the innocent belief that all things were possible, and proved it before noon one spring morning across the Channel. The great gift of those Americans, as the British see it, was not their blood or their bravery, but their innocence.

—June 1969

HELL'S HIGHWAY TO ARNHEM

by STEPHEN W. SEARS

Operation Market-Garden promised to lay an airborne red carpet to victory.

I t would have taken considerable effort to locate an Allied fighting man on the battle line in Western Europe on September 10, 1944, who doubted that the end of the war was just around the corner. To American GI's and British Tommies up front, heartened by six weeks of unrelieved victory, the chances of being home home by Christmas were beginning to look very good indeed.

Those six weeks had been spectacular. Since late July, when the Anglo-American armies had burst out of their Normandy beachhead, the vaunted German army had fled for its life. Narrowly escaping encirclement at Falaise, nearly trapped against the Seine, harried out of Paris, driven pell-mell toward the Siegfried Line, which guarded the borders of the Third Reich itself, the German forces in France had lost a half million men and 2,200 tanks and self-propelled guns. It was a rout, a blitzkrieg in reverse.

The optimism buoying the combat troops was not entirely shared by the Allied High Command, however. Supplies were critically short, and the enemy showed signs of getting himself sorted out. A hot inter-Allied argument—soon to be christened the Great Argument—was raging over the next strategic step. On September 10 the debate hit one of its peaks. The setting was the Brussels airport, the scene the personal aircraft of the Supreme Commander, Dwight D. Eisenhower. The principal debater was British Field Marshal

Bernard Law Montgomery.

The meeting went badly from the start. Eisenhower, who had recently wrenched his knee in a forced landing during an inspection flight to the front, was confined to his plane. On arriving, Montgomery arrogantly demanded that Ike's administrative aide leave while his own stayed. Ever the patient conciliator, Eisenhower agreed. Montgomery then delivered himself of an increasingly violent attack on the Supreme Commander's conduct of the war. Rather than continuing the advance on Germany on a broad front, Montgomery argued for a halt to all offensive operations except for "one really powerful and full-blooded thrust" in his own sector, aimed toward the great German industrial complex in the Ruhr Valley and beyond.

"He vehemently declared," Eisenhower was later to write, "that . . . if we would support his 21st Army Group with all supply facilities available he would rush right on to Berlin and, he said, end the war."

Eisenhower's temper rose with Montgomery's intemperance. Finally he leaned forward, put his hand on the Field Marshal's knee, and said: "Steady, Monty! You can't speak to me like that. I'm your boss!" Montgomery, who calculated his outbursts for effect, saw that he had gone too far and contritely apologized. Their discussion continued calmly enough, but their strategic differences remained.

When he left the meeting, however, Montgomery carried with him Eisenhower's approval of a plan code-named Operation Market-Garden. If he had gained less than he sought, Montgomery at least had in Market-Garden what British war correspondent Chester Wilmot has described as "the last, slender chance of ending the German war in 1944."

In those early days of September the Allies had simply outrun their supply network. Armored units were stalled without gasoline. Replacements, food, ammunition, and spare parts were far below even minimum needs. Yet only by applying hard, continuous pressure on the enemy could the Allies hope to breach the Siegfried Line and win a bridgehead across the Rhine before winter—and perhaps even force a complete Nazi collapse.

Supply problems could not be solved overnight. The Allies had reached the German border 233 days ahead of their preinvasion timetable, and it would take weeks for logistics to catch up. In Eisenhower's view, just trying to reach the Rhine on the present supply shoestring was gamble enough. To approve Montgomery's "full-blooded thrust" without a solid logistic base and without the capability of making diversionary attacks elsewhere on the front was to invite its destruction. Better to advance to the Rhine on a broad front, Ike believed, and then pause to regroup and resupply before plunging on into the Third Reich at full strength.

Ike conceded that the strategic opportunities in Montgomery's northern sector were attractive—the vital Nazi arsenal of the Ruhr, the good "tank country" of the north German plain—and had granted supply priority to the 21st Army Group. Yet he was unwilling to rein in completely U.S. Lieutenant General Omar Bradley's 12th Army Group to the south, whose advance was aimed at the industrialized Saar region.

The Supreme Commander also carried a burden of quite a different sort: mediating between two eccentrics of towering military reputation. On the one hand, spearheading Bradley's army group, there was the flamboyant George Patton, a familiar sight in newsreels and on front pages throughout the Allied world. His Third Army tankers had covered the most ground and grabbed the most headlines in the race across France, and to the American public they seemed unstoppable.

Then there was Bernard Montgomery, victor of El Alamein and Britain's great hero, with an acrid manner and an insufferable ego that invariably grated on his American colleagues. To halt either Patton or Montgomery at the other's expense might open a serious fissure in the Anglo-American coalition. Dwight Eisenhower was too good a student of coalition warfare to allow that to happen.

In any case the issues that September were clear: how to keep the pursuit from bogging down; how to break the barrier of the Siegfried Line; how to gain a bridgehead across the Rhine. Operation Market-Garden offered to resolve all three.

By September 10 the staging area for Market-Garden was secure. At dusk that day elements of Montgomery's 21st Army Group crossed the Meuse-Escaut Canal in Belgium, close to the Dutch border. Most of Belgium was in Allied hands, including Antwerp, the great port so badly needed for logistic support of Eisenhower's armies. Antwerp was useless, however, until German troops were routed from the banks of the

Schledt estuary that linked the port with the North Sea.

Operation Market-Garden, scheduled for September 17, involved a sudden, one-hundred-mile thrust from the Meuse-Escaut Canal almost due north into Holland, crossing the Lower Rhine at the city of Arnhem and reaching all the way to the Zuider Zee. If successful, it would completely outflank the Siegfried Line and win a coveted Rhine bridgehead. In addition, it would cut Holland in two, trapping thousands of German troops and isolating the chief launching sites of the deadly V-2 ballistic missiles that were pummelling London.

With these objectives in hand Montgomery was confident that Eisenhower would have no choice but to fully support his plan to seize the Ruhr and drive on toward Berlin. Thus, the Field Marshal declared, the war could be won "reasonably quickly."

Eisenhower was less sanguine. He cautioned Montgomery that the opening of Antwerp could not long be delayed. Much would depend on Market-Garden succeeding quickly and at minimum cost.

As bold as the plan was the technique designed to carry it out. The Dutch countryside was ideally suited to defense, marshy and heavily wooded and cut by numerous waterways: in the span of sixty-five miles the single highway running north from the Belgian border to Arnhem crossed no less than three canals, two small rivers, and three major streams—the Maas, the Waal, and the Lower Rhine. Montgomery proposed to lay a "red carpet" for his ground forces over this difficult terrain by using Eisenhower's entire strategic reserve, the paratroops of the First Allied Airborne Army. Their mission was to seize the bridges over these eight waterways in a massive surprise invasion from the sky. This airdrop was to be coordinated with a "rapid and violent" thrust by a British armored column along the Arnhem highway.

Previous airborne operations had shown that the effectiveness of paratroopers varied in inverse proportion to the time they had to hold their objectives; in a long fight they were invariably overmatched in firepower. On the face of it, then, laying down a carpet of paratroopers and glider-borne infantry up to sixty-five miles ahead of the ground forces, as Market-Garden proposed to do, was a very high-risk tactic. Eisenhower and Montgomery counted on the condition of the German forces in Holland to even the odds. Allied intelligence was confident that behind a thin crust of resistance along the Meuse-Escaut Canal, there was hardly any organized enemy at all.

Opposing the Allies in this northern sector was Field Marshal Walther Model, working with his characteristic furious energy to patch together a defensive line. Model was a stocky, roughhewn character, a favorite of Hitler's who had performed well in crises on the Eastern Front and who liked to call himself "the *Führer's* Fireman." His command had been so badly shattered in France, however, that facing Montgomery in early September there was only a mixed bag of stragglers, garrison troops, and *Luftwaffe* ground units, braced by a few green paratroop regiments and some fanatical but inexperienced SS men. Line infantry and armor were in very short supply.

A few days before Market-Garden was scheduled to begin, fragmentary reports came in from the Dutch underground of two German armored formations that had just bivouacked north of Arnhem, apparently for refitting. Allied intelligence surmised that these must be the 9th and 10th SS Panzer divisions. Both were known to have been decimated in the French debacle, and intelligence discounted them as a threat to the operation.

In England U.S. Lieutenant General Lewis H. Brereton's First Allied Airborne Army, honed to a fine edge, was spoiling for a fight. The three divisions slated for Market-Garden—the U.S. 82nd and 101st Airborne, veterans of the Normandy airdrop, and the 1st British Airborne, which had fought in Sicily and Italy—had seen eighteen scheduled drops canceled in a period of forty days as the ground forces advanced too fast to need them.

The mission of Maxwell Taylor's 101st Airborne was a drop near Eindhoven to seize that city and key river and canal bridges. Farther along the road to Arnhem would be James Gavin's 82nd Airborne, assigned the big bridges over the Maas at Grave and over Waal at Nijmegen, plus a ridge line to the east that dominated both bridges. The farthermost objective, the bridge over the Lower Rhine at Arnhem, was allotted to Robert E. Urquhart's 1st British Airborne, assisted by a brigade of Polish paratroops.

In tactical command was British Lieutenant General Frederick Browning, dapper and brusque, the husband of novelist Daphne du Maurier. Browning had his reservations about the operation. Montgomery assured him he had to hold the Arnhem airhead only two days. "We can hold it for four," Browning replied. "But I think we might be going a bridge too far."

The ground forces, led by the Guards Armoured Division of the British Second Army, were to begin their northward push as the airdrop began. In command was Brian Horrocks, tall and white-haired and with something of the manner of a Biblical prophet about him. He had served Montgomery in North Africa and was both energetic and capable. Unlike Browning, Horrocks radiated optimism about the speed his forces would make. "You'll be landing on top of our heads," he warned the paratroops in mock seriousness.

Market-Garden lacked the "tidiness"—a substantial margin of superiority—that Montgomery usually demanded in operation. There were few reserves in case of trouble and, with Patton embroiling the Third Army in battle to the south to keep his supplies coming, only minimum supporting stocks of gasoline and ammunition. Nevertheless, the plan was bold and imaginative; if the Germans were indeed on the brink of collapse, a victory at Arnhem just might provide the extra shove to keep the pursuit rolling and measurably shorten the war.

The opening phase of the largest airborne operation in history was, in the words of an RAF pilot, "a piece of cake." D-day, September 17, 1944, was clear and windless, ideal for an airdrop. Shortly before 1 P.M.—following a softening-up of German defenses by 1,400 Allied bombers—some 1,400 transport planes and 425 gliders, plus swarms of escorting fighters, blackened the skies over Holland.

Edward R. Murrow had wangled a place in one of the 101st Airborne's C-47's to make a recording of his impressions for CBS Radio. "Now every man is out . . .," Murrow reported. "I can see their chutes going down now . . . they're dropping beside the little windmill near a church, hanging there, very gracefully, and seem to be completely relaxed, like nothing so much as khaki dolls hanging beneath green lampshades. . . . The whole sky is filled with parachutes."

On the ground below, a few miles from the 101st's drop zones, German General Kurt Student watched the sight with frank envy. Student was a pioneer of airborne warfare who had led the aerial assaults on Rotterdam and Crete. "How I wish that I had ever had such a powerful force," he remarked wistfully to an aide. Dutch civilians returning from church cheered the awesome sight. As the paratroopers landed, the Dutch rushed out to meet them with offers of food from their Sunday tables.

Max Taylor's 101st Airborne in the Eindhoven sector had been assigned the longest stretch of the Arnhem road—soon to be christened Hell's Highway. Meeting little opposition, Taylor's units formed up and seized their objectives one after another. However, as they approached the bridge over the Wilhelmina Canal at Zon, a few miles north of Eindhoven, they were pinned down by the accurate fire of a pair of German 88-mm guns in a nearby forest. The 88's were finally destroyed by bazooka fire, but the delay was costly. As the paratroopers tried to rush the Zon bridge, it was blown up in their faces.

Farther up Hell's Highway Jim Gavin's 82nd Airborne was also finding both success and frustration. The 82nd's assault on the long, nine-span bridge over the Maas River at Grave was the most neatly executed strike of the day. Paratroopers landed close to both ends of the bridge. Using irrigation ditches as cover from the fire of a flak tower guarding the bridge, Gavin's men worked their way to within bazooka range. Two rounds silenced the flak tower, and they rushed the bridge and cut the demolition wires. A second key bridge, over the Maas-Waal Canal, was taken in much the same manner. Gavin's two regiments that dropped astride the dominating heights of Groesbeek Ridge southeast of Nijmegen dug themselves in securely on the wooded slopes.

The frustration came at 8 P.M. when, with the division's three primary objectives in the bag, a battalion of the 508th Regiment under Lieutenant Colonel Shields Warren made a dash into Nijmegen to try for the big highway bridge across the Waal. It ran head-on into a newly arrived battalion of the 9th SS Panzer Division. There was a sharp clash in the growing darkness. Warren's men gained the building housing the controls for the demolition charges on the bridge, but the superior firepower of the Panzers drove them away from the span itself.

The Red Devils of the 1st British Airborne executed an almost perfect drop at Arnhem on D-day. It was here, however, that a serious tactical error on the part of Market-Garden's planners caught up with them. The drop zones were six to eight miles west of the city. The need to hold the drop zones for later reinforcements—there were too few aircraft to deliver the full strength of any of the divisions in the D-day lift—meant that General Urquhart could spare but a single battalion to go after the bridge in Arnhem.

That evening five hundred men under Colonel John Frost slipped into the city along an unguarded road and seized the north end of the bridge. At almost the same moment that the 9th SS Panzer was halting Gavin's bid for the Nijmegen bridge, another unit of the same division arrived in time to prevent Frost's men from crossing the Arnhem bridge and taking its southern approach. A second battalion sent to aid Frost was cut off by the Germans on the outskirts of Arnhem.

All in all, the airborne situation at the end of D-day was reasonably satisfactory. Montgomery's red carpet was twenty thousand men strong. The landings had been unexpectedly easy, the easiest in fact that any of the divisions had ever made, in combat or in training. Except for the blown bridge at Zon and the failure of Gavin's coup de main at the Nijmegen bridge, all objectives had been taken or, as at Arnhem, at least denied to the enemy.

The progress of the ground forces was less satisfactory, for the German crust beyond the Meuse-Escaut Canal was thicker and tougher than Allied intelligence had predicted. General Horrocks was forced by the marshy terrain to attack on the narrowest of fronts—the forty-foot width of Hell's Highway. His armor was immediately in trouble. Concealed antitank guns knocked out eight of the Guards Armoured's tanks in rapid succession. Infantry finally flushed the enemy from the woods on the flanks, but it was slow work.

Supported by the rocket-firing Typhoon fighter bombers, the Guards battered their way forward, greeted in every village by the cheering Dutch. Portraits of Princess Juliana appeared magically in shop windows. But by nightfall the armored column was still a half dozen miles short of Eindhoven and a linkup with the 101st Airborne.

Heavy rain fell during the night, and in the morning of D-day plus 1—Monday, September 18—there were thick clouds over the Continent and fog over the Allied airfields in England, delaying the second day's lift of glider infantry and supplies. By noon the 101st's paratroopers had liberated Eindhoven, but not until seven that evening did the Guards Armoured link up with them. British engineers went to work building a prefabricated Bailey bridge to replace the blown canal bridge at Zon.

Model and Student began to put in counterattacks. Soon the two American divisions were embroiled in what Max Taylor characterized as "Indian fighting." The fourteen thousand U.S. paratroopers had to control over forty miles of Hell's Highway, which meant a constant scurrying from one threatened sector to another. An example was the fight for the big bridge at Nijmegen. This span was fast becoming the key to the whole Market-Garden operation, and both sides knew it.

The bridge across the Waal in Nijmegen was well over a mile long, with a high, arching center span. Five streets cut through a heavily built-up section of the city to converge on a traffic circle near the bridge's southern entrance. Between the traffic circle and the bridge was a large wooded common known as Hunner Park, where elements of the 9th and 10th SS Panzer divisions had dug in automatic weapons, mortars, self-propelled guns, and at least one of the deadly 88's. Their fire was directed from a massive stone tower in the center of the park.

Just after dawn 82nd Division paratroopers deployed for their second attack on the bridge. The heavy-caliber German fire quickly drove them from the streets. Advancing through alleys and from doorway to doorway, the Americans worked their way to within a block of the traffic circle. That was as far as they got: reinforcements slated for the bridge attack had to turn back to meet a German thrust threatening to overrun the landing zones south of the city where gliders carrying Gavin's artillery battalions were scheduled to land at any minute. The thrust was beaten off and the gliders landed safely—but the Nijmegen bridge remained in German hands.

A planned night attack on Hunner Park was canceled by General Browning, who was disturbed by reports of a German buildup in front of Groesbeek Ridge to the southeast. If the Germans ever drove the thin line of paratroopers from the ridge, their guns would control both the Maas and Waal bridges, ending any chance of Market-Garden's success.

Colonel Frost's British troopers continued to cling to the

north end of the Arnhem bridge, but the enemy repulsed every effort to reinforce the tiny bridgehead. The rest of the Red Devils were besieged at their landing zones west of the city. Communications had completely broken down. The first news from Arnhem was a clandestine telephone call placed by the Dutch underground. Recorded in an 82nd Division intelligence journal, the message was brief and blunt: "Dutch report Germans winning over British at Arnhem."

The chief topic of conversation on the third day of battle, Tuesday, September 19, was the weather. A glider pilot complained of fog so thick that he could see "only three feet of towrope" in front of him. Less than two-thirds of the reinforcements and supplies due the 101st arrived, and only a quarter of the 82nd's. A resupply effort at Arnhem was a disaster. Model's troops had finally driven the Red Devils from the drop zones, and a glider pilot on the ground watched in anguish as the C-47's came in and the flak caught them. "They were so helpless! I have never seen anything to illustrate the word 'helpless' more horribly," he recalled. Over 90 percent of the parachuted supplies fell into enemy hands.

As viewed by a Red Devil in the rear ranks, the situation at Arnhem "was a bloody shambles." The bad weather scrubbed the scheduled drop of the Polish brigade at the south end of the bridge. Every effort to break through to Colonel Frost's battalion failed. Toward evening, in the rain, several German Tiger tanks approached the British bridgehead. To Frost the Tigers looked "like some prehistoric monsters as their great guns swung from side to side breathing flame. . . . We drove these monsters back, but . . . as we prepared for yet another night Arnhem was burning."

Guards Armoured tanks made good progress during the day, jumping off from the new Bailey bridge at Zon at dawn, linking up with Gavin's 82nd Airborne, and reaching the outskirts of Nijmegen by early afternoon. Horrocks met with Gavin and Browning to work out a combined assault on the Nijmegen bridge. Time was a critical factor: the ground forces were now more than thirty-three hours behind the operation's schedule.

The third attack on the Nijmegen bridge jumped off at 3 P.M. Gavin could spare only a battalion from his hard-pressed forces on Groesbeek Ridge. The British contributed an infantry company and a tank battalion. A smaller force of paratroopers and tanks moved against a railroad bridge downstream.

This latter column fought its way through Nijmegen's streets to within five hundred yards of the railroad bridge before it was halted by heavy enemy fire. Every effort to advance farther was stymied, and when an 88 knocked out one of the British tanks, the attackers withdrew.

Meanwhile, the battle for Hunner Park guarding the highway bridge reached its crescendo. Horrocks's tanks had little maneuvering room in the narrow streets, and four of them were set ablaze by antitank fire. The German gunners kept the foot soldiers pinned down. In desperation, paratroopers attempted to advance along rooftops and through buildings, knocking out the connecting walls with explosives. But the enemy fire was too heavy and too well directed. As darkness fell, the third assault on the Nijmegen bridge sputtered out.

News from the 101st's sector to the south was ominous. Student was moving up powerful forces to try to cut Hell's Highway behind Horrocks's armored spearhead. In the late afternoon a squadron of Panther tanks broke through to the road and shot up a British truck convoy. General Taylor himself led a pickup force against the interlopers, and with their single antitank gun they knocked out two Panthers and drove off the rest.

That night the *Luftwaffe* made a devastating raid on Allied-held Eindhoven. "Half a dozen trucks carrying shells were hit directly," reported war correspondent Alan Moorehead, "and at once the shells were detonated and began to add a spasmodic stream of horizontal fore to the bombs which were now falling at a steady rhythm every minute. Presently a number of petrol lorries took fire as well. . . . In the morning one saw with wonder how much of bright Eindhoven was in ruins . . ."

On Wednesday, September 20, the Market-Garden planners expected the Second Army's tanks to be rolling toward the Zuider Zee. Instead they were stymied at Nijmegen. The bombing of Eindhoven and the German shelling of Hell's Highway were having their effects. Ammunition and reinforcements were held up, and the assault boats needed for a new attack on the Nijmegen bridge were delayed almost eight hours. While they waited for the boats, the 82nd Airborne and the Guards Armoured whittled away at the bridge defenses and fought off savage enemy attacks on Groesbeek Ridge. Finally, in midafternoon, the assault boats arrived.

Gavin's plan was to force a crossing a mile downstream from the railroad bridge and take the defenders of both the railroad and highway bridges in the rear. A battalion of paratroopers of the 504th Regiment, commanded by Major Julian A. Cook, was picked to make the crossing. In concert with the amphibious attack, Gavin and Horrocks would hurl every man and tank they could lay their hands on against the southern approach to the highway bridge. H-hour was set for 3 P.M.

As the U.S. Army's official phrased it, ". . . an assault crossing of the Waal would have been fraught with difficulties even had it not been so hastily contrived." At this point the Waal is four hundred yards wide, with a swift, ten-mile-an-hour current. The assault boats were unprepossessing plywood and canvas craft nineteen feet in length. There were only twenty-six of them. German strength on the northern bank was unknown; in any case, the paratroopers could not count on surprise, for the crossing site was completely exposed to enemy observers.

Fifteen minutes before H-hour, Allied artillery, tanks, and mortars began to batter the German defenders on the north bank, climaxing their barrage with smoke shells. The wind blew the smoke screen to tatters. At precisely 3 P.M. the 260 men of Major Cook's first wave waded into the shallows, hauling and shoving their awkward craft. They scrambled aboard and with paddles flailing pushed out into the deep, swift stream. Then the Germans opened fire.

Mortars, rifles, machine guns, 20-mm cannon, and 88's thrashed the water until it looked (as a paratrooper described it) like a "school of mackerel on the feed." Shrapnel tore through the canvas sides of the boats, knocking paratroopers sprawling. Of the twenty-six craft in the first wave, thirteen made it across.

Stunned by the ordeal, the paratroopers huddled in the lee of the north bank, retching and gasping for breath. But these men were veterans, trained as an elite force, and as they recovered physically they recovered their poise as well. Although unit organization was hopelessly scrambled, they took stock of the situation and began to move against their tormentors with deadly precision.

They raced forward to seize a sunken road, killing or scattering its German defenders and smashing machine-gun positions with grenades. A pickup platoon stormed an ancient Dutch fortress that dominated the shoreline. With this strongpoint silenced, the paratroopers hurried along the roads leading to the rail and highway bridges.

Meanwhile, weary engineers paddled reinforcements across the Waal. Two more of the flimsy assault boats sank under the enemy's guns. By late afternoon, however, after repeated round trips by the eleven surviving craft, the 504th Regiment had two of its batallions ranged in a solid bridgehead on the north bank of the river.

A mile and a half upstream, the Anglo-American attack on Hunner Park was well under way. During the previous night Model had reinforced the bridge defenders with a battle group from the 10th SS Panzer Division, and several 88's were newly dug in along the north bank, sited to fire into the streets converging on Hunner Park. By now, however, the paratroopers had control of the buildings fronting on the park and were pouring a devastating fire down into the German weapons pits from the rooftops. About an hour and a half after the attack began, an all-or-nothing tank-infantry assault was launched. Charging two and three abreast, the British tanks burst into the park, closely followed by paratroopers. The stone observation tower and a heavily wooded piece of high ground were quickly overwhelmed. The defenders of the park began to withdraw.

It was now dusk, and in the dim light and drifting battle smoke an American flag was seen flying high above the north bank of the river. Taking this as a signal that the far end of the highway bridge was secured, five British tanks raced onto the bridge ramp. In fact the flag was flying from the northern end of the railroad bridge downstream, but no matter: paratroopers were just then overrunning the defenses of the highway bridge as well. German bazookamen hiding in the girders knocked out two of the tanks, but the remaining three clattered across the span, shot their way through a barricade, and just after 7 P.M. were greeted by three grinning privates of the 504th Regiment. The great prize was intact in Allied hands at last; as darkness fell, the final stretch of Hell's Highway lay ahead.

However, the situation of the British paratroopers at Arnhem to the north had grown desperate during the day. Attempts to reinforce Colonel Frost's men at the north end of the bridge were broken off; facing an estimated six thousand German troops, Urquhart could do no more than try to retain a bridgehead on the Lower Rhine a half dozen miles to the west of the city with the remnants of his force. That night a grim message from the Red Devils was received by the British Second Army: "Enemy attacking main bridge in strength. Situation critical for slender force . . . Relief essential. . . ."

Arnhem is only ten miles beyond Nijmegen, but on Thursday, September 21, it might just as well have been ten light years away. The Guards Armoured Division was immobilized in Nijmemgen due to shortages of ammunition, gasoline, and replacement tanks. It had virtually no supporting infantry. The 82nd Airborne was stretched near the breaking point containing attacks on its flank. And to the south on Hell's Highway thousands of supply vehicles were enmeshed in a huge traffic jam.

Thus, the fifth day of Operation Market-Garden was frittered away, much to the frustration of the conquerors of the Nijmegen bridge. Only a trickle of tanks and other fighting vehicles crossed the hard-won span; Allied gains beyond Nijmegen were slight. And at Arnhem the last of Colonel Frost's men, out of ammunition, had been routed from their strongholds and forced to surrender. Allied reconnaissance planes reported seeing German armored units and infantry convoys rolling south, headed toward Nijmegen, across the Arnhem bridge.

The road between Nijmegen and Arnhem runs some six feet above the low fields and orchards flanking it, making the British tanks that tried to advance northward on the next day, Friday, September 22, sitting ducks for the enemy gunners. The advance soon foundered at a roadblock in the village of Ressen, seven miles short of Arnhem.

Although the Germans now held the Arnhem bridge in strength, Horrocks believed a crossing of the Lower Rhine might still be possible by building a bridge downstream, where the Red Devils had their slender bridgehead. Horrocks's troops eventually reached the river over back roads late in the day, but it was too late. German forces arrived on the north bank in too much strength for Horrocks to attempt a bridging operation.

Thirty miles to the south, Student's tanks slashed across Hell's Highway, bringing all traffic to a halt. Continued bad weather made aerial support and resupply impossible. "Waiting and waiting for the Second Army," wrote one of the Red Devils in his diary. "The Second Army was always at the back of our minds. The thought of it made us stand up to anything. . . ."

On Saturday the Second Army refused to release the reserve division scheduled to be airlifted to the support of the Arnhem airhead. It is an old military maxim to reinforce success, but with each passing hour Market-Garden was looking less and less like a success. Paratroopers of the 101st Division and British tanks managed to reopen Hell's Highway by afternoon, but not enough assault boats could be brought forward to the Lower Rhine to effectively reinforce Urquhart's shrinking perimeter. The Red Devils were critically short of ammunition, food, water, and medical supplies; air resupply was all but impossible, although C-47 pilots repeatedly braved the German flak to try it.

On Sunday, as the Allied command groped for a way to save the battle slipping away from them, Urquhart radioed the Second Army: "Must warn you unless physical contact is made with us early 25 September [Monday] consider it unlikely we can hold out long enough." That evening Student's tanks cut Hell's Highway once more.

At 9:30 A.M. on Monday Generals Browning and Horrocks made it official: Market-Garden had failed; the Arnhem airhead would be evacuated. When night fell the Red Devils began to slip away toward the river, boots and equipment muffled in rags, each paratrooper holding on to the belt of the man in front of him. In a pouring rain rescue boats hurried back and forth across the dark river under the cover of a steady bombardment by Horrocks's guns. Hundreds of wounded had to be left behind.

Only 2,400 of the nine thousand Red Devils who had fought in and around Arnhem were rescued. When there was time for a count, it was found that in the nine days of fighting the 82nd Airborne had lost over 1,400, the 101st over 2,100. Another fifteen hundred men and seventy tanks were lost by Horrocks's ground forces. Close to three hundred Allied planes were downed.

The Arnhem bridge—the last bridge—stayed firmly in German hands. There it would remain for seven months, until the final few weeks of the war.

Operation Market-Garden came tantalizingly close to success—a few hours saved here, a different decision made there, and everything might have been different. The weather was certainly an important factor in the failure, limiting aerial resupply and reinforcements and hampering air support. The decision to drop the Red Devils so far from Arnhem was a costly one. The pace of the Second Army's rear echelons carrying supplies and reinforcements was hardly what Montgomery had in mind when he called for a drive of "the utmost rapidly and violence." Allied intelligence fumbled badly in not taking reports of the presence of the two Panzer divisions more seriously. And there was pure misfortune in Market-Garden's taking place on the very doorsteps of Model and Student, two of the most skilled German generals on the Western Front.

Most of all, however, Market-Garden failed because it was conceived on the assumption that the German army was about to collapse. The Nazis were not as close to the brink as they seemed: to push them over the edge required a far stronger force than Market-Garden was given. "Perhaps," writes the military historian Charles B. MacDonald, "the only real fault of the plan was overambition."

But if it was a failure, it was a gallant one. If boldness, imagination, and sheer raw courage deserve the reward of victory, then victory should have gone to the men of the First Allied Airborne Army. The fighting record of the 1st British Airborne in Arnhem has been justly celebrated as an epic. Yet the exploits of the two American airborne divisions that defended Hell's Highway against all odds and brilliantly won the great bridge at Nijmegen have too often been overlooked. As General Brereton put it: "The 82nd and 101st Divisions . . . accomplished every one of their objectives. . . . In the years to come everyone will remember Arnhem, but no one will remember that two American divisions fought their hearts out in the Dutch canal country and whipped hell out of the Germans."

"I think we might be going a bridge too far," General Browning had warned a week before the airdrop. Unwittingly, he had framed the epitaph of the greatest airborne assault in history.

—June 1971

LET SLIP THE BATS AND BALLOONS OF WAR . . .

The strangest secret weapons of World War II.

I. The Fu-Go Project

by CARMINE A. PRIOLI

On August 3, 1976, a retired Japanese scientist made a pilgrimage to a World War II battlefield shrine. Accompanied by a small group of Americans from the nearby lumbering community of Bly, Oregon, Sakyo Adachi climbed a secluded woodland slope and stopped before a monument built of native stone. While the others watched, Adachi placed a floral wreath below an inscription that reads:

THE ONLY PLACE
ON THE
AMERICAN CONTINENT
WHERE DEATH RESULTED
FROM ENEMY ACTION
DURING WORLD WAR II.

Then he stepped back, pressed his palms together in a gesture of prayer, and bowed. His American companions grasped his hands in friendship.

The people being memorialized had been killed by a weapon that linked the technology of twentieth-century warfare with an ancient object of fragile grace.

In the early daylight hours of April 18, 1942, the carrier *Hornet*, steaming several hundred miles off the Japanese coast, headed into the wind as, one by one, sixteen B-25's lifted off her rolling deck. Flying low and in brilliant daylight, all sixteen planes reached their targets and unloaded incendiary bombs on Kobe, Nagoya, Yokosuka, and Tokyo. The physical damage inflicted by James H. Doolittle's spectacular raid was negligible, but it shook the Japanese Imperial High Command: the homeland had been violated, and honor demanded retaliation upon America.

For more than a decade Japanese meteorologists had been aware of air currents high overhead that traced a serpentine pattern eastward. Would it be possible for these currents, later to be called "jet streams," to carry free-floating balloons that could bomb the forests, farm lands, and cities of the United States? The idea seemed preposterous. But Japanese scientists had been experimenting with hydrogen-filled balloons since the early 1930s, and they had solved some formidable technical problems. So by 1943, when military leaders ordered a face-saving counterattack, the balloon specialists already had their "Fu-Go" project under way. They were close to perfecting a weapon that would travel sixty-two hundred miles toward a target area, drop its payload of bombs, and then destroy itself, entirely under its own power.

The first bomb-laden balloon lifted off the Japanese mainland on November 3, 1944. If all went as planned, heat from the sun's rays would cause the hydrogen in the bag to expand, raising each balloon to its highest altitude, approximately thirty-eight thousand feet. There it would meet the winter winds coursing northeastward at speeds often exceeding two hundred knots. At night, when temperatures dropped to minus 50 degrees Centigrade and the contracting gas pitched the craft about three thousand feet, a specially developed altitude-control device would discharge enough ballast to lighten the balloon, maintaining a minimum altitude of thirty thousand feet. Next day the sun would again warm the gas and the balloon would ascend to repeat its vaulting cycle. By the time the craft reached the American Northwest, all its ballast would have been dropped. The altitude mechanism would then begin discharging bombs instead of sandbags. The estimated sailing time from Japan to the United States was sixty hours.

During the last weeks of 1944 the U.S. Western Defense Command began receiving reports of paper balloons, or fragments of them, landing in scattered areas across the American Northwest. At first they were thought to be Japanese weather or antiaircraft barrage balloons that had accidentally drifted across the Pacific. By the end of December, however, sightings grew more frequent, and the Naval Research Laboratory and the FBI set out to determine the origin and objective of the balloons. Investigators already knew that the balloons were Japanese and, in some cases, when they were constructed and even where they were launched. Early in the new year they would discover their purpose.

On January 4, 1945, two men working in a field about a mile southwest of Medford, Oregon, were startled by a strange aerial whine. Within seconds there was an explosion nearby, and a thirty-foot column of flames shot skyward. When investigators arrived, they found a charred hole six inches wide and twelve deep and the remains of an incendiary bomb. Since no aircraft had been heard, the source of the bomb remained a mystery until someone found a hook nearby, identical to ones discovered among fragments of the peculiar balloons now being reported in alarming numbers. The origin of the mysterious bomb became apparent: Japanese balloons were bombing the United States.

The U.S. Office of Censorship immediately quashed the story. News agencies were requested to refrain from publishing reports of the balloon operations for fear that if the Japanese knew their bombs were reaching North America, they would redouble their attacks.

A few days after the Medford, Oregon, explosion, a Navy P-38 Lightning was dispatched to intercept a balloon drifting high over Alturas, California. Employing British antibuzz-bomb tactics, the pilot used his plane's slip stream to force the balloon to a lower altitude, where he laced the bag with machine-gun bullets. It gradually lost gas, settled gently, and was recovered with all its remaining ballast, bombs, and release mechanisms intact. The entire balloon was shipped to Moffett Field, Sunnyvale, California, where it became the basis for the Western Defense Command's first detailed report on the new weapon.

The confidential study noted that the bags were made of sections of paper, layered and glued with a paste manufactured from *konnyaku*, a common potatolike vegetable. The bags, which measured a shade under thirty-three feet in diameter, were connected to the undercarriage by nineteen 49-foot shroud lines. The undercarriage contained a single-cell 2.3-

volt battery, an altitude-control device, a ballast-discharging mechanism, a ring of thirty-two sandbags, and five bombs—including four incendiaries and one fragmentation. Each undercarriage carried a two-pound demolition block of picric acid designed to destroy the mechanism in midair after it had completed its mission. Finally each balloon bag carried a flash bomb attached to the undercarriage by a 64.5-foot fuse. When the undercarriage exploded, this long fuse would burn until it ignited the hydrogen, producing a brilliant airborne explosion.

The ordnance they carried suggested the balloon bombs' primary strategic mission was to wage an incendiary war against the rich forests of the American Northwest. Upon impact, each fire bomb would disperse a flaming chemical and had the potential of destroying hundreds of acres of woodland. If the Fu-Go mission had been entirely successful, the Imperial Command would have unloaded fifteen thousand antipersonnel bombs and sixty thousand incendiary bombs on the United States. But although more than three hundred and fifty balloons were documented as having reached the continent, few caused any significant fire damage, for their targets were frozen and often snow covered. Only during the winter were the westerly winds powerful enough to sweep the balloons across the Pacific in the three days the craft could be expected to remain aloft.

But what if physical destruction was not the primary objective of the balloon bombs? Even the most idealistic of Japan's wartime planners knew that their balloons could not destroy the American military machine. But as they observed the psychological effects of American bombing raids on their civilian population, they became increasingly aware of how vulnerable a nation under stress could be. Enemy bombers coming out of the sky are fearsome weapons; but at least their coming can be seen and heard. The Fu-Go balloons, on the other hand, were capricious: they drifted silently, unpredictably, far beyond sight of the naked eye. Their bombs descended mysteriously, from an unknown, faceless enemy, presumably leaving their victims prey to hidden fears, to vague suspicions, and even to mass hysteria.

And they *were* mysterious, these weapons. After the balloons had dropped the last of their payload, they would ignite themselves in a celestial grand finale. This fashioned a blazing extraterrestrial phenomenon, and throughout the winter months of 1944-45, Western farmers and ranchers reported seeing bright, stationary fireballs in the skies, while, on December 8, 1944, the *Northern Wyoming Daily News* reported that a "Phantom Plane" was being sought after a series of explosions illuminated the night sky. The mystery was later solved when Naval Research Laboratory investigators determined that bomb and paper fragments found in the area had Japanese origins.

The balloons failed to inspire widespread panic but they did succeed in stirring grave fears among U.S. government officials, who foresaw the possibility of a disaster of unimaginable scope. One military historian, who believes the primary purpose of the balloon bombs was to spread fire, describes their "second most logical purpose" as the introduction of biological warfare. "The intense cold (minus 20 to minus 50 degrees Centigrade) at the altitude of the balloon flights," wrote Cornelius W. Conley in the February/March 1968 issue of *Air University Review*, "would facilitate the transmission of bacteria, and disease germs affecting humans, animals, crops and forests could be transported. . . . It would be theoretically possible to infect the vast U.S. culcine (mosquito) population and establish a permanent endemic focus of an agent."

Consequently, state health officers, veterinarians, agricultural agents, and 4-H Clubs were among those mobilized, under the code name "Lightning Project," to be on the lookout for possible epidemics or poisonings. Decontamination squads were trained, and the government set up detailed procedures for collecting information, for dealing with reports, and especially for keeping a tight lid on the story.

There is no evidence that the Japanese loaded the balloons with harmful bacteria. General Sueki Kusaba and Technical Lieutenant Commander Kiyoshi Tanaka, leaders of the balloon bomb project, have consistently maintained that they never planned to engage in biological or chemical warfare.

T he Fu-Go project ended early in April 1945 after thousands of launchings. Historians have extolled American newspaper and radio editors for their discretion, which allegedly prevented the Japanese from knowing that their balloons were reaching the United States. On May 29, 1947, *The New*

York Times declared: "Japan was kept in the dark about the fate of the fantastic balloon bombs because Americans proved during the war they could keep their mouths shut. To their silence is credited the failure of the enemy's campaign."

That silence did not long survive the six American deaths near Bly, Oregon, on May 6, 1945—nearly a month after the last balloons had lifted off Japanese soil. On May 7 the Klamath Falls (Oregon) *Herald and News* reported that Elsie Mitchell and five children had been killed while on a fishing trip by an explosion of "unannounced cause." "One of the party found an object," it continued, "others went to investigate, and the blast followed." There were no other details. There was no speculation in the news media about the cause of the explosion. Further reports were limited to a single account of a mass funeral for four of the blast victims. Two weeks later the government abandoned its censorship campaign and the Navy and War departments issued a joint statement describing the nature of the balloon bombs, and warning people to avoid tampering with strange objects. Because the attacks were "so scattered and aimless," it was believed they posed no serious military threat to the United States. The announcement stressed "that the possible saving of even one American life through precautionary measures would more than offset any military gain occurring to the enemy from the mere knowledge that some of his balloons actually have arrived on this side of the Pacific."

In 1949 the soundness of the censorship campaign was further questioned when the U.S. Congress approved a bill providing compensation of twenty thousand dollars to the families of those killed at Bly. Although the Senate Judiciary Committee maintained that no Army personnel were directly responsible for the deaths, it insisted that the Army and other services were "aware of the danger from these Japanese bombs and took no steps, for what may have been valid reasons, toward warning the civilian population of the danger involved."

Although the American news blackout rendered it difficult for the Japanese to assess the effectiveness of their Fu-Go project, it was not the principal cause for the termination of the mission.

By April of 1945 Japanese ground crews suspended further balloon launchings because American B-29's were destroying important hydrogen sources. General Kusaba reported: "To my great regret, the progress of the war was faster than we imagined. Soon after the campaign began, the air raids against our mainland were intensified. Many factories that manufactured various parts were destroyed. Moreover, we were not informed about the effect of Fu-Go throughout the wartime. Due to the combination of hardships we were compelled to cease operations."

In the five months that they drifted over American soil, what did the balloon bombs accomplish? Was the mission, as *The New York Times* described it, a "humiliating failure" that should have been awarded "first prize for worthless war weapons"?

The total cost of the Fu-Go project has been estimated at $2,000,000, with each balloon estimated at $920. Thus, in comparison with other military weapons, the balloon bomb was remarkably inexpensive, and one historian has assessed the campaign as an economic success that "gave the Japanese a good return on their investment." The bombs, he continues, "were a headache for Canadian and American military and security people and created more paperwork and disrupted more routine than any other Japanese attack against the North American mainland. . . . The money, material, and effort expended in defense and investigation caused more time and monetary damage to the Allied war effort than the two million dollars the Japanese spent to build, equip, and launch the balloons."

The Army had to train a large number of soldiers for the "Fire Fly Project," an extensive plan to combat forest fires. By May of 1945 American Forest Service personnel in the Northwest were supported by three thousand Army troops, including the 555th Parachute Infantry, a battalion of three hundred combat-ready paratroopers, backed up by thirty-nine airplanes.

And in one instance, the Fu-Go project came close to achieving an effect beyond the wildest hopes of the Japanese.

At the Hanford Engineering Works in the state of Washington, a project of utmost secrecy was taking place: huge reactors were turning out radioactive uranium slugs that were to be used to manufacture plutonium for atomic bombs. Engineers had taken extraordinary precautions to prevent a variety of possible mishaps, but the one they most feared was a cutoff of water needed to keep the reactors at safe operating temperatures. Electrical power for the cooling pumps came from generators at the Bonneville or Grand Coulee dams. Interruption of flow for even a fraction of a second would create such a build-up of heat that the reactor might collapse or explode.

Suddenly, on March 10, 1945, the worst happened: a power failure occurred. Immediately, safety controls were triggered and current resumed, but the entire plant was shut down for one-fifth of a second. It took scientists three days to bring the reactor piles back up to full capacity, but they welcomed the incident because, as one witness later reported, "it proved that all safety arrangements, never before tested in actual crisis, were working beautifully."

An accident of calamitous proportions had been averted, but what caused the mysterious shutdown? A Japanese balloon, descending upon the Hanford area, had become tangled in electrical transmission lines, short-circuiting the power for the Hanford reactor pumps.

The Japanese could scarcely have suspected how their simple Fu-Go campaign disrupted the Manhattan Project, the most complex and expensive scientific enterprise yet conceived. It was a single paper balloon that nearly unleashed the furies of the nuclear age on the United States only months before they were visited upon the cities of Hiroshima and Nagasaki.

II. Bats Away!

by JOE MICHAEL FEIST

It is early 1945. An American bomber crew is anxiously nearing the now familiar islands of the Japanese Empire. Flak begins to burst around the plane as the target comes into view. The bombardier releases the payload, and the crew watches as thousands of incendiary bats plummet toward the paper cities of Japan.

The bizarre event never actually occurred, but it very well could have—largely through the enthusiasm of an unlikely war planner by the name of Lytle S. Adams, a Pennsylvania dental surgeon. It seems he was on his way back from a visit to Carlsbad Caverns, New Mexico, when he learned of the

Japanese attack on Pearl Harbor. He immediately thought of the millions of bats that lived in Carlsbad: why not arm the little beasts with tiny incendiary bombs? The following January he somehow got the ear of President Franklin Roosevelt and convinced him that the idea warranted investigation.

Next Adams approached Dr. Donald R. Griffin, a distinguished Harvard zoologist. Griffin was intrigued by the concept and agreed to accompany Adams on a return trip to the bat caves of Carlsbad.

The pair arrived late in July 1942 and covered the entrance to the cave with netting wire. This snagged some five hundred of the Mexican free-tailed bats, which were transferred to cold-storage chests. The low temperature, it was hoped, would impel the bats to hibernate, thus making transportation easier and eliminating bothersome feeding. Unfortunately the system did not work too well, and only about three hundred bats survived the flight back to Cambridge. There Griffin found that the survivng bats could be kept in hibernation for a period of up to two weeks at a temperature of 10 degrees Centigrade and that each could carry a weight of three to five grams.

By this time the National Defense Research Committee had become acquainted with the "Adams Plan," so much so that Earl P. Stevenson, a top NDRC official, suggested that bats could conceivably be released from submarines as well as from bombers. Stevenson was of the opinion that the use of bats would be very demoralizing, especially when used against a "superstitious people."

Toward the end of 1942 the Adams Plan bogged down in bureaucratic indecision. The main drawback was the fact that Griffin's preliminary experiments indicated bats could carry only a slight weight. But when later tests showed that the creatures could support fifteen to eighteen grams, the Army Air Force asked to push ahead with the bat bomb. So the Army's Chemical Warfare Service and the NDRC joined forces on the project.

The incendiary unit was produced by a noted Harvard chemist, Dr. Louis F. Fieser, who was also an NDRC consultant. With a celluloid case three-quarters of an inch in diameter and two and one-half inches long, the bomb was shaped so that it could easily be dragged into a small crevice. It was filled with a concentrated napalm gel, equipped with a fifteen-hour delay mechanism, and attached to the loose skin of the bat's chest with a surgical clip and a string. Moreover, Dr. Adams had designed a case that would slow the falling of the bats as they were dumped from the plane, allowing them to recover from hibernation gradually. Once fully awake, they would supposedly seek refuge in buildings, gnaw through the strings, and leave the incendiary units behind.

T he first experiments, conducted at Muroc Lake, California, on May 15, 1943, were an unaltered disaster. Fieser, Adams, and their associates found that the bats were harder to capture, more awkward to handle, and more difficult to force into hibernation than anyone had expected. Adams's container did not sufficiently slow the descent: many bats broke their wings, and some never awakened at all. And all the bombs were too heavy. Luckily the bats released from the plane were not armed with incendiary units. Much to the chagrin of Adams and Fieser, however, the units *were* tested. Several bats on the ground that had incendiaries attached to them managed to escape. The hangars and outlying buildings of the small airport, as well as a general's automobile, were the first victims of the American bat bomb.

After the May 15 fiasco, many recommended scrapping the project; indeed, no work was done on the delay device between May and September of 1943. Finally Dr. Harris M. Chadwell, chief of the NDRC's Division 19—which handled the development of the delay mechanism—wrote Fieser that "it would be unwise for NDRC to spend any more time, money, and effort on the bat problem unless NDRC's aid was solicited by some recognized branch of the service."

Not wishing to see his brainchild cast aside, Dr. Adams began a vigorous public relations campaign. He explained to every general or admiral who would grant him an interview that bats are very robust and strong in any season except spring, when the tests had been conducted. Though the Army had given up hope on the bat bomb, Adams succeeded in attracting the attention of the Navy. In October 1943 Rear Admiral D. C. Ramsey, the chief of the Navy's Bureau of Aeronautics, asked the Chemical Warfare Service and the NDRC to keep going with the Adams Plan.

Problems soon arose, not the least of them the confusion among those working on the bomb. Because of the project's highly secret nature (even today the blueprints of the incendiary unit remain security classified by order of the CIA), researchers struggling with one aspect of the device were unaware of the activities of their counterparts. Adams himself turned out to be a problem, too. In December 1943 Dr. William G. Young, a UCLA chemist and NDRC consultant, complained that the dentist skipped an appointment with him on November 19: "He did not arrive either that day or the next; and at the time I phoned his home I learned that he had left at 5 o'clock in the morning for parts unknown. Apparently, he just chases around from one part of Southern California to another without staying put long enough for anyone to corner him.

"Last Saturday Lieutenant Charles J. Holt of the Marine Corpos Air Station at El Centro came to Los Angeles to see me, and we had a very interesting talk. . . . Everyone in the project seems to be in agreement that Adams cannot accept responsibility for the project and have it function. For example, he ordered Lieutenant Holt to prepare for a test to be held on the desert in which ten thousand assemblies were to be used. When Holt pointed out the tremendous hazard involved to the whole of Southern California by such a program, Adams was most indignant, and the lieutenant finally had to tell him that such an experiment would not be performed even if he, Holt, had to stand in front of the arsenal with a machine gun to prevent it."

By the middle of December, Adams had been squeezed out of the Adams Plan—which the Navy then renamed "Operation X ray." Further tests, held at the Dugway Proving Grounds in Utah on December 15, were quite promising. In fact, on a weight-to-weight basis, the tiny bat incendiary was more effective than any other such bomb in our arsenal; one estimate had it that a typical planeload of bat bombs would set anywhere from 3,625 to 4,748 fires, as opposed to from 167 to 400 with a planeload of regulation incendiaries.

It finally seemed that the time had come to use the bat bomb against Japan. The last day for all design changes was March 15, 1944; extensive tests of the finished product were scheduled for late April, and large-scale production, as many as 1,000,000 units, was set to begin in May.

But then, in March 1944, Operation X ray came to an abrupt end, twenty-seven months and $2,000,000 after its conception. After the war, rumor had it that X ray had been terminated for fear the Japanese would charge the United States with having waged biological warfare. In fact, the chief of naval operations called a halt to X ray because of what he termed the "uncertainties" surrounding the behavior of the bats and the length of time before an actual strike could be launched.

So the bats of war never got there.

—April 1982

THE FIRST FLAG-RAISING ON IWO JIMA

by RICHARD WHEELER

A single great photograph has become an indelible symbol of the Marines' heroic fight for the Japanese island. But hours earlier a now-almost-forgotten platoon had raised the first American flag on Mt. Suribachi's scarred summit—and under enemy fire.

I wo Jima was a gray silhouette in the dawn of February 19, 1945, when we got our first look at it. The naval guns that would support our landing had started to thunder, and the target areas teemed with red perforations. From the deck of our transport we forty-six men of the 3rd Platoon of Company E, 2nd Battalion, 28th Marines, scanned the island apprehensively. We knew that its seven and a half square miles held more than 20,000 of Japan's best troops and a multitude of ingenious defenses. Its highest point was Mount Suribachi, an extinct volcano that made up its southwestern tip. This heavily fortified elevation would be our regiment's first objective.

Although we had no way of knowing it, our platoon was destined to play a vital role in Mount Suribachi's capture. Those men who managed to avoid death or injury would plant the first American flag on the volcano's summit. Unfortunately, a few hours after the flag was raised it would be replaced by a larger one, and a dramatic photograph taken of this replacement would become so popular that it would doom our unit's exploit to obscurity.

It was about seven thirty when our platoon, along with the other assault troops of the 4th and 5th Marine Divisions, took to the sea in our landing craft and began to await the signal to head for shore. We were scheduled to land with the twelfth wave. The naval bombardment had been stepped up and was now raising thick columns of smoke and dust. At 8:05 several groups of carrier-based planes roared to the attack, and a little later a fleet of Seventh Air Force bombers from Saipan droned over the island and added to the destruction.

The first wave of troop-carrying amphibian tractors churned out of the water along the two-mile landing zone at 9:05, and succeeding waves began to beach at five-minute intervals. Under cover of the barrage, which had shifted inland, the units quickly organized and prepared for action.

Our platoon, in two tractors, was still some distance from the island when Mount Suribachi began to loom up forbiddingly on our left front. The craft I occupied soon took a burst of machine-gun fire that almost hit our coxswain. Then as we neared shore the booming of a large weapon could be heard over our engine's clatter, and some of us thought we were under pointblank, heavy-caliber fire. "It's one of our own! It's one of our own!" shouted our young platoon sergeant, Ernest Thomas. As our tracks touched bottom we passed an armored tractor whose 75-millimeter gun was striking toward the left, at Suribachi.

We hurried from our craft as soon as it clacked to a stop and a few moments later were lying on our stomachs about fifty feet from the water's edge. Artillery and mortar shells were whooping along the beach, and small-arms fire was weaving an invisible crisscross pattern just above it. We shortly lost two men. Pfc. John Fredotovich took serious mortar wounds in the torso and thigh, and Pfc. Bert Freedman was hit in the foot.

The sandy terrain that sloped up sharply a few yards ahead of us was crowded with 2nd Battalion Marines. Our regiment's 1st Battalion was already pushing across the island in an attempt to isolate Mount Suribachi. Iwo was only 700 yards wide in our zone. About half the distance was barren sand, while the remainder held a sparse covering of subtropical brush and a maze of bunkers, pillboxes, and other emplacements. The medleys of detonations issuing from the scrubwood indicated the fierceness of the 1st Battalion's struggle. Our company was to follow these men when it became practicable, and occupy the ground they had captured. The other two companies of the 2nd Battalion were to swing to the left and start attacking the Japanese holding the volcano. Our

3rd Battalion was kept in floating reserve, but would soon be ordered to the Suribachi front. The volcano had to be taken with all possible speed: it served the Japanese not only as a fortress but as an observation post that commanded a view of two-thirds of the island.

Our platoon leader, First Lieutenant John Wells, shouted above the din, "Let's move out!" and began to lead us toward our company rendezvous area. Wells was an enthusiastic Marine who once told us in training: "Give me fifty men who aren't afraid to die, and I can take *any* position!" This heroic pronouncement had bothered us a little ever since.

We had to travel 200 yards along the crowded beach to the right and then another 200 yards inland, and we divided the hazardous trip into short jumps. Our way was marked with shocking sights: a dismembered leg trickling blood into the sand, a number of ashen-faced casualties being treated by Navy hospital corpsmen, a blinded man being led toward the water for evacuation. An amphibian tractor with its landing party was hit by an artillery shell as we passed it, and a little farther on we saw a Marine blown high into the air by a shell that had burst directly under him.

The strain of being under fire was already beginning to show on the faces of most of our men. Some displayed a definite anxiety, their brows drawn into a deep frown. Others had a blank look, as though their facial muscles had gone numb.

We remained in our rendezvous area for about two hours. Although we were surrounded by noisy action we were in a zone of comparative quiet. The height of our position gave us a good view of the beach behind us. Enemy resistance to our landing was increasing: useless landing craft, jeeps, trucks, and other pieces of heavy equipment were settling haphazardly into the surf-soaked sand; around them lay a growing number of torn and bleeding bodies.

It was about one o'clock when our company commander, Captain Dave Severance, gave Lieutenant Wells the order to start taking us across the island. The 1st Battalion had reached the western beach, on the far side, but had suffered many casualties. Our unit was one of those that would be needed for the night defense of the ground already taken. We picked our way through the scrubwood slowly and cautiously, the trip taking several hours. Since the area had been only partly neutralized, we drew considerable fire. Fortunately a network of abandoned Japanese trenches and antitank ditches helped to screen our progress, but once we were pinned down by machine-gun fire from a pillbox and were unable to move until its diehard crew had been blasted by two Sherman tanks.

It was late afternoon when we reached the 1st Battalion's front, a zone that held numerous unassaulted Japanese defenses. Our lieutenant deployed us along a brushy rise that overlooked the beach. Then he took Pfc. Donald Ruhl, who was serving as his runner, and joined a 1st Battalion unit in attacking an artillery bunker. It was first hit with a shaped charge and a thermite grenade. Then Wells and Ruhl gunned down three Japanese who were trying to break from one of the smoking entrances. Ruhl, his rifle emptied, finished off one of the fallen men with his bayonet. These were the first enemy soldiers our platoon accounted for.

As darkness settled over the island it seemed almost to have physical weight, for it was an added threat to our lives. The Navy began to send up illuminating shells, and this made the brush around us cast moving shadows that gave us a start when we mistook them for skulking Japanese. The large-scale counterattack we were expecting failed to develop, but in keeping with their reputation the enemy made many individual attempts to infiltrate our lines. One of these occurred in the zone occupied by my own squad. With a hand grenade in readiness, a Japanese came creeping toward us along a trench that Pfc. Edward Kurelik was covering with his Browning automatic rifle (BAR). Thinking it might be a Marine, Kurelik held his fire and called out a challenge. This was immediately followed by an exclamation in Japanese and a flashing explosion in our midst. Kurelik and Pfc. Phillip Christman were hit, Kurelik seriously. The rest of us leapt up with raised rifles as the Japanese darted away. We opened fire, and there were two orange explosions in the brush as Sergeant Howard Snyder, our squad leader, threw hand grenades. But the Japanese escaped.

The gray arc of dawn was by far the most beautiful sight most of us had ever seen. As the platoon began to stir I heard our right guide, Sergeant Henry "Hank" Hansen, say: "God, what a long night!"

We had new orders to follow this second morning. We were to start working our way back across the island toward our own battalion's zone on the left of the lines facing Suribachi. By late afternoon we would be needed at the unit's front. The 1st Battalion would spend the day reorganizing and mopping up the scrubwood, while the 3rd Battalion would operate on the right of the attack on Suribachi.

As we moved out, swooping groups of Navy and Marine planes were beginning to smash at the volcano with bombs, rockets, and machine-gun bullets. From destroyers and gunboats lying close offshore came shells and more rockets. Our artillery batteries on the island added their own heavy missiles to the deafening, earth-shaking barrage. We who had to face the enemy with light weapons were dramatically reminded that we had some powerful assistance.

It was about noon when we reached the eastern edge of the scrubwood and took cover along a line about 200 yards behind the units attacking Suribachi. Some of us began to nibble K rations at this point, though our stomachs were almost too tense to accept the nourishment. It was the first food we had eaten in thirty hours.

We got our orders to head for the Suribachi front about four o'clock. The assault had made some gains during the afternoon, and the line was now about 300 yards ahead of us. As we rose from our concealment and began to plod across the open sand we felt very conspicuous. But except for a few close shellbursts and the sporadic whine of small-arms fire, our advance did not encounter any notable resistance. Two tanks were sent to cover our final hundred yards. Although only a few men fell in behind them, the rest of us were encouraged just by having them with us. Suribachi was monstrously close now, and some of us began to spot enemy movement in the brush covering its approaches. Now and then one of our riflemen would stop briefly and let go a few shots. When we finally halted we were part of a line that was a scant 200 yards from the volcano's first emplacements. Fortunately a generous scattering of bomb craters and shell holes enabled us to set up our night defense without delay.

During the first hour the Japanese gave us little trouble. Then they hit us with an intensive mortar barrage, the worst we had yet experienced. Up and down our lines the exploding shells walked, spewing steel and sand in all directions. The fire came from cleverly concealed positions, and we could do nothing about it but cower in our holes and pray that we'd be missed. We were infinitely relieved when it finally let up. Lieutenant Wells had thought the platoon was being torn apart, but our good fortune was still holding. Only one man had been hit, taking a blast of small fragments in the chest.

With the coming of darkness the Navy once more began to illuminate the island, and the volcano took on a ghostly aspect. The shells hurled against it burst vividly among its restless shadows, while enemy flares called artillery fire down on us from the north. One Japanese shell eventually hit an ammunition dump on the beach and set off a spectacular fireworks display. Suribachi and the reaches of sand about us were lit by a red glow that flickered eerily. It seemed as though our evil little island had suddenly been transported to hell.

The Japanese made one attempt to counterattack. They began to mass and organize on a plateau that lay along the volcano's left flank. But a destroyer covering this area closed in, switched on a searchlight, and thwarted the attack with a thunder-and-lightning concentration of shells and 20-milli-meter tracers.

Our second dawn on the island was not quite so welcome a sight as the first had been. As Suribachi's gray hulk began to outline itself against the sky we became starkly aware of what we were up against. We were now going to have to make a frontal assault, across a 200-yard open stretch, into the vol-cano's main defenses. Again, the 2nd Battalion would attack on the left, and the 3rd Battalion on the right. The 1st Battalion, having finished its job of mopping up the scrub-wood, had now been assigned a one-company front on the attack's extreme right flank.

The pre-attack bombardment was a repetition of the one the morning before, but we were closer to the volcano now and its effects seemed even more violent. We had to keep our heads down during the air strikes, for some of the rocket bursts sent clouds of debris winging toward our lines.

As the last group of planes droned away from the target, Sergeant Snyder, beside me in our shell hole, stood up and looked toward the rear. "Where's our tank support?" he asked with a frown. It turned out that the tanks had been delayed by refueling and rearming difficulties. Lieutenant Wells decided not to wait for them.

A few minutes later he launched our platoon's attack. Climbing out of his crater, he signaled with a sweep of his

Thompson submachine gun for us to follow him, and began to trot toward Suribachi. By this time we had learned that Wells's courage was not just talk. As we forced ourselves to rise from our holes and imitate his example, I could feel the fear dragging at my jowls. We seemed to be heading for certain death.

For the first few moments the volcano was unresponsive. Then it erupted. Rifle and machine-gun bullets snapped and whirred about us, and crashing shells began to kick up savage funnels of steel and sand. The Japanese were making a desperate attempt to stop us. Men started to fall, and the entreating cry, "Corpsman! Corpsman!" became a part of the action's jumble of sounds. Pfc. Raymond Strahm went down a few yards to my left, a piece of shrapnel above his ear. His helmet slowed the fragment and saved his life. Then another man near me fell with a leg wound. And next it was my turn. Corporal Edward Romero and I caught it from the same shell; Romero was hit in the back, and I had my jaw broken and two molars smashed. Corpsman Clifford Langley reached us, but as the attack swept on, a second shell hit all three of us. Romero was killed, Langley took several small fragments of shrapnel in the torso, and a large piece laid my left calf bare and cut its main muscle in two. Langley bandaged my leg and then followed the platoon. I crawled into a shell hole to await evacuation— which came within half an hour. What happened to my platoon after that I was to hear later, in many conversations with the survivors.

Although shells and bullets continued to menace them, our unit's darting groups soon neared Suribachi's first fringe of brush. They had begun to find a degree of hope in the destruction our planes and guns had wreaked along the volcano's belt of defenses, but as they rushed the first line they found it harboring plenty of live defenders. Hank Hansen and Donald Ruhl, who had been up ahead with Wells, ran to the summit of a large, flat-topped pillbox and promptly clashed with a unit of Japanese located in a network of trenches just behind it. While the two Marines were firing point-blank into the trenches, a demolition charge came flying through the air and landed in front of them. Yelling a warning to Hansen, Ruhl dived on the charge and absorbed its full blast. Hansen had recoiled off the pillbox as the charge exploded, and now, with the emplacement between him and the enemy, he reached up and grasped Ruhl by the foot. Wells, who was crouching nearby and could see that Ruhl's whole chest had been blown away, quickly ordered, "Leave him alone. He's dead." Ruhl had sacrificed himself to save a comrade, and was posthumously awarded the Congressional Medal of Honor.

Howard Snyder and the first squad were moving up on the left flank of the pillbox now, and they took up the fight. The Japanese had begun to scurry back and forth through the trenches and appeared to be trying to organize for a counterattack. Snyder and Corporal Harold Keller quickly began to lob grenades among them, and Pfc. James Robeson and Pfc. Louie Adrian, our squad's full-blooded Spokan Indian, took turns firing with their BAR'S. After Snyder and Keller had thrown all the grenades the squad was carrying, Lieutenant Wells tossed them his own and ordered more passed up to them. The combination of grenades and BAR fire took its toll of the scampering enemy, and no counterattack developed. But now the Indian, while standing upright and firing into the trenches, got a bullet through the heart. His BAR kept chugging as he crumpled to the sand. Our platoon's second and third squads, led by Corporal Robert Lane and Sergeant Kenneth Midkiff, were by this time close behind the leading attackers, and one of Midkiff's BAR men, big Leo Rozek, hurried forward and took up the firing.

Now a Marine carrying a light machine gun moved into the platoon's area, and Wells placed him on the line. The man began to fire into the entrenched Japanese with deadly effect, but he was soon killed. Several other men tried to operate the machine gun, but all were shot away from it. During these moments a Japanese bunker that lay just ahead of the platoon began to spew hand grenades. Many of our men were pinned down by these blasts, and there wasn't much they could do about them. Rifle fire proved ineffective, and the platoon had used up its own grenades. Corporal Charles Lindberg's squad, with its flame throwers and demolitions, had not yet made its final break through the heavy mortar barrage that was still being laid on the open sand. Corporal Wayne Hathaway, a quiet-spoken veteran of several Pacific campaigns, volunteered to go back for more grenades, and Wells consented. Hathaway took with him Private Edward Krisik, an eighteen-year-old who was seeing his first action. The pair had not gone far before they were cut down by Japanese bullets. Both were wounded fatally.

Several men of the assault squad had moved up with demolitions now, and Hank Hansen told Wells that he thought he could get to the bunker with a charge. "Give it a try!" Wells ordered. With some help, Hansen rigged a heavy charge and equipped it with a time fuse. Then he ran at the bunker. But instead of placing the charge at an aperture, he threw it—and missed. The blast that followed rocked the area but served only to make the enemy grenadiers more active. To further complicate the platoon's problems, enemy mortar shells were starting to burst alarmingly close.

Chuck Lindberg had brought up the rest of the assault squad by this time, and Wells prepared to direct our flame-thrower men against the bunker and the other menacing defenses. But the effort was impeded by mortar fire, which now had our range. One of the shells soon scored a bull's-eye. It burst among Wells and four other Marines. Wells was hardest hit. His legs were filled with shrapnel, his trousers were shredded, and one of the canteens at his belt was exploded. As he said later, at first he had no feeling in his legs, being conscious only of a burning sensation along his spine. But he did not relinquish command of the platoon. By the time a medical corpsman had given him first aid, the feeling had crept back into his legs. Discovering that he was still capable of movement, he disregarded his wounds and turned his attention once more to the platoon's difficulties. The situation had become critical. Our unit had lost seventeen men since the attack began; those who were still in action were being tried to the limit of their endurance and had only a precarious hold on the section of enemy line they had hit.

But then things began to look up. Braving the mortar shells, hand grenades, and small-arms fire, our two flame-thrower men, Lindberg and Private Robert Goode, started to move against the troublesome defenses. The results they achieved were dramatic—and terrible. Squirting streams of fire at every opening they could find, they began to destroy dozens of the enemy. The bunker and the pillboxes were turned into furnaces. Ammunition exploded, and shell casings, bullet casings, grenade fragments, and other pieces of debris came flying out through the smoking apertures. As the Japanese died, the platoon could smell their roasting flesh. Some of our men said later that the circumstances made the odor seem the sweetest they had ever smelled.

Tanks were moving up all along the line now, and the assault on the first defenses was assured of success. By this time our tattered and bloody lieutenant had got his wounds full of sand and was groggy from two morphine injections. He knew he was no longer fit to command. Turning our unit over to Platoon Sergeant Thomas, he crawled painfully to the rear. For his leadership that morning, Wells was awarded the Navy Cross. Thomas, who was only twenty years old, had the same sort of spirit, and he too won the Navy Cross for his work against Suribachi. It was he who discovered the soft spot that enabled our battalion to make a relentless drive toward the volcano's base.

The push through the fortifications meant a hodge-podge of encounters accompanied by a great racket and many moments of confusion. Hand-to-hand fighting developed as enemy soldiers suddenly darted from cover, some to attack and others to race for the safety of more remote defenses. There were a number of knife killings and bayonetings. One Marine, attacked by a saber-swinging Japanese officer, caught the sword with his bare hands, wrested it from the officer, and hacked him to death with it. I saw this Marine later. He stopped by my hospital-ship bunk and told me his story. Both his hands were badly gashed—but he still had the Japanese sword.

Three days after our landing on Iwo Jima, Suribachi was surrounded and the fight for the volcano was largely won. There were still substantial numbers of Japanese in obscure caves and other holes, but hundreds had been slain and the power of the fortress had been broken. Our platoon, its thin ranks bolstered by replacements, was chosen to secure the summit. By this time our unit had more than proven its combat efficiency. Our high-spirited lieutenant had come pretty close to having the fifty men he wanted—the fifty who weren't afraid to die.

The next morning our company's executive officer, First Lieutenant Harold G. Schrier, led our platoon to 2nd Battalion headquarters, which had been set up near the volcano's northeast base. While Schrier consulted with our battalion commander, Colonel Chandler W. Johnson, our men were issued extra ammunition and were joined by a radioman, two teams of stretcher-bearers, and a photographer, Staff Sergeant Louis Lowery of *Leatherneck* Magazine.

As the patrol prepared to move out, the colonel handed Lieutenant Schrier a folded American flag, one that our battalion adjutant had been carrying in his map case. He had acquired the flag from the *Missoula*, the transport that had carried our battalion to Saipan, our staging area. Colonel Johnson's orders were simple: the patrol was to climb to the summit, secure the crater, and if possible, raise the flag. Our men hoped feverently that their mission would prove as uncomplicated as the colonel made it sound.

Falling into a irregular column, the patrol headed directly to the volcano's base. When the route became steep and difficult, Schrier sent out flankers to guard the vulnerable column against surprise attack. Some slopes of the volcano were so steep they had to be negotiated on hands and knees. Although several cave entrances were sighted, no resistance developed. Far below, the Marines posted in a semicircle around the northeast base observed the patrol's laborious ascent. Also watching, through binoculars, were numerous men of the U.S. fleet.

Within half an hour after leaving battalion headquarters the patrol reached the summit. The scattered caves and the yawning crater remained silent, so Schrier ordered the men to start moving over the rim. Howard Snyder took the lead, Harold Keller was second, and Chick Robeson was third. Then came Schrier, his radioman, and Leo Rozek. Robert Leader was seventh—and fully expecting to be fired upon, he hoped that number 7 was really the lucky number it was supposed to be. The men fanned out and took up positions just inside the rim. They were tensed for action, but the caves about them and the reaches below them were strangely still. Finally one of the Marines stood up and urinated down the crater's slope. But even this insulting gesture did not stir the Japanese to action.

While half the patrol stayed at the rim, the other half now began to press into the crater to probe for resistance and to look for something that might serve as a flagpole. Keller, moving in the lead, made the first contact with the enemy. He spotted a man climbing out of a vertical hole, his back to the Marines. Keller fired three times from the hip, and the Japanese dropped out of sight. Now enemy hand grenades began to explode among our men. Those closest to the caves from which they came took cover, and replied with grenades of their own.

While these duels were being fought, Leader and Rozek discovered a long piece of pipe, apparently a remnant of a rain-catching system, and passed it up to the summit. Waiting with the flag were Schrier, Thomas, Hansen, and Lindberg, and they promptly set about affixing it to the pole. It was about 10:30 A.M. when the pole was planted and the Stars and Stripes, seized by the wind, began to whip proudly over Mount Suribachi. The date was February 23, 1945. This achievement by the 3rd Platoon had a unique significance. Mount Suribachi was the first piece of Japanese-owned territory—not counting mandates like Saipan—to be captured by American forces during World War II.

The planting of the colors brought a great swell of pride and exultation among Iwo Jima's combat-weary Marines. Those who were watching from below raised the cry, "There goes the flag!" The electrifying word quickly spread to all the units about the volcano's base and to the regiments that were fighting the main battle to the north. The cry was also taken up by the fleet. Aboard my hospital ship I thrilled to the news as it came over the public-address system—though I was not aware at the time that it was my own platoon that had raised the flag. Soon, word of the accomplishment would also be cheering the people at home, who had been following the progress of the battle anxiously and had been disheartened by the reports of our mounting casualties.

The flag was barely up before it was challenged. A Japanese rifleman stepped out of a cave and fired at photographer Louis Lowery and BAR-man Robeson. He missed, but Robeson didn't. He swung his BAR up for a long burst, and the man dropped heavily. The body was quickly seized by the feet and dragged back into the cave. But now an officer stepped out. Grimacing bitterly, he charged toward the flag-raising group, brandishing a sword that had only half a blade. By this time a dozen Marines were alerted to the cave threat, and a volley of bullets turned the one-man charge into a headlong tumble.

Several additional caves now came to life, and enemy grenades once more started to fly. Lowery had another narrow escape. A grenade landed near him and he was forced to leap down the side of the volcano, tumbling fifty feet before he was able to catch hold of a bush, and breaking his camera.

Our men once more met the grenade threat with grenades of their own. They flanked the caves and kept tossing them inside until the occupants were silenced. Some of the caves were then also assaulted with flame throwers and blown shut with demolitions. The cave that had produced the rifleman and the swordsman was one of these. It would later be dug open by souvenir hunters who would discover that it held no less than 150 decomposing enemy bodies. Many of these men died by detonating grenades held to their chests. They had chosen suicide over suffocation.

Other units soon joined the 3rd Platoon at the summit and began to assist with the crater mop-up. Similar operations were still going on at the volcano's base and had also been started on its outer slopes.

It was about three hours after the flag was planted that Colonel Johnson made the decision to replace it. The 3rd Platoon's flag measured only 54 inches by 28 inches, and was hard to see from a distance without binoculars. Since the sight of the flag was important to the morale of our troops, who still had a lot to do before Iwo was secured, Johnson felt that a larger one was needed. He got a bigger flag from LST 779, a vessel beached near Suribachi's eastern base. As the new flag was being carried up the volcano, Joe Rosenthal, a civilian photographer covering the Iwo operation for the Associated Press, spotted the move and decided to follow. This resulted in the now-famous photograph. Although about half the 3rd Platoon was present at the second raising, only one of our men, Corpsman John Bradley, is in Rosenthal's picture. So much has been written about the second event that it need not be discussed here. But let me say this: the photograph deserves to be popular; it depicts an authentic combat scene, even though the circumstances were less impromptu and dangerous than those of the earlier flag-raising.

By the time Suribachi was finally secured, the 28th Marines had lost more than 900 men. But the grimmest part of the tale is that our regiment's ordeal was only beginning. On February 28 it was ordered to Iwo Jima's northern front. There, during several weeks of the bitterest kind of fighting, it was cut to pieces. As for the 3rd Platoon, it was virtually wiped out. Only four of our original forty-six men got through the battle unscathed. Among the dead were two of our flag raisers, courageous Ernest Thomas and Hank Hansen.

I don't suppose this telling of the 3rd Platoon's story will make much difference to history. But maybe it will help to keep my former comrades from being forgotten entirely. I hope so. After all, they were Iwo Jima's *real* flag-raising heroes.

—June 1964

THE AGONY OF
THE *INDIANAPOLIS*
by *KENNETH E. ETHRIDGE*

She was the last major American warship sunk during World War II, and her sinking was the single worst open-sea disaster in our naval history. How could it have happened?

On July 16, 1945, the heavy cruiser *Indianapolis* departed the California coast for the Pacific island of Tinian. On board was a heavily guarded top-secret cargo destined to end the war. Only hours before the *Indianapolis* began her high-speed journey, the first successful atomic detonation had ushered in the nuclear age. The cruiser itself carried vital elements of the atomic bomb that would be dropped on Hiroshima. Even Captain Charles B. McVay III, in command since November 1944, did not know the contents of his mysterious shipment. He had been assured, however, that every hour he cut from travel time would shorten the war. Captain McVay took this admonition seriously, and the vessel made the five-thousand-mile voyage in only ten days.

After delivering her lethal cargo to the American base at Tinian on July 26, the *Indianapolis* proceeded to Guam and prepared for the final leg of her voyage across the Pacific to the Philippine island of Leyte. There the ship was to complete two weeks of training in preparation for joining Naval Task Force 95 at Okinawa, where plans were under way for the expected invasion of Honshū in November of 1945.

While at Guam, Captain McVay inquired about an escort for his ship to the Philippines; naval headquarters replied that none was needed. The response was not considered unusual:

the *Indianapolis* was a fast cruiser and had traveled alone before; she would be sailing through a rear area where danger was considered minimal; and in any event, escort vessels were scarce, due to heavy kamikaze attacks at Okinawa and the extensive preparations for the invasion of Japan. On the other hand, the cruiser had no sonar gear to detect enemy submarines; she had to rely solely on radar and lookouts. And during a recent inspection, Admiral Raymond Spruance had warned that were the ship torpedoed, her "top-heaviness" would make her "sink in short order." The *Indianapolis* left Guam on July 28. She was due to dock at Leyte July 31.

On Sunday evening, July 29, the *Indianapolis* was traveling at seventeen knots through the Philippine Sea, thirty-nine hours out of Guam. The day had been overcast, and by evening the sea had become rough. Just before 8:00 P.M. Captain McVay instructed the officer of the deck, Lieutenant Charles B. McKissick, to cease the zigzag course the ship was maintaining, because of poor visibility. Although zigzagging was of dubious value—many submariners claimed a ship could be sunk despite it—standing fleet orders specified that a ship should zigzag during good visibility. Usually, zigzagging ended at twilight "except on clear nights and in bright moonlight." Lieutenant McKissick thought nothing unusual of the captain's order; he too believed visibility was limited. When McVay retired to his emergency bunk twenty feet from the bridge at 11:00 P.M., he noted that visibility was still poor despite the moonrise. Nevertheless, he issued orders that officers could resume zigzagging at their own discretion and were to wake him if there were any weather changes.

Aboard the *Indianapolis* that torrid Sunday evening, most crew members slept on deck. Commissioned in 1932, the cruiser originally had been intended for service in the Atlantic. Therefore, the ship did not have air conditioning as did other vessels in the Pacific, and many crew members preferred a hammock or blanket above deck to their sweltering quarters below.

By 11:30 P.M. individual watches began to change throughout the ship, some men heading above deck or below, some making for the showers before turning in. Commander Stanley W. Lipski replaced Lieutenant McKissick as officer of the deck. The cruiser sailed on into the night on true course, with more than one hundred men on watch, while officers on the bridge remarked on the lack of visibility.

That same Sunday evening Lieutenant Commander Mochitsura Hashimoto, skipper of the Japanese submarine I-58, decided visibility had so deteriorated by 7:00 P.M. that his vessel could not continue on the surface. Hoping for improved conditions at moonrise, Hashimoto raised his periscope at 10:00 P.M., but his view "was pitch black," and the Japanese commander, like his American counterpart, retired to his bunk for a nap. Returning to the conning tower at 11:00 P.M., Hashimoto found the visibility improved; in his own words he "could almost see the horizon." Ordering the I-58 to surface and bringing his crew to battle stations, the Japanese skipper made for the bridge just in time to hear his navigator exclaim, "Bearing red 9-0 degrees, a possible enemy ship." Despite the heavily overcast sky, Hashimoto could see the black spot on the horizon silhouetted by one of the intermittent rays of moonlight. The Japanese immediately ordered his vessel to dive. Keeping close watch on his target through the periscope, Commander Hashimoto ordered torpedo tubes and his one-man human torpedoes, called *kaitens*, readied for firing. The time was 11:08 P.M.

Although Hashimoto could make out the distant outline of a ship, he was unable to determine the type of vessel. At first the submariner believed it might be a destroyer making a depth-charge run, since it was sailing toward the I-58. When the approaching ship slowly veered away from the submarine, however, the Japanese commander decided he could easily sink it. Now the Japanese skipper believed he had either a cruiser or battleship of the *Idaho* class in his sights.

On board the *Indianapolis*, no telltale "blip" appeared on the radar screen; the I-58's periscope did not protrude far enough above the surface to be detected by the cruiser's main antisubmarine defense. Scanning the horizon for the escorts he believed must be following such a large ship, Hashimoto gave his orders. Despite the pleas of his *kaiten* crews that they be used, the captain decided on conventional torpedoes. He waited until the vessel was fifteen hundred yards away and then fired a spread of six torpedoes. The projectiles hurtled toward the unsuspecting ship at a speed of forty-eight knots, each carrying a lethal 1,210-pound explosive charge.

Hashimoto saw the dark sky erupt as huge columns of water and bright red flames enveloped the cruiser's number-one turret, followed by another explosion amidships. Then a final column of water rose from the number-two turret and appeared to cover the entire ship. "A hit, a hit!" Hashimoto shouted as crew members danced jubilantly. Several secondary explosions followed, resounding enough to make the submarine's crew believe they were being depth-charged.

The first blast shook the *Indianapolis* at 11:35 P.M. The tremendous explosion sent a column of water rising higher than the bridge; seconds later the next burst closer to the bridge. Because of the explosions that followed, it is unclear whether two or three torpedoes struck the vessel; some survivors remembered three initial blasts, others only two.

Two would have been enough. The first blew off the ship's bow forty feet back to the forward turret, while the second knocked out the vessel's power center, touched off an ammunition magazine and supply of aviation fuel, and tore away great sections of the cruiser's bottom. Everywhere on board men found the ship's communication system dead. With the bridge unable to contact the engine room, the cruiser continued plowing ahead at seventeen knots, scooping up tons of seawater through the gaping hole forward.

As secondary explosions rocked the vessel, the *Indianapolis* began listing to starboard. On the bridge the officer of the deck, John I. Orr, ordered a coxswain to "go below and pass the word, 'All hands topside.' "

Thrown from his bunk by the second torpedo blast, Captain McVay scrambled to the bridge to receive a report from Lieutenant Orr. Although informed that communications were dead, the skipper's first thought was to send a distress signal; he sent Orr below to relay the ship's position and report its torpedoing. Returning to his emergency cabin for clothes, McVay ordered that additional damage reports be carried by runners. When the captain made his way back to the bridge, dressing as he went, he received his first report from Lieutenant Commander K. C. "Casey" Moore. Commander Moore explained that most forward compartments were flooding quickly, then asked the dread question, "Do you want to abandon ship?"

Captain McVay believed the vessel's list was still slight and that she could possibly be saved. He ordered Moore to make a further check below. The commander obeyed—and was never seen again. With no word yet from Radio Shack I,

McVay ordered Commander John H. Janney to the ship's communications center to make certain a message was sent. Janney, too, disappeared.

Radio I, containing the ship's receivers, was a shambles after the second hit. "We can neither send nor receive—no power," watch officer Lieutenant Dave Driscoll reported to the ship's radio officer, Lieutenant N. P. Hill. Despite this, Hill ordered the transmitters warmed up and a distress signal sent. Although the message was dutifully tapped out on the brass keys, no one believed the signal was transmitted.

After sending Janney to Radio I, Captain McVay spoke with Commander Joseph A. Flynn, just up the ladder from below deck. Flynn's advice: abandon ship. He told McVay that the bow was down and the ship taking water fast, with extensive damage elsewhere. Unable to see from the bridge because of flames and smoke, the captain agreed with his trusted subordinate. "Okay, pass the word to abandon ship."

With communications knocked out, orders from the bridge had to be sent by messenger. Most men had reported to their battle stations or gone topside with the initial blasts. Many had to abandon ship, however, before being given the order to do so. Seaman Richard P. Thelen did not have to leave the ship. "The ship left me," he recalls. Sleeping topside near the number-one turret, Thelen could see immediately that the *Indianapolis* had been dealt a mortal blow. While he and other shipmates quickly donned kapok life jackets, the cruiser began turning nose-down into the sea. Cutting loose life rafts and throwing them over the side, Thelen and those about him felt water swirling first around their ankles and then their knees. Men near the bow were the first to be forced off the ship.

Other officers felt the ship was sinking and, with no way of communicating with the bridge, decided on their own authority to give the order to abandon ship. Seaman Robert J. McGuiggan was nearly rolled out of his hammock by the shock of the explosions. Rushing to his gun position sixty feet away, McGuiggan and others were issued life jackets at their battle station. Stationed aft, where damage was least visible, he thought the ship could be saved. But the cruiser quickly listed to almost forty-five degrees. Life rafts nearby could not be cut loose, and several men attempting to free one of the cruiser's two 26-foot motor whaleboats were killed when the ship lurched to starboard at an even greater angle and the lifeboat crushed them against the deckhouse. Ordered by the battery officer of his antiaircraft gun to abandon ship, McGuiggan and other crew members walked down the vessel's keel and jumped into the water. Not all of them made it. Seaman McGuiggan saw more than one shipmate mangled in the spinning blades of the number-three screw. No message had reached the engine room to cut power.

The lack of communications increased the chaos. At some stations officers and enlisted men took it upon themselves to issue the men kapok jackets and give the order to abandon ship; at others it was a different story. One seaman guarded two stacks of four life rafts with a .45 automatic, decreeing they be left alone until official word came to abandon ship. Men on the starboard side, however, needed no order; as the ship rolled over, they were pitched into the sea.

Crew members above deck when the torpedoes hit were better off than those below. Pitched from his bunk onto his desk by the first explosion, Lieutenant Commander Lewis L. Haynes, ship's medical officer, got to his feet only to be knocked down when the second torpedo burst beneath him. Everywhere there was smoke and flame: the doctor could hear his hands sizzle as they touched the burning deck. Clad in pajamas, he rose and stumbled aft toward a wardroom already filled with acrid smoke. As he sank into an armchair, gasping for breath, the doctor heard a voice cry, "My God, I'm fainting," and a body fell across him. Realizing he too would soon be overcome, Dr. Haynes heard someone shouting, "Open a port! Open a port!" and forced himself up to grope for a porthole. His hands were too badly burned to force the catch, but he finally discovered an open one and thrust his head through to suck in the fresh air. A rope dangling from a floater net above him slapped against his face. Despite the agonizing pain in his hands, Haynes climbed overhand up to the fo'c'sle deck. Hearing the cry of "Doctor!" from the quarterdeck, he picked his way toward it through the shambles topside. He could see that the cruiser's bow was gone and that the crippled vessel was dipping lower and lower to starboard.

Arriving in the port hangar, the doctor found thirty badly burned men being treated by Chief Pharmacist's Mate John A. Schueck. As the ranks of the injured continued to swell—many suffering from burns caused by the exploding aviation fuel—

the doctor and pharmacist's mate could do little more than inject morphine into those "most crazed with pain." When a sailor arrived with kapok jackets for the wounded, one horribly burned seaman, folds of skin hanging from his arms, pleaded, "Don't touch me! Don't touch my arms, doc! Please don't!" Haynes ignored the pleas, tying the life jacket on. Others screamed in agony as jackets were put around them.

Like Haynes, Ensign John Woolston had to crawl out a porthole to escape the inferno below, and other officers were also burned severely in their quarters just above where the second torpedo hit. Lieutenant Richard B. Redmayne scorched his hands after being thrown to the deck by the blast, while Lieutenant McKissick, wrapping a wet towel about his face to avoid being overcome by smoke and flames, burned his hands climbing a ladder to get above deck.

Yet others abaft and distant from the tremendous damage in the bow and amidships were able to escape safely and even to take time for last-minute niceties. One sailor packed a ditty bag with valuable possessions; another continued clipping his toenails; a third finished writing a letter and sealed it in an envelope. Electrician's Mate André Sospizio, after helping burn victims coming from the forward deck, heard a verbal order to abandon ship and immediately went to his quarters. Determined to prepare himself properly, Sospizio retrieved six hundred dollars in cash, a pair of flashlights, and two life jackets. He swallowed a sandwich whole, washing it down with as much water as he could consume; then, believing a can of lard would be valuable in the sea, he made his way to the galley. However, an internal explosion rocked the cruiser, showering the electrician's mate with cans. Deciding at last that it was time to leave, Sospizio finally went overboard.

With the stricken vessel in its final agony, crewmen struggled to cut loose life rafts and kapok jackets. Seaman Louis P. Bitonti was thrown from his bunk by the torpedo blasts but quickly put on clothes and went above to cut loose bags of life jackets and pass them out to his shipmates. Seaman Henry T. McKlin and others around him threw jackets, rafts, and kegs of fresh water overboard, hoping shipmates could retrieve and use them. Dr. Haynes saw several sailors vainly fighting against the ship's severe list to release life rafts. Seeing men going over the side without life jackets, Captain McVay ordered two seamen to free floater nets stored near the bridge.

But the sailors couldn't do it. In the end only a dozen life rafts and six floater nets were released from the cruiser before she went down.

From the beginning the captain's prime concern had been to send out a distress signal. When no one returned from the radio shack, the skipper went himself. But before he got there, the ship rolled over to a full ninety-degree list. Clinging to lifelines from the vertical communications deck, McVay pulled himself up to one of the bulkheads and hung there, looking down at the massive, red-painted bottom of the ship. In a few seconds the vessel dipped farther into the water, and Captain McVay was washed into the sea.

The men near the bow and on the starboard side of the cruiser slid or were swept off. Seaman McKlin found that sliding down the oil-covered deck and over the side into the water was similar to going down a ski slope. Men stationed on the port side had to walk onto the keel and then jump clear of the ship's hull; several were caught in the screws. Many leaped into the water in total darkness, but Electrician's Mate Sospizio waited until the moon came into view for a few seconds before jumping clear. Most of the men who had been in the cruiser's gang showers when the torpedoes struck had no choice but to go into the water naked. Some seamen left the ship clad only in underclothes; a supply officer abandoned ship with a bathrobe and a bottle of Scotch.

Of the ship's company of 1,196 men, approximately 850 were able to get clear before she sank. Spread out over thousands of yards because the cruiser continued moving after she was hit, many sailors did not see the ship go down. But the majority of her crew left the vessel at the very last and saw the ship's stern rise vertically a hundred feet from the water before plunging down. Many, including Captain McVay, thought the towering hulk would fall on them, but she did not; the cruiser vanished in a wisp of smoke. As the ship slid under, many heard a sound they would never forget: the screams of their shipmates inside the hull.

The cruiser had sunk in only thirteen minutes. It was a little before midnight, Sunday, July 29, 1945.

The sea around the men was covered with thick fuel oil from the ship's tanks; it burned their eyes, clogged their nostrils, and choked their throats. Unable to swim away from this slick area of the sea and lashed by twelve-foot swells, the men could not avoid swallowing water and oil. Soon there was violent retching throughout the scattered groups, and as men vomited, the hateful scum kept splashing into their mouths.

While most of the sailors had kapok jackets, some swam unaided. Soon those more fortunate paired off with their helpless shipmates. For the most part the men were dazed and quiet, though when a few wondered aloud if an SOS had been transmitted, a radioman near Dr. Haynes shook his head. The medical officer began to wonder how long the men would have to remain in the water before they were rescued.

At first most men were chiefly afraid of being left alone. They gathered into groups, some of only a few dozen sailors, but three containing more than a hundred. By far the largest group was made up of the men who were last to leave the ship, among them Dr. Haynes, the ship's chaplain, Father T. M. Conway, and the assistant medical officer, Lieutenant Melvin W. Modisher. Haynes estimated that there were between three and four hundred men around him. Although this group had no rafts, a cork life ring with a long line attached was found. Soon one hundred and fifty men had gathered about it. A severely injured sailor was placed across the ring, and for no apparent reason the lifeline slowly coiled itself around his resting place. Two officers swam around the group, preventing those who fell asleep from drifting away. Commander Lipski, his eyes burnt to a crisp and the flesh on his hands seared to the tendons, was held above the salt water and oil by a dozen men.

The cries of the wounded were everywhere. Seaman Robert McGuiggan, with another group of men, spent the entire night beside his division officer, who had been burnt beyond recognition when the aviation fuel ignited. Sailors like him watched helplessly as their comrades endured the effects of the salt water on their already hideous wounds. By daybreak, however, death had freed most of the wounded from their suffering.

While men in the largest group of survivors were compelled to hang onto the lifeline or drift alone in their kapok jackets, several smaller groups gathered around floater nets released before the cruiser sank. Each of these nets had buoyant blocks of canvas-covered balsa wood attached around the edge. Seaman McGuiggan and one hundred and fifteen shipmates collected in a double circle around one floater net.

The sailors put the wounded in the center to give them a chance to rest, then gave themselves more support by tying their life jackets to each other and to the net.

Electrician's Mate Sospizio found himself in a group of nearly one hundred and forty men gathered around a single raft and floater net. The canvas-covered rafts were designed to hold sixteen men. The wounded went on the raft while those in better condition clung to its sides or to the floater net.

Seaman Henry McKlin and his close friend Seaman Sam Lopetz gathered with another dozen sailors around a small net. There, as nearly everywhere, what little talk there was centered around the hope that a distress signal had been transmitted. One seaman maintained that this was improbable, since all power had been knocked out; but another insisted that batteries existed for just such an emergency. Seaman McKlin and others chose to put their faith in the latter's logic; hope was as necessary as a kapok jacket.

While most men had only a jacket or net, a few were luckier. A sailor had pulled Seaman Louis Bitonti to the surface by the hair after he jumped from the ship. As Bitonti and four others clung to a floater net, a raft appeared not far away. The men swam to the small craft and hoisted each other aboard.

Captain McVay, swimming away from the ship as she went down, soon came upon two empty life rafts. Shortly after climbing into one, the skipper helped a sailor haul in two seamen nearly overcome with oil and salt water. Several hours later they spotted another raft containing five men, and McVay ordered the three tied together. Paddles, rations, flares, and other emergency gear were secured to the rafts, and this offered some solace. At this point Captain McVay believed he and the nine other men were the only survivors of the *Indianapolis.*

Another group of four rafts and nineteen men, hundreds of yards away from McVay, was commanded by Ensign Ross Rogers. Those in the rafts were unable to see the vast majority of swimmers. Because a man low in the water can see very little, the twelve-foot swells diminished the likelihood of discovery. In addition nearly all the survivors were partially or totally blinded by the fuel oil. By daybreak the possibility of those in the rafts sighting the large groups of swimmers had vanished: the swimmers were carried in a southwesterly direction by the current, while the men on rafts were sent to the northeast by a ten-knot wind.

As Monday morning dawned clear and sunny, most groups found their ranks thinner. Some sixty men had died during the first night; their life jackets were removed and their bodies allowed to slip away. Many were happy to see the sun rise, but with no breeze the sea was calm and soon the day became intolerably hot. The rays of the sun reflecting on the fuel oil created a new affliction: photophobia. Dr. Haynes remembered it as worse than snow blindness. Even when men closed their eyes, they still felt "two hot balls of fire" burning through their eyelids.

A new terror was added to the group containing Seaman McGuiggan. With daylight men could see flotsam about them: ammunition cans, a toilet seat, and some bits of food. A seaman near McGuiggan left the group, swimming toward a crate of potatoes nearby. The sailor never reached his destination. As men stared in horror, a shark attacked their shipmate, and he disappeared.

Sharks were lurking everywhere. Dr. Haynes's group discovered that as long as the men remained grouped together, the sharks would not attack. Yet every group's experience with the predators was different. In one group every sailor splashed and flailed the water to frighten the attackers away; in another the decision was made to remain perfectly still and quiet. Seaman Donald McCall's common sense as a fisherman told him to remain motionless whenever a shark approached. He remembers many coming so close he could have reached out and touched them, but he was never once harmed.

Seaman Henry McKlin's fourteen-man group also chose to remain quiet and still. Clinging to their floater net, with one knife their sole defense, the seamen determined the weapon would be passed to the man closest to the shark if one approached. When McKlin saw a dorsal fin slicing toward him, he held his breath; none of his companions uttered a sound. The twelve-foot-long intruder came close but left the sailors unmolested.

Electrician's Mate Sospizio had drifted away from his group when he saw a shark approach and then dive, apparently intending to come up under him. Sospizio swam toward the group as the seamen beat the water to frighten the attacker away. He never has fully understood how he did it, but

Sospizio was in the midst of his companions before the shark could get him.

Many crew members were not so fortunate. Seaman Richard Thelen remembers seeing some twenty-five men attacked, while, in the largest group, Dr. Haynes eventually counted eighty-eight of the dead mutilated by the creatures. A few seamen actually survived attacks. One sailor swam up to Seaman McKlin, showing him the wound he received from a shark. McKlin remembers the huge pie-shaped gash in the man's side. The sailor later swam away, never to be seen again.

Lone swimmers seemed to be most susceptible to the sharks. A man would disappear with a startled cry in the midst of thrashing water. One sailor lost both his legs to a shark and, suddenly top-heavy, turned upside down in the water to drown. Seaman Joseph Dronet saw several shipmates snatched screaming from their floater net and pulled beneath the surface. Dronet remained motionless when the attackers approached, and he lived.

The threat of being devoured by sharks was only one misery. Under the sun's blinding rays, men tore strips of cloth from their scant clothing to bind their eyes or shield their heads. Seaman McGuiggan ripped his pants legs off to cover the head of a naked sailor delirious from the sun. On board the rafts men soon returned to the water to avoid the intense heat. The hated diesel oil now was appreciated as a sunscreen. Dr. Haynes recalled the tropical sun failing "to burn through the fuel oil coating our bodies."

While most soon suffered greatly from sunburn—eyelids swollen, lips puffed and cracked—the most urgent problem was thirst. Having retched out much of their body fluids, the men suffered from dehydration. But thanks to repeated warnings in training, no one had yet been tempted to drink salt water.

Despite sharks, thirst, and sunburn, most men expected rescue that first day in the water. Many still believed a distress signal had been sent. Those who knew that no SOS was sent nevertheless felt help would be forthcoming when the cruiser was missed on Tuesday morning.

In fact, on that first day U.S. patrol planes did pass directly over the survivors. Flying at more than a thousand feet and by instrument, not eyesight, the pilots and crew never noticed the frantic men in the water. One sailor shouted,

"Blind aviators, mates! Just a bunch of blind aviators!" Soon others picked up the call, which lifted their spirits slightly. But the stark reality was inescapable; no one had seen them, and no one appeared to be looking for them.

That Monday evening most men were glad to see the sun go down, but the choppy sea made sleep impossible, and men clung to each other, fearful of becoming separated.

During the night another plane flew overhead. Captain McVay and others in the rafts with flares fired them into the darkness. Above them Captain Richard G. LeFrancis, piloting an Army Air Force C-54, saw the flares but thought they were star shells, tracers, and heavy gunfire. After landing at Guam the pilot reported to his superiors that he had seen a naval action involving three ships. He was told, "If it was a naval action, the Navy [knows] about it." Incredibly this attitude was not unusual; naval battles were not the concern of the Army Air Force. Thus the survivors of the *Indianapolis* were seen but not seen. If only a Navy plane had sighted the flares, a tremendous number of lives could have been saved.

With the dawning of Tuesday morning, the groups of survivors were smaller still. Despite the efforts of those who patrolled groups looking for strays, some had drifted away during the night. Many more had died of their wounds, while others had been taken by sharks, which appeared most often at night or in early morning.

Tuesday brought a calmer sea and still hotter sun. In the water for more than thirty-six hours, the men were exhausted. Thirst obsessed everyone.

"Doctor, if I hold this water in my hands to the sun and evaporate it a bit, will it be safe to drink?" a man asked Dr. Haynes.

"No, son, that will only make it more salty. You must not drink."

Tuesday, they hoped, would at least bring the search planes; surely they would be missed after not arriving at Leyte. But no planes flew overhead. As the day progressed, hopes grew dimmer.

The kapok jackets were becoming increasingly water-logged. Dr. Haynes remembered they were designed to hold a man in the water for only forty-eight hours. As time went by, chins sank closer and closer to the surface. Some men had left the ship with rubber life belts strapped around their waists rather than life jackets. The belts were old, and the deteriorating effect of the fuel oil caused them to rupture and deflate. Many of the panic-stricken men were able to don a kapok jacket recovered from a dead shipmate, and Dr. Haynes recalls one man in his group, who was labeled a misfit before the sinking, taking it upon himself to help those desperate sailors find a jacket to wear.

Although some of the men drifting on the rafts had a smattering of rations—a few malted-milk tablets, biscuits, or Spam—no one had any drinking water. On Tuesday the hallucinations began. Some aboard the rafts wanted to "go below deck" for some milk or take a swim with the Hollywood beauties they saw nearby.

Despite warnings from Dr. Haynes and others, some thirst-crazed swimmers gave in to the temptation to drink the sparkling clear water surrounding them. The saline solution soon brought on severe diarrhea, which in turn caused further dehydration and an even greater craving to drink. The vicious cycle brought on acute dehydration and delirium. "Those who drank became maniacal and thrashed violently," said Haynes, "until the victims became comatose and drowned." Even some who did not drink the water lost their lives struggling to save their raving shipmates.

As Tuesday drew to a close, the strain on the men was painfully evident. Bickering started over whose turn it was to be on board the rafts, where it was possible to rest a bit and not worry about sharks.

By the evening of the second day photophobia from the blinding sun and infections caused by salt water and fuel oil had rendered nearly all the swimmers blind. Skin exposed to the sun had been terribly burned, and even the lifesaving kapok jackets added to the misery: they rubbed the men's flesh raw, and soon the swimmers were covered with immersion ulcers.

After nearly forty-eight hours in the water, their bodies drained by exhaustion and dehydration, the men faced a third night at sea. Not long after sunset they were plagued by severe chills. In André Sospizio's group men fought to get aboard the single raft. He remembers the loud chattering of teeth as chills wracked their bodies. Sospizio put a rope between his teeth, which he found he had nearly chewed through by daybreak. As for the rest of the night: "It was so awful, I don't even want to talk about it."

Everywhere the night was one of incomprehensible horrors. "High fever gripped our shaking bodies," said Dr. Haynes. "It consumed our reason, and in a little while we became a mass of delirious, screaming men." Men who only a short time before had aided and supported their shipmates now saw the oil-covered unrecognizable brings beside them as the enemy returned to finish the kill.

"There's a Jap here! He's trying to kill me!"

"There's Japs on this line!"

"There he goes! Get the Jap! Kill him!"

Fights broke out, and more than one man was stabbed by others who had knives.

When Dr. Haynes attempted to calm the ravings of the wildest men, two of them thrust him under the water, and he had to fight his way to the surface. While the shrieking and babbling continued, the ship's doctor swam away from his group for safety.

"They weren't themselves," Donald McCall, then a seaman first class, remembers. Among his group he heard the cries, "He's a Jap! There's a Jap!" as men attacked each other. He, too, swam away from his group.

With dawn the men began their third day in the water. It was Wednesday, August 1. Again the sea was like glass, with a merciless sun overhead. After more than fifty hours in the water, most men spoke gibberish or hallucinated.

There was no more talk of rescue. Most had passed from reality into a world of delusions. Seaman Thelen described his mental condition as a semiconscious state, like coming out of anaesthesia. The all-pervading thought was the need for water.

"Doc, if I dive down real deep will the water be less salty?" a sailor asked Dr. Haynes. The doctor had barely answered when another seaman shouted to him: "I've found her! The ship hasn't really sunk! She's right beneath the surface! I swear she is!" Others gathered around him. The seaman explained how the ship's fountains, called scuttlebutts, still worked and poured forth fresh water.

"I dove down and turned on the scuttlebutt. Honest, I did—and it works. When you drink from it, the water is fresh. Fresh water, men! Fresh water!"

While many took off their life jackets to dive down to the ship, Haynes himself saw the vessel. Yet some instinct prevented him from following. But the doctor and others who were still lucid could not dissuade many who dived under for a lethal drink. Another sailor who still had his wits listened to enthusiastic shipmates describing how they had dived down to the ship and "had a good drink." Donald McCall heard but did not believe; trying to stay calm was his plan for survival, and he had not yet begun to hallucinate. Later McCall watched those men die in the agony of saltwater poisoning.

The mass hallucinations continued throughout Wednesday. Richard Thelen saw some around him remove their kapok jackets and begin swimming for the "island." This particular fantasy affected many. One sailor complained to Dr. Haynes of a stomachache caused by drinking too much tomato juice while on the island. Others saw Seabees on the island drinking tomato juice. Dozens of men swam off in the direction given to them by those who had "visited" the island.

Dr. Haynes came upon a long line of men waiting patiently to take their turn in a one-room hotel "up ahead." The doctor was urged to get in line, for each man was allowed only fifteen minutes in the sack.

While many men found the *Indianapolis* or went to a mythical island, others engaged in individual fantasies. Yeoman Victor R. Buckett spent all day Wednesday in a store filled with watermelons where he could eat all he wanted. Lieutenant John Reid sought to retrieve his car keys in order to drive to New Hampshire for some cold milk. Some seamen decided not to wait for rescue any longer; they would simply swim the five hundred and fifty miles to Leyte.

Everywhere men died. They died from the salt water they drank, from the sharks, from exhaustion, exposure, and dehydration—and from being dragged under by their own waterlogged life jackets. By Wednesday morning most men had only their heads above water. As the day progressed, men watched in horror as a few struggled to free themselves after their jackets had reached the saturation point. But more than once the knots were swollen and a seaman fatally trapped.

Some crew members knowingly took their own lives. Thinking rescue would never come, they gave up all resistance. "They haven't missed us . . . let's get it over with in a hurry." Electrician's Mate Sospizio saw many allow themselves to die. One shipmate approached him saying, "I can't take this," and beseeched Sospizio to take his wallet and go to his father to explain what happened. The seaman also asked the electrician's mate to marry his sister. Sospizio tied the man on a line attached to a raft and encouraged him to hang on. The next morning, however, the sailor was gone.

As many succumbed to the ordeal, some found extraordinary reserves of strength and hope. Those with families and other responsibilities struggled to endure. Officers and enlisted men alike expended energy they could have reserved for their own survival encouraging and helping others. When someone died nearby, Dr. Haynes would lead others in the Lord's Prayer before removing the kapok jacket and allowing the body to sink slowly into the water.

On board his group of rafts, Captain McVay also led seamen in the Lord's Prayer each evening. Everywhere men prayed, seeking deliverance from their living hell. Despite the dead and dying around them, Dr. Haynes recalled, "We [had] not lost everything. To the contrary, we ... found one comfort—a strong belief to which we could cling. God seemed very close." The ship's doctor attributed much of their faith to the *Indianapolis*'s young chaplain. Although not physically a strong man, Father Conway swam from "one group to another to pray with the men." The encouragement and good will he offered appeared limitless. Yet, like so many others giving help and solicitude, the ship's chaplain literally laid down his life for those around him. He died delirious Wednesday night. Captain Edward L. Park, commander of the cruiser's Marine detachment, also slipped beneath the surface that night after wearing himself out trying to hold his group together.

The surviving men endured Wednesday night, their fourth evening in the water, with chills, fever, and still more delirium. While some in rafts fared slightly better because of a few rations, those men in the three rafts led by Lieutenant Redmayne were piled on top of each other to such a degree that some were smothered.

Thursday morning, August 2: For most the nightmare had ended. In the largest group, fewer than one hundred of the original three hundred and fifty seamen were alive. That morning, a quartermaster led twenty-five men in an attempt to swim to Leyte. A few tried to dissuade them, but they swam away. The rest waited for the end. Only by the bumping into a sailor to see if he opened his eyes could Dr. Haynes determine who still lived.

Shortly after 11:00 A.M. they heard a plane overhead. Dr. Haynes and three others prayed they were not suffering another "tortuous dream." Overhead, Lieutenant W. Charles Gwinn, U.S.N., and two crew members of his PV-1 Ventura, attempting to repair an antenna in the rear of the plane, noticed an oil slick on the water. Believing he might have spotted an enemy sub, Gwinn turned the Ventura as the crew readied for action. Diving to one thousand feet, Lieutenant Gwinn saw heads bobbing in the water and men feebly waving and splashing. At last the crew of the *Indianapolis* had been found. It was 12:05 P.M., August 2, more than eighty-four hours after the cruiser had gone down.

As the Ventura circled, some of the swimmers motioned for drinking water. Soon life jackets and cans of water tumbled from the aircraft, and the seamen mustered their remaining strength to swim to the jackets and recover the cans—which, they found, had burst after hitting the surface. Continuing to circle, Gwinn and his crew counted more and more men in the water. Their first message to the base at Peleliu reporting the sighting was garbled by the plane's faulty antenna. However, as the Ventura continued sending reports, it became apparent something big was under way. At 12:40 P.M. a huge amphibious PBY commanded by Lieutenant R. Adrian Marks took off from Peleliu carrying a full load of survival gear.

While Gwinn continued circling, other planes arrived. A PBM flew overhead dropping three life rafts and radioing Guam about the men in the water. Another Navy Ventura relieved Gwinn, who was low on fuel, at about 2:15 P.M. While Lieutenant Marks flew north, he was contacted by the destroyer escort *Cecil J. Doyle.* Informed by Marks of the situation, Lieutenant Commander W. Graham Claytor decided not to wait for orders but changed course and steamed full speed toward the survivors. By late afternoon, seven vessels were sailing to the rescue.

Beneath the planes the survivors' reactions were much alike; those still aware knew rescue was now at hand and sought desperately to hang on, some praying, "God, give us strength." Electrician's Mate Sospizio remembers seeing Gwinn's plane overhead and crying out, "I don't believe it . . . it's an angel!"

As life rafts, kapok jackets, and other survival gear

dropped from the planes, the men attempted to retrieve the precious material. Rescue was certain now, but another twenty-four hours would pass before naval vessels could pluck the survivors from the sea, and many died in those last hours.

Seaman Robert McGuiggan and three other shipmates left their floater net and swam to a life raft dropped nearby. McGuiggan hoisted himself in and looked back to see dorsal fins all around and his companions gone. Seamen who were pulling shipmates aboard their rafts had them snatched from their hands by sharks.

Some could not grasp what was happening around them. One sailor believed the Japanese were about to take them prisoner; another thought the survival gear was plane parts being dropped so the men could assemble their own rescue craft.

Those who reached the life rafts could barely manage to inflate them. Dr. Haynes and others in the largest group found two rafts and hauled eleven seamen who were suffering the most into them. Once aboard, the "naked, emaciated" forms reminded the doctor of "cadavers in the dissection room." Both rafts were pulled together, and those unable to come aboard hung onto the sides. Finding a pint can of water, Dr. Haynes distributed an ounce of fluid to those in most need. He was amazed that the small plastic cup passed from hand to hand with no one giving in to the tremendous temptation to cheat. Other survivors were not as restrained. Seaman Richard Thelen swam to a nearby raft to find that those who had arrived before him had destroyed the food and water containers in their delirium.

All suffered from mental anguish. In his enfeebled condition, Dr. Haynes was unable to operate the saltwater converter in the raft and he even overlooked additional cans of drinking water. A sailor on another raft that had been dropped by the planes did manage to detoxify some salt water with a converter. Seaman McCall remembers the foul-tasting liquid: "It was terrible, but it was wet."

Though he saw that some men had reached the supplies dropped to them, it was clear to Lieutenant Marks in his PBY that many could not help themselves and would perish before the rescue ships arrived. At 4:25 P.M. Marks radioed his base that he would attempt a landing on the open sea. Although the PBY was an amphibious craft, she was not built for landing in rough water with twelve-foot swells. Nevertheless the Navy pilot brought down his huge plane between the swells. The seaplane disappeared in a cloud of spray, bounding three times before coming to a halt, but she remained afloat. Damaged by the rough landing and taking on water, the PBY still managed to taxi around while the copilot, Ensign Morgan F. Hensley, reached from the plane's port blister to pluck in swimmers.

Passing by groups of survivors who appeared able to endure a few more hours, Marks sought out the most desperate. André Sospizio heard the pilot explain that help was on the way and to remain in the water if possible. Sospizio obeyed, although he was only a few feet from the plane, and soon had a life raft to himself as others went aboard the PBY.

By midnight Lieutenant Marks had collected fifty-six survivors. Soon they had kicked holes in the wings and fuselage of the overcrowded seaplane. In a short time the sixteen gallons of drinking water aboard the craft had been consumed.

At 9:30 P.M. the *Doyle* was still sixty miles from the area. Despite the threat of enemy submarines, Commander Claytor ordered a twenty-four-inch searchlight turned on. Pointed to the sky, the beacon became literally a ray of hope to those awaiting rescue.

Although there were visible signs of coming rescue, the survivors continued to hallucinate. As Seaman Henry McKlin and those around him went through their fifth night clinging to their floater net, the young seaman decided to "go below deck" where he could see coffee brewing in one of the ship's large urns. Fortunately for McKlin, his close friend Sam Lopetz was at hand to slap him back to reality and point out the light shining from the *Doyle*. "There's a boat out there with a spotlight. They're going to get us." Like so many others, McKlin credits a fellow shipmate with saving his life.

Shortly after midnight on Thursday the rescue ships reached the survivors. After four full days in the water, a total of ninety-six hours, the pitifully small number who remained were beginning to be rescued.

Scanning the sea with searchlights and putting out whaleboats to comb the area, the *Doyle* began picking up men suffering from blindness, pneumonia, shark bites, and acute dehydration; their bodies were covered with immersion ulcers, and in some cases the flesh was so badly burned by sun and flame that it fell away in the rescuers' hands.

At approximately 4:00 A.M. on Friday, August 3, the *Doyle* located Dr. Haynes's group of survivors. The men stared in silence as a searchlight shone on them; most were unable to comprehend what was happening. A naked sailor called to an officer on the bridge, "Y-you-you got any drinkin' water aboard?" When told there was plenty, the disbelieving seaman asked, "You sure you got water—you ain't foolin' me?" Assured he could have all he could drink, the man concluded, "If you ain't got no drinkin' water just shove off and leave us alone." After persuading the sailor to come aboard, the doctor reported to Commander Claytor, "This is all that is left of the *Indianapolis*." Claytor was stunned.

The crewmen of the rescue vessels did all in their power to ease the suffering of the survivors. Many rescuers leaped into the water to retrieve those too weak to move or those who had left their rafts and were floundering toward the rescue craft. For many the rescue vessels were just another fantasy. Men from the U.S.S. *Bassett* came upon one sailor riding a pyramid of cork rings and told the seaman to come aboard. "No thanks," he replied. "I'm waiting for a friend to come by."

By Friday afternoon Captain McVay and those who had spent the ordeal on life rafts were picked up, and the three hundred and eighteen crew members of the *Indianapolis* still alive were aboard vessels bound for Leyte and Peleliu. Later, two who survived the ordeal in the water died in Navy hospitals.

Aboard the rescue ships the survivors were carefully showered and then carried to bunks and spoon-fed as much fluid as they could tolerate. One survivor remembers the water given to them as tasting "so sweet . . . the sweetest thing in your life." But while those who had been plucked from the edge of death were resting and beginning their long recuperation, everywhere the bodies of those who had not survived floated face-down in the water. As he held a dead man in his arms, one young seaman broke down. "We're sorry, Mac," he sobbed. "If we had've know you were out here like this, we would've come sooner."

How could the Navy not have known? This question haunted all of those immediately affected by the tragedy. It seemed impossible that an overdue warship would not be missed and never looked for. Yet the impossible had happened. Within hours of learning of the sinking, Fleet Admiral Chester Nimitz ordered a court of inquiry to investigate the tragedy. On August 13, 1945, the court convened.

A week earlier the *Enola Gay* had dropped the first atomic bomb on Hiroshima, Japan, and only then did the crew members of the *Indianapolis* learn the nature of their secret shipment to Tinian. While recovering from their experience, the survivors were individually interviewed to determine the sequence of events surrounding the sinking. An air of secrecy covered the proceedings: medical personnel were warned not to divulge any details of their patients' ordeal. Wartime censorship was still in effect, and the Navy did not immediately release news of the sinking. But with the war's end in sight, it was held especially crucial to determine who, if anyone, was responsible for the tragedy. The American public would soon learn of the sinking and would demand an explanation.

The court of inquiry met from August 13 to 20, 1945, interviewing Captain McVay and nineteen other officers and enlisted men. Other "interested parties" were questioned as well, among them Leyte's port director and various operations officers. The court's primary concern was determining why the cruiser had not been missed for four days.

On Tuesday evening, August 16, President Harry S. Truman announced Japan's unconditional surrender; that same evening the Navy finally released a twenty-five-word communiqué stating that the *Indianapolis* had been lost to enemy action. The newspapers of August 17, 1945, heralded the news of Japan's surrender, but the bottom of page one in *The New York Times* contained an article describing the greatest sea disaster in U.S. naval history: "Cruiser Sunk, 1,196 Casualties."

While Americans celebrated V-J Day, hundreds of families received word that a son or husband was "missing in action." Soon other publications provided accounts of the disaster, stressing the irony of the doomed cruiser delivering the weapon "which sealed our victory."

As the story of the *Indianapolis* competed with news of the war's end, the court of inquiry concluded and recommended letters of reprimand for Captain McVay, Lieutenant Commander Jules C. Sancho, port director at Tacloban, Leyte, and Lieutenant Stuart B. Gibson, Sancho's operations officer. McVay's reprimand referred to his failure to order a zigzag course the night of the sinking and his not exerting "every effort at [his] command to cause a distress message to be sent." The latter two officers were reprimanded for not alerting their superiors that the *Indianapolis* was overdue.

When Captain McVay came home to Washington in September, he began the sad task of answering the letters and calls of bereaved families. Dr. Haynes also helped console those who wanted to know how and why the tragedy occurred. But their explanations did not suffice. Soon letters poured forth to President Truman, Secretary of the Navy James Forrestal, and members of Congress. All wanted to know how it could have happened. One heartsick mother wrote: "How can we draw any comfort from their sacrifices when we know his life . . . could have been saved if the Navy had been alert. I have tried hard not to shadow the sacrifices these boys made . . . but those agonizing hours my child suffered will not let me rest."

The clamor for an explanation continued, and on November 28, 1945, the Navy announced that Captain McVay would be court-martialed upon recommendation of the court of inquiry. Of four hundred and thirty-six American commanders whose warships went down during World War II, only Captain McVay was brought to trial for losing his vessel to enemy action.

The unprecedented event began December 4, 1945. The charges against McVay were: "Failure [to zigzag] during good visibility after moonrise on the night of July 29" and failure "to insure and see effected such timely orders . . . to cause said vessel to be abandoned." The Navy explained that an investigation into the affair was continuing with "other courts-martial . . . possible."

McVay pleaded "not guilty" to the charge of negligence and inefficiency. The trial continued through December with the Navy trying to determine conditions of visibility at the time of the sinking. Lieutenant McKissick, one of the cruiser's few surviving officers, testified that visibility was limited when McVay ordered the zigzag course halted, and he did not think the order unusual. Yet the prosecution cited the captain's own written disposition of July 29, in which he remembered "intermittent moonlight at which time visibility was unlimited." McVay, however, sought to amend that document, stating he had been under duress and still suffered from his ordeal while composing it.

The prosecution also pressed home the allegation that McVay's "inefficiency" in issuing the order to abandon ship had "contributed to the high death toll." Many crew members of the cruiser rallied to their skipper's defense. Testifying that he had given the order but that the sound system had failed to perform, seamen told the court how they passed the word from man to man. Several witnesses stated they would gladly serve under McVay's command again.

Halfway through the trial, in a most dramatic and controversial move, the prosecution summoned Commander Hashimoto from Japan to testify as to whether McVay's decision not to zigzag was justified. Bringing a fallen enemy to bear witness against an American officer ignited a storm of protest, including several condemnations from Congress.

Hashimoto's testimony both before and during the trial indicated that he would have been able to sink the *Indianapolis* whether or not she was zigzagging. Later, one of the U.S. Navy's most decorated submariners, Captain Glynn R. Donaho, substantiated Hashimoto's claim. Submarines expected ships to zigzag, Donaho said, and he stated before the court that the maneuver was of "no value to surface ships."

The final witness was Captain McVay himself. The cruiser's skipper testified upon his own request, reiterating his claim that poor visibility prompted him to rescind the order to zigzag. McVay also testified that his officers had standing orders to resume zigzagging or report any weather changes to him. The captain also related the impossibility of passing the "abandon-ship order by other than word of mouth."

Acquitting him of the charge of untimely orders to abandon ship on December 20, 1945, the court later found Captain McVay guilty of negligence in the loss of the *Indianapolis* because "he failed to cause a zigzag course to be followed in dangerous waters." The court sentenced McVay "to lose 100 numbers in his temporary grade of captain and also his permanent grade of commander" but recommended clemency "in view of his outstanding previous record." Secretary Forrestal remitted the sentence upon the recommendation of Admirals Nimitz and King.

At the same time McVay's sentence was announced, the Navy released its "Narrative of the Circumstances of the Loss of the U.S.S. *Indianapolis*," a forty-five-hundred-word document representing the Navy's final statement on the tragedy. In the narrative four Navy officers were publicly reprimanded: Commodore N. C. Gillette, former acting commander of the Philippine Sea frontier; Captain A. M. Granum, Gillette's operations officer; Lieutenant Commander Jules C. Sancho, former acting port director at Leyte; and Sancho's operations officer, Lieutenant Stuart H. Gibson. These officers were cited for their "failure to report that the ship had not arrived in Leyte as scheduled."

Admiral Nimitz, holding a press conference upon release of the Navy's findings, stated it would be "unlikely that Captain McVay would again have a command of great responsibility." Nimitz read one letter of the many received from families of those lost in the sinking: it questioned whether the tragedy was "being whitewashed." Nimitz expressed his sorrow and said, "I must bear my share of the responsibility for the loss." The admiral explained that the cruiser's course was on the plotting boards in the Philippines and Marianas, but "plotting ceased at the time of her expected arrival at Leyte, without verification that she had in fact arrived." Operations officers Sancho and Gibson had failed to keep themselves informed of such matters, Nimitz continued, and he blamed Commodore Gillette and Captain Granum for not giving "sufficient supervision" to their subordinates.

The narrative was released on a Saturday, and Sunday newspapers and newscasts were full of the story. The publicity painted a picture of four officers at Leyte idling on the beach while hundreds of men died in agony. Commodore Gillette, in a letter to the Navy chief of personnel, defended himself and eloquently summarized the true cause of the disaster. Navy directives, he pointed out, provided that "Arrival Reports shall not be made for combatant ships" and "since the directive was not explicit, it led to misunderstanding and misinterpretation." Indeed, after the tragedy this proviso was altered to require reports of overdue combatant vessels. Gillette concluded: "I do not blame anyone. There is no definite clear-cut fact that points in one direction. The investigations disclosed many interrelated circumstances . . . incompletely defined or misunderstood responsibilities, matters subject to more than one interpretation . . . and the activities of many organizations and persons. It was the almost impossible that happened. It was the unbelievable coincidence of many circumstances that combined in an unbelievable manner to produce delay in rescue."

On December 9, 1946, the Navy withdrew the letters of reprimand, this time without public fanfare. Captain McVay never held command of a ship again, and retired from the Navy in 1949, after thirty years of service.

In August 1960, at Indianapolis, Indiana, most of the cruiser's survivors gathered together for the first time in fifteen years. The reunion was highly charged with emotion; many saw shipmates they thought had perished long ago; all were moved by Captain McVay's address to his former crewmen. And the parents of those who had not survived went from man to man asking, "Did you know my son?"

On August 2, 1980, ninety survivors met for the thirty-fifth anniversary of the sinking. The youngest men are in their fifties now, while others are unable to attend because of age or ill health. There is little remorse or bitterness among them, though many still bear scars, both physical and emotional, from their ordeal, and many quickly refer to the "raw deal" given their skipper. Also attending this most recent reunion were crew members of the new U.S.S. *Indianapolis,* a recently commissioned nuclear submarine. Wives and children of the survivors were there, too, many listening in awe as a husband or father related his harrowing experience.

Thirty-five years later they still remembered and supported each other, much as they did during those days in the water. The story of the *Indianapolis* is one of tragedy, pathos, and brutal irony. Yet above all, we should remember the courage and perseverance of those who survived and the sacrifice of those who did not.

—August 1982

CONTRIBUTORS

STEPHEN E. AMBROSE is Boyd Professor of History at the University of New Orleans and the author of a biography of Richard Nixon.

PETER ANDREWS is a contributing editor of *American Heritage*. He is at work on a biography of William Tecumseh Sherman.

MARTIN BLUMENSON was formerly with the Army's Office of the Chief of Military History, and is the author of several books on World War II.

COLONEL T.N. DUPUY is a West Point graduate and a combat veteran of the Burma Campaign.

KENNETH E. ETHRIDGE is a junior high school teacher and freelance writer in Royal Oak, Michigan.

MICHAEL FEIST is a freelance writer in Texas.

THOMAS FLEMING is a novelist and historian whose works include *Time and Tide*.

JOHN LORD is a British writer-producer. In World War II, he was an infantry platoon commander and fought in Normandy.

JOHN LUKACS is the author of many books, including the recent *The Duel*.

GEORGE MCMILLAN is a former Guggenheim Fellow who served in the Pacific theatre as Marine combat correspondent.

JOHN MCDONOUGH has written on contemporary cultural history for *The Wall Street Journal*, *The New York Times*, and other publications.

CARMINE A. PRIOLI teaches English at North Carolina State University.

STEPHEN W. SEARS is a former Book Division editor at American Heritage. His books include *The Automobile in America* and *Landscape Turned Red: The Battle of Antietam.*

W.A. SWANBERG has written biographies of William Randolph Hearst, Joseph Pulitzer, and Henry Luce.

ROBERT L. VARGAS is a freelance writer in El Paso, Texas

RICHARD WHEELER is a freelance writer and poet.